D1175156

NATURE'S
SECRET WORLD

ARCO PUBLISHING, INC.
New York

CONTENTS

STRATEGIES FOR SURVIVAL

ADAPTING TO THE ENVIRONMENT

SPECIALISED STRUCTURES

Published 1984 by Arco Publishing, Inc.
215 Park Avenue South
New York, NY 10003

Editor: James Harrison
Designer: Chris Walker
Production: Richard Churchill

Produced by Marshall Cavendish Books Limited
58 Old Compton Street
London W1V 5PA

© Marshall Cavendish Limited 1982-84

All rights reserved. No part of this publication
may be reproduced, stored in a retrieval system, or
transmitted in any form or by any means, electronic,
mechanical, photocopying, recording or otherwise,
without the permission of the publisher.

**Library of Congress Cataloging in
Publication Data**

Main entry under title:

Nature's secret world.

   Includes index.
   1. Natural history — Miscellanea.
QH45.5.N36815   1984   574   84-9169
ISBN 0-668-06213-4

Printed in Italy by New Interlitho SpA, Milan.

STRATEGIES FOR SURVIVAL

In the continuous struggle of life and death between predator and prey, animals and plants have evolved clever and curious ways of surviving the odds . . .

574
Nat
c.1

MADISON COUNTY
CANTON PUBLIC LIBRARY SYSTEM
CANTON, MISS. 39046

ALL CREATURES GREAT AND DIFFERENT

Scientists are adding to our understanding of why Nature is so marvellously diverse

Identikit pictures – of all things – are a paradoxical reminder of one of the most extraordinary scientific facts of Life. A single, crude jigsaw of standardized facial features can go a long way towards singling out one human being from millions upon millions of others. The system works, of course, on the principle that the differences between facial features are sufficiently minor to be boiled down to a manageable selection of standard types.

But the reality underlying this creation of modern criminology is startlingly different. Every human being is utterly different, not just in appearance but in every way conceivable. The scientific term for the phenomenon is diversity; and not only human beings, but every species of plant and animal inhabiting the globe has the same remarkable characteristic.

Geneticists – scientists who specialize in the study of heredity – have been asking some fundamental questions about diversity. Why, for instance, is it necessary? All the animal species – including *homo sapiens* – alive on Earth today have brilliantly survived through millions of years of evolution.

Moreover, they have done so through natural selection: so why bother to go on diversifying when the case, as it were, has been proven by the best test of all – survival? Why not just select, for instance, a single, fine specimen of leopard and make every other leopard in his (or her) image?

The simple answer is that diversity seems to be essential for the continued success of a species, despite the fact that it is itself responsible for creating occasional weak specimens, incapable of surviving individually. And this greatly helps our understanding of not only the animal world, but our own, too.

Far left **An albino peacock.** *Left* **An albino zebra stands out from the herd. Albinism – absence of pigmentation – is one of the more curious manifestations of genetic diversity. It occurs on the relatively rare occasions when an individual inherits a chance double dose of a particular recessive gene.**

The heron family provides one of Nature's most magnificent examples of diversity. *Below* **are mainly tropical species:** *1* **Intermediate egret.** *2.* **Agami or chestnut-bellied heron.** *3.* **Black heron** *4.* **Western reef heron.** *5.* **Little egret.** *6.* **Swinhoe's egret.** *7.* **Snowy egret.** *8.* **Reddish egret.** *9.* **Eastern reef heron.** *10.* **Little blue heron.** *11.* **Pied heron.** *12.* **Great white egret.** *13.* **Tri-coloured or Louisiana heron.** *14.* **Slaty egret.**

The language of genes

The *genes*, totalling well over 30,000 in a human being, are the biochemical 'blueprints' which control its development and maintenance, as they also do in every plant and animal. Added together, all an organism's genes make up its *genotype*. What the genes produce by directing the body's biochemistry – what you actually see – is the organism's *phenotype*. Unlike the genotype, which undergoes few changes during an organism's lifetime, the phenotype is able to change enormously, both naturally and artificially. The genotype may direct the production of mouse-coloured hair, for example, but its phenotype may be blonde, thanks to the effects of the sun or chemicals from a bottle.

In the vast majority of organisms, the genes are arranged on pairs of threadlike *chromosomes*, one member of every pair coming from each parent. And, even before the members of each pair meet up with each other, the genetic material is given a thorough shuffling. As a result of chromosome pairing, the genes

John Francis

are doubly represented. But the two members of each paired gene need not be identical. They can exist as alternative forms called *alleles*.

Dominant or recessive

In the simplest genetic terms, one allele is usually *dominant* over its alternative. The genes determining skin pigmentation in humans are a classic example. The gene for normal skin pigmentation, written *A*, is dominant over the gene for the disease albinism, *a*, in which the skin lacks proper pigmentation: *a* is said to be *recessive*.

Children inheriting the genetic make up *aa* – that is, an *a* gene on the chromosomes from each parent – will be albinos. But if they inherit the genetic make up *Aa* or *AA*, their skin will be normal because in the case of *Aa* the *A* gene is dominant and effectively 'blots out' the activity of the *a* gene. In the language of genetics, individuals with a double dose of a gene, in this case *AA* or *aa*, are said to be *homozygotes*, while the *Aa* individuals are *heterozygotes*.

Simple dominance of this kind operates for many genes, but in many other cases, the situation is more complex. Sometimes, for example, whole series of alternatives can exist for a single gene. In the dog, there is a gene *E* which acts to vary the amount of dark pigment in the animal's coat. This gene can occur as any one of four *multiple alleles*. The most dominant of the four is called E^m. This allele produces a black mask on the dog's face. Next most dominant is *E*, which gives the dog all black colouration. After that is the recessive e^{br}, which produces a brindled coat, in which each hair is striped black and yellow. The most recessive of the four is *e*, the allele for an all-yellow coat. Thus an $E^m E$ dog will have a black mask, an Ee^{br} one will be solid black, and an $e^{br}e$ one will have a brindled coat. Only the *ee* combination will give a dog with a yellow coat.

Permutations and combinations on the theme of genetic diversity increase as new research identifies more and more of the genes present in each species, and discovers new sorts of genes and gene activity. *Polygenes*, for instance, are genes which act together, each contributing a small part to a single inherited characteristic or trait. Added together, they can determine the amount of milk a cow produces, the size of an ear of corn or the weight of a human being.

Polymorphism

As far as the promotion of genetic diversity is concerned, one of the most vital genetic phenomena is that of *polymorphism*. In polymorphism, two or more forms of a species exist side by side in a population. These forms are not just the extremes of a series of multiple alleles. Instead they are 'discontinuous': there is no series of intermediate forms to fill in the gaps.

The different forms, or *morphs*, in a series of polymorphs may, like other genetically diverse characteristics, be governed by

Right **Many insects mimic each other in order to fend off predators. The row of butterflies on the left are unpalatable generally; those on the right generally taste good. Ability to develop diversely enables the latter to copy the former's appearance, and fool predators into leaving them alone.**

Herons of the world continued from previous page. *Below* **are mainly temperate species:** *1.* **Malagasi heron.** *2.* **Sumatran heron.** *3.* **Cattle egret.** *4.* **Cocoi heron.** *5.* **Great blue heron.** *6.* **Goliath heron.** *7.* **Capped heron.** *8.* **Grey heron.** *9.* **White-faced heron.** *10.* **Black-headed heron.** *11.* **Purple heron.** *12.* **Imperial heron.** *13.* **White-necked heron.** *14.* **Green heron.** *15.* **Whistling heron.**

genes which are heterozygous or recessive, but often depend on the action of more than one gene pair. The two different forms of primrose flowers, one with a long stigma, the other with a short one, are a well-known example of polymorphism, as are the different banding patterns of *Cepaea nemoralis* snails. In primroses, however, the different forms of the flowers depend on the action of at least *seven* pairs of genes.

The system is thought to work because the genes are controlled by a 'supergene', which not only assures that the relevant genes are 'glued' together — and stay together even despite the shuffling that goes on during sexual reproduction — but actually 'switches on' the genes. Switching on ensures that the correct phenotype develops, and maintains the discontinuity.

By their very number and arrangement, genes make for diversity, and being shuffled every generation adds to the vast potential for variation. So how is it that this variability can exist

Graham Smith

John Francis

Jean-Paul Ferrara/Ardea London

side by side with the stability that maintains the unique identity of species over millions of years. What is the use of diversity?

The importance of genetic diversity lies in its nature. It is the raw material fuelling both day-to-day survival and the long-term process of evolution. In any population, the individuals most likely to survive are those that tolerate a wide range of prevailing environmental conditions. Those individuals that live long enough to reproduce will pass their genes on to the next generation – all their genes, if they reproduce asexually, half of them if they reproduce sexually. In terms of a whole population, the best survival chances arise when individuals in that population are diverse enough to occupy the largest number of specialized environments, or *niches*. So the more diverse a population, the more niches it can occupy and the better its overall chances of survival in the face of disasters which wipe out some of those niches and their occupants.

Turning a theory round

So are the individuals most likely to survive the ones with the most diversity? Until the late sixties, biologists thought that diversity was closely associated with success, provided that it did not go too far. Heterozygote genes were thought to be advantageous as long as there were not too many of them. However, it was also considered essential for an individual to have a large proportion of genes homozygous for 'wild type' traits, provided they were tried, tested and proved successful over several generations. If there were too many heterozygotes, it was argued, then the chances of two unacceptable recessives – like the albinism genes – coming together was dangerously high.

However, experiments begun in the late sixties and continuing today have turned this theory on its head. Analysis of the proteins made as a direct result of gene activity show that there are far more heterozygous genes in individual animals and plants than ever imagined. Added to this, a great number of the genes operate in polymorphic systems. One researcher even concluded that Man was so variable he should be extinct.

The neutralists

Attempting to absorb these results into evolutionary theory, many biologists adopt a neutralist stance. They maintain that the various proteins made by the heterozygous genes are so minutely different that they could not have any effect on survival.

The neutralists also argue that the observed variations fit perfectly with the idea of the 'protein clock', a scale which reflects the random changes in proteins which have taken place by chance over millions of years. They say, for instance, that changes in blood proteins of mammals and fish have remained constant in rate since the two groups diverged onto different evolutionary paths some 350 million years ago.

A closer study of the rate of change of proteins which has taken place in recent years shows clear flaws in this line of argument. Rates of change in proteins have been revealed as much greater than those indicated by the sluggish hands of the protein clock. And in-depth studies on how proteins work reveal that even small changes in their structures are highly significant in biological terms, because these proteins work as enzymes, catalyzing (speeding up) biological reactions within living organisms.

The inevitable conclusion from these results must be that it is an advantage to be variable. Statistical studies bear out the fact that the presence of a high proportion of heterozygous genes in any organism tends to have a stabilizing effect on that organism and increase its chances of survival.

Survival chances seem to increase still further when the effects of being heterozygous lead to a situation in which different forms, polymorphs, of the same organism are created. Because they provide many different alternatives with which to exploit an environment, polymorphs tend to increase the fitness – the survival potential – of a population and at the same time, through the action of the supergenes, provide a means of combining stability with variability.

If diversity is the key to success, then is there any way in which we can tap this diversity and use it to even better advantage? Attempts to provide more food for an ever hungrier world could well look to the use of the genetic diversity inherent in the organisms themselves. For many years, plant breeders have produced new, more productive strains by mixing the genetic complements of plants. Now, with the advent of genetic engineering, there exists a prospect of increasing the genetic diversity of both animals and plants in an entirely new way. We can now create our own recipe for diversity and carry it out – who knows with what results?

Dogs' coats are a familiar example of genetic diversity in its more complex forms. One gene theoretically governs the amount of dark pigment in the coat, but it occurs as a multiple, with four different forms. Most dominant is one giving a black mask, *top left.* **Next dominant is all black. A brindle coat,** *left,* **is given by a recessive gene, as is a 'yellow' coat,** *far left.* **If a husky happens to inherit the black mask gene from one parent and the all yellow gene from the other, it is bound to have a black mask.** *Right* **Snails** (Cepaea sp.) **exemplify the phenomenon of polymorphism in colour pattern.**

Heather Angel

Jane Burton/Bruce Coleman Ltd.

Heather Angel

NATURE GOES TO TOWN

Tower blocks and monolithic office buildings conspire to shut out daylight. The traffic noise and petrol stench are overpowering; concrete pavements carpet the Earth. No hope for Nature, you would think. But look closer, and a whole world of wildlife reveals itself

Until recently, urban wildlife was largely ignored by naturalists, who preferred to travel to rural habitats and remote wildernesses to study animals and plants. Today, however, there is a surge of interest in the ecology of cities and towns. Urban councils are starting to realize the wisdom of making room for Nature, setting aside havens such as the William Curtis Ecological Park in London or the Jamaica Bay Wildlife Refuge in New York. It is not only the animals and plants that benefit: city dwellers have new 'mini-wildernesses' in the midst of the concrete and noise.

In 1982, the Greater London Council (GLC) appointed its first ever Senior Ecologist, attached to their Department of Transport and Development. David Goode's task is 'to infiltrate ecological thinking into all aspects of London planning and functioning'. Goode insists that this does not mean setting up élite enclaves to protect rare species and keeping out everyone but a select bank of scientists (though such schemes are of great value in the countryside). Instead, it should involve setting up a programme of creating or maintaining environments in which both city dwellers and wildlife can coexist. Of necessity, the wildlife involved must consist mainly of common, tough and adaptable species.

As naturalists began to take the study of urban wildlife seriously, they realized that they were studying complex communities of plants and animals, with diverse origins. First,

there are native species that have moved into towns and cities to exploit habitats that are basically similar to their original ones. Many woodland birds have done this – blue tits, blackbirds and jays have all established themselves in parks and gardens, mainly in the suburbs.

Other bird invaders such as house martins and swifts were originally cliff-nesters; although they occasionally nest in natural sites, they have largely deserted their natural homes for the manmade 'cliffs' formed by the eaves and roofs of houses.

Foreign invaders

The European black redstart is a relative of the robin which has made successful invasions of towns and cities from its natural habitat of mountain screes and rocky outcrops, flying across the English Channel to colonize London and other southern British cities in the 1930s and 40s. Bomb sites seemed to suit it perfectly, but since these have largely disappeared, it has switched to living and breeding in power stations, gasworks and railway sidings.

Together with small mammals, the varied populations of urban birds form a rich source of food for the few predatory birds that have managed to survive the harsh urban habitat and the presence of their main enemy, humans. Notable among the hunters is the kestrel, which has successfully invaded the heart as

Mike Leach/NHPA

A. J. Deane/Bruce Coleman Ltd.

Keystone Press Agency

Top left **Foxes are becoming increasingly successful urban dwellers. Here a red fox scrounges for food in a dustbin.** *Far left* **Cows are common town dwellers in India. This one is sharing refuse with a Sind house crow in Kashmir.**

Above **A flock of Maribou storks feeding at a refuse tip in Kenya.** *Top right* **The most successful adaptors are the most successful survivors. Here, a spotted flycatcher makes its home in a discarded baked bean tin.**

Right **The feral pigeon is one of the most successful and adaptable urban birds, being found in almost every city in the world. But its population often overflows to nuisance – in Venice pigeons were fed contraceptive pills.**

well as the suburbs of many European cities, nesting and hunting on office blocks as well as in gardens, parks, and along motorways. Kestrels have even nested on London's Houses of Parliament and Westminster Abbey, and as many as 20 pairs have bred in Richmond Park, rearing 54 young. One of the most spectacular birds of prey, the peregrine falcon, nests on skyscrapers in New York's Manhattan, and can be seen around urban areas in Europe such as the outskirts of Paris.

It is not only the highly mobile birds that have successfully moved in from the country. A wide variety of native wild flowers have established themselves in cities as big as London or Paris. Red deadnettle, goosegrass, woody nightshade and knapweed, among others, have managed to set up home, growing from seeds borne on the wind and carried in by birds or on the shoes of visitors to the country returning to the city. These plants, in turn, attract a whole world of insects, including such colourful species as elephant hawkmoths and peacock and red admiral butterflies.

River and lake dwellers

River and lake dwelling animals have penetrated deep into cities, though the increasing pollution of urban waters has resulted in their disappearance in many places. However, stricter

laws and improved treatment methods have helped: during the last 25 years, a 'clean-up' programme has resulted in more than 100 species of fish recolonizing the River Thames in London. Park lakes and urban reservoirs, too, can be havens for wildlife. They attract wild fowl to rest and feed, particularly in winter, and some of the birds may stay to breed if they can find enough privacy. Garden ponds are sanctuaries for animals such as frogs and newts whose natural habitats are being threatened by pollution or drainage schemes.

Reptiles

In warmer countries, urban dwellers may share their homes and streets with reptiles. Geckoes – stout, large-headed nocturnal lizards – use sucker-like discs on their feet to walk up and down walls and across ceilings. They are a common sight in cities as far apart as Bangkok and Cairo. Various species of snake hunt rats and mice that infest the cities of India and South-East Asia, and these include poisonous snakes such as cobras as well as harmless ones like the northern brown snake of North America.

Mammals, too, have taken to the towns. In Europe, foxes are becoming increasingly successful urban dwellers. In Bristol, England, over 200 litters of fox cubs have been recorded. Urban

Brian Hawkes/NHPA

Brian Hawkes/NHPA

Left **The blackbird is a typical example of a native bird that has moved from the woodlands into an urban habitat. This one is nesting on top of a 'general purpose' gasmeter. City life offers comfort in terms of warmth and rich food supply.** *Above* **Kittiwakes find the manmade 'cliffs' of a brewery an ideal home, suiting them far better than their natural, coastal nests.**

Top right **A tenacious grey squirrel steals from a peanut feeder meant for garden birds.** *Bottom right* **Hard-to-see peppered moths rest on lichen-covered bark.** *Bottom, far right* **Bury Hill, a wildlife reserve near Birmingham where Nature has reclaimed exhausted marl pits, giving a huge variety of vegetation a chance to flourish and offer a home to insects and animals.**

foxes are often spotted in broad daylight, in parks, gardens and wasteland, and even on streets or along railway lines. Hedgehogs live in many suburban gardens, and even though cars take a heavy toll, manage to survive and prosper.

Like foxes, North American racoons raid urban garbage bins. Other American town visitors are coyotes, which have established themselves in Chicago, Detroit and other cities, and Virginian opossums (North America's only marsupial mammals), which are sometimes involved in violent fights with domestic cats.

Surprise visitors

Although many species of animals and plants cannot tolerate the harsh urban world, there have been some surprising visitors. Polar bears pay regular visits to the garbage dumps of townships in subarctic Canada, and workers have had to travel an indirect route by bus to avoid encounters with these potentially dangerous animals. During the expansion of Miami, Florida, alligators were discovered by alarmed residents in their backyards, swimming pools, golf courses and even the streets: the urban sprawl had encroached upon their habitat.

In contrast to these occasional exotic visitors, a small but tenacious group of animals and plants have made a real success out of city life. The brown and black rats are formidable survivors,

thriving on our waste. A recent estimate by the US Department of Agriculture is that there are as many rats as people in a large number of cities. They have even been caught gnawing the feet of elephants in city zoos – several elephants had to be destroyed at Hamburg Zoo after one attack.

House mice are even tougher and more adaptable than rats. They have been found living very well in cold stores of wholesale meat markets. The average weight and size of the cold-store mice is bigger than that of free-living animals, and they produce more litters in their self-imposed icy prisons. In total darkness, in a temperature that never exceeds −10°C, and with no food apart from frozen meat, the mice live, breed and die. They make nests of hessian or other material used to wrap the meat, or use feathers and fur from the stored carcasses. They may even burrow into the frozen meat and nest inside it.

City birds

Several species of birds, too, have become true city dwellers. Starlings have spread worldwide, mainly with human help. Their phenomenal success is typified by their spread in North America after introduction there. In 1890, 100 starlings were released in Central Park, New York: 50 years later, there were an estimated 50 million starlings in the USA and they had spread throughout most of the country.

I. R. Beames/Ardea London

Urban starlings are commuters, flying in from their feeding grounds up to 30 kilometres away to roost in huge numbers on buildings in the heart of the city, seemingly undisturbed by traffic noise, which they almost equal with their loud chuckles, whistles and many other sounds, or by the neon 'daylight'. Some roosts contain hundreds of thousands of birds.

Feral pigeons

Another extremely successful and adaptable urban bird is the feral pigeon – the street pigeon of cities from New York to Berlin, from Madrid to Bangkok. Many feral pigeons owe their origins to escaped racing pigeons, others to birds kept in dovecotes; all are originally descended from the wild rock dove of coastal cliffs. During the last century of urban expansion, there has been a huge explosion of pigeon numbers. Today, feral pigeons are such sophisticated urbanites that they can be seen hitching rides on London underground trains.

Despite all the problems of an urban existence for many plants and animals, city life is relatively easy, and even offers some advantages. People, industry and traffic all generate heat, which becomes trapped by the city's buildings. Urban areas are generally up to 5°C warmer than the surrounding countryside. Plants may start growing earlier and for longer, and birds may breed earlier. Our buildings, parks, gardens and wastelands provide shelter and breeding sites for wildlife, and there is usually a rich supply of food in cities and towns, from the discarded office worker's sandwich to the local garbage dump.

Wildlife is extremely resilient. However much we alter our environment, however hard we try to dominate it and control Nature, wild animals and plants will exploit the new habitats we unwittingly create. Despite this sobering resilience, urban wildlife needs our help, and it would benefit city dwellers as much as the animals and plants they share their lives with if we were to devote more energy to encouraging them to survive and prosper.

Heather Angel

DEAD OR ALIVE?

Tongue lolling, a grass snake lies dead. So you might justifiably believe, but what the camera cannot reveal is that under the snake's skin, its heart beats on. This is not death but a mere sham, aimed to make an approaching predator give up the chase, and the last line of defence for this possum amongst reptiles. Without the advantage of poisonous fangs with which to fight their foes, grass snakes go in for several ploys to save themselves from being eaten by birds, badgers, hedgehogs and other carnivores. Speed of escape is the grass snake's number one ally, but if it should be approached by an attacker, the snake first begins to

hiss and puffs itself up behind the head just as many poisonous snakes do. Again imitating its venomous relatives, the grass snake then thrusts forward, making as if to strike. But instead of lashing out with its jaws, the snake tries to turn its attacker off course by emitting a foul-smelling liquid. Once it becomes obvious to the snake that the predator is not going to be put off lightly, then it coils up, turns on its back and plays dead. With remarkable efficiency, this behaviour can jam the predator's instinctive patterned programme of attack and it turns away to find sustenance elsewhere.

Allan Power/Bruce Coleman Ltd.

SEA SERPENTS

One of Nature's strangest anomalies: snakes that
have adapted to life at sea so well that they
are helpless on land

The most poisonous snakes in the world give no sign of their lethal nature – neither the rattle of the American desert snakes nor the hiss of the striking cobra herald their approach. For these venomous creatures are sea snakes – a collection of some 50 species of ocean-going snakes that thrive throughout the tropical waters of the world.

The sea snakes, in the family *hydrophiidae*, are probably closest to cobras by descent, but their precise relationship to the terrestrial snakes is uncertain. Some millions of years ago they took to the water and are now the most completely aquatic of all air-breathing vertebrates. Most never come ashore and have evolved a host of striking adaptations to marine life.

For a start, their bodies are flattened vertically, making them streamlined in the water. Their tails are elongated and compressed so that they resemble the blades of oars, and a flat fold of skin stretches along the belly of the snakes to form a rudimentary fin. They move through the sea with great ease and can swim as fast as fish. In fact, filmed studies show that they swim much like fish – by undulating their bodies from side to side.

Sea snakes are active predators. They eat mostly fish and eels and have improved their ability to strike at prey by another modification of the standard snake body. Several species, such as *Microcephalophis gracilis*, have bodies much thicker than their heads and necks. This allows the trunk to absorb the opposing forces that occur when the neck is stretched out to bring the head to the prey. Their smaller heads and necks – less than a quarter of the mass of the trunk and tail – provide them with greater stability when striking prey. The thick abdomen may also serve as a firm base for launching an attack on their favourite prey, the numerous eels that surround them.

The small heads and necks also allow the snakes to keep the front of the body near the centre line of forward movement, making undulating swimming more efficient. Inspite of their diminutive heads, they still manage to eat fish much larger than their own bodies. The nostrils of the sea snakes are also well suited to life at sea. Located at the top of the snout, the nostrils have valves (opercula) that the snake opens when it comes to the surface to breathe. They also have specially adapted lungs.

One lung is much reduced but the other

is enlarged so that it extends down most of the body. The lung has a fluted inner surface which increases the area available for storing oxygen. At its farthest end, the long lung is just a simple air sac with no alveoli (microscopic pockets, lined with tiny blood vessels, for transferring oxygen into the blood). This part of the lung seems to be a hydrostatic organ, used to give the snake buoyancy in water. It allows the snake to lie quietly at the bottom for at least 10 minutes before coming up for air.

Sea snakes, in common with many other marine animals, also possess a special salt gland, called the natrial gland, in the bottom of the mouth. The gland excretes the excess salt they take in with their food. The sea snakes also have unusually smooth scales. Land snakes rely on their rigid scales, especially the scutes (the large, overlapping scales on their underside) to grip surface irregularities when they move. Most sea snakes have lost these scales and are helpless on land. One species, *Laticauda oviparous*, has kept its ventral scales; these sea snakes are in fact amphibious. They may leave the sea to warm themselves on rocks or grass along the coast and come ashore to lay their eggs in the sand. These snakes can move easily on land. The solely marine snakes, however, bear live young – an obvious necessity for an air-breathing animal totally committed to life at sea. A pregnant female of *Lapemis hardwicki* produces three or four young, 25-30 cm long at birth, that grow to be 90 cm as adults.

Habitat

Sea snakes are widespread throughout the warmer parts of the world. They are found along the shores of Asia, between the Tropics of Cancer and Capricorn, and along the Pacific islands. They also lurk around the islands of the Indo-Malayan Archipelago, much of Australia, the east coast of Africa and the western shores of Central America. One species, the yellow-bellied or pelagic sea snake, *Pelamis platurus*, is found in almost all these places. Its geographic range is wider than any other reptile, save some of the more adventurous sea turtles. This snake is dark brown or black with a bright yellow belly, and is usually about a metre long.

The sea snakes often prefer shallow coastal waters which allow them to rest on the bottom and still be within easy reach of air at the surface. They sometimes gather in estuaries, especially in the rainy season when large amounts of organic detritus is washed into the sea by swollen rivers. The snakes may migrate to the estuaries at these times in large numbers, swimming in shoals at the surface with their heads out of water. This input of nutrients causes the fishes that the snakes eat to flourish. The snakes can even venture upriver into fresh water. One species, *Hydrophis semperi*, lives in Lake Taal in Luzon in the Philippines, while *Laticauda crockeri* lives in Lake Te Nggano on Rennel Island, in the Solomon Islands.

Walter Deas/Seaphot Ltd.: Planet Earth Pictures

Bill Wood/Bruce Coleman Ltd.

Ken Lucas/Seaphot Ltd.: Planet Earth Pictures

Above right **An olive sea snake (***Aipysurus laevis***) resting on the sea bed, its colour blending well as it waits for a passing fish. The venom of the sea snake is one of the most powerful toxins known to man. The fangs are small and hollow and usually hidden by a fold of skin in the gums. To milk the venom the snake must be immobilized and the fangs carefully exposed (***top***). A plastic tube is then pushed over one of the fangs (***above***) and the natural biting of the snake pumps about 20 mg of slimy, ropy fluid into the tube for collection.**

The snakes use their powerful venom to kill their prey. The small fangs are fixed in the front of the jaw and are almost completely tubular, rather like hypodermic needles. Normally they are hidden in the gums by a fold of skin but emerge readily to penetrate the victim's flesh. An attacking sea snake seizes a fish in the middle of its body and then 'nibbles' at it while keeping its hold, slowly pumping the venom into the fish. In a few minutes the struggling fish becomes paralyzed. Then, without loosening its grip, the snake manoeuvres the fish around in its jaw and swallows it head first.

Venom

A single bite can produce about 20 mg of venom (dry weight) which emerges as a slightly slimy, ropy fluid. When dried, it forms light yellow crystals. The venom is extremely toxic to fish. In experiments, the LD50 of the venom of *Enhydrina schistosa*, the beaked sea snake, for goldfish — the dose of venom that kills half the fish tested — is only 40 μg/kg body weight; a very small amount.

The bite of a sea snake can be fatal to Man as well. The venom is a curare-like poison that paralyzes its victim by disrupting the transmission of the impulses from nerves to the muscles. It also contains en-

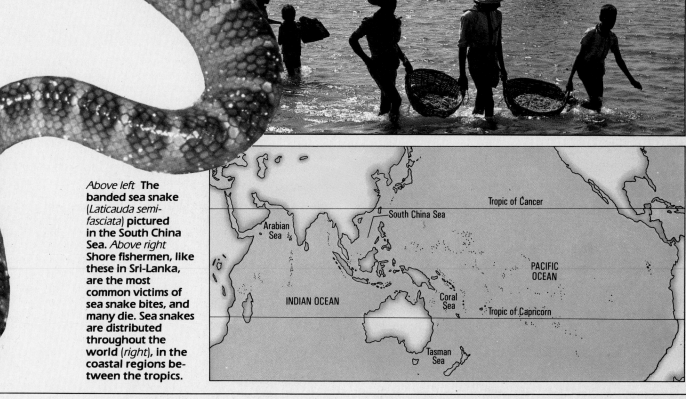

Above left **The banded sea snake** (*Laticauda semifasciata*) **pictured in the South China Sea.** *Above right* **Shore fishermen, like these in Sri-Lanka, are the most common victims of sea snake bites, and many die. Sea snakes are distributed throughout the world** (*right*), **in the coastal regions between the tropics.**

Sally and Richard Greenhill

Simon Roulstone

zymes which prevent the clotting of blood and destroys the red blood cells. The human victims of the snake develop red-coloured urine, stained by this degraded blood. However, bites to humans are not always fatal – perhaps because it takes several days for the snake to re-arm with a full complement of venom, and so the amount of venom in the bite may be quite small if the snake has recently eaten.

Human victims

Most of the human victims of the snake are local fishermen. The snake's bite is particularly insidious because it is usually painless. A fisherman standing in turbid water, pulling in nets, may not know he has been bitten. The fang punctures are inconspicuous and there is no local swelling or bleeding. But a few hours later, the victim will begin to find movement difficult, and numbness and paralysis increase until death results from respiratory failure. The muscles of the eyelids are paralyzed early, making the immobilized man or woman seem to be asleep. Villagers in Vietnam say 'when someone has been bitten he falls asleep and dies' – but the victim is actually conscious until death. In Malaya, probably as many as 30 per cent of people bitten by the snake die, usually within 24 hours.

Folklore

Some sea snakes, such as *Laticauda colubrina,* seem to be rather docile and do not usually bite even if handled or trodden upon. But *Hydrophis cyanocinctus* in the Indian Ocean is very aggressive and will bite fishermen even after it has escaped from their nets. Bathers are apparently rarely victims of sea snakes. A seaman whose ship was anchored off the Pacific side of the Panama canal decided to swim ashore. He found himself surrounded by a shoal of sea snakes, but came to no harm.

It is difficult to calculate the toll in human life taken by sea snakes, not least because

Above left **The typical small head of an** *Aipysurus duboisii* **pictured off the Marion Reef in Australia.** *Above right* **The nostrils are seen clearly here on an olive sea snake.** *Right* **A yellow-bellied sea snake** (*Pelamis platuris*) **unusually on City Beach, Perth in Western Australia.** *Below* **The flat fold of skin, resembling a fin, can be seen on the belly of this sea snake swimming in the Coral Sea off the coast of north-east Australia.**

the fishermen of Malaya and Vietnam are forbidden to speak of people who have been killed by the snakes. Their folklore has it that the King of Snakes, who rules over sea snakes, will send snakes to attack men who talk of such deaths. An antidote to the specific venom of sea snakes, in the form of antivenom serum, has been developed by Michael Barme of the Pasteur Institute in Paris and Dr H A Reid, working at Penang Hospital. But sadly such treatment is rarely available to people living in remote villages.

Still, these remarkable creatures are not entirely a bane to human existence. In Japan, one of the largest sea snakes, some 2.5 metres long, *Laticauda semifasciata,* is a great delicacy and there is a thriving trade in the creatures. Japanese cooks thread the snakes onto a bamboo spit and roast or smoke them. In the Philippines, sea snakes are fished commercially, largely for their skins; but local people also eat them or feed them to livestock.

Carl Roessler/Seaphot Ltd.: Planet Earth Pictures

Left Beteenthe larval form of today's horseshoe crab and the fossil (*below*) of a Cambrian age trilobite stretch millennia of geological time. But the resemblance between the two creatures is plainly apparent and the newly hatched *Xiphosura* (*Limula*) polyphemus is rightly named a trilobite larva. In the horseshoe crab, Nature hit on a design that she has seen no reason to change.

THE ULTIMATE SURVIVOR

This 'living fossil' helps doctors diagnose disease and physiologists discover the way human vision works

For over 300 million years – since long before the period when dinosaurs ruled the Earth – horseshoe crabs have dwelt somewhere in the brackish waters of the world's oceans. Studying them gives scientists what amounts to a telescopic view back through the ages because, in all the millennia since they first appeared, these bizarre-looking creatures have remained virtually unchanged.

To etch further detail onto this prehistoric picture, the newly-hatched horseshoe crab goes through a developmental stage called a *trilobite larva* with an outward appearance similar to that of the fossil animal whose name it bears. Extinct more than 200 million years ago, after a spell on Earth of about twice that length, the trilobites were segmented creatures which crawled or burrowed on the seabed. They gave rise to some of the first creatures ever to live on land, and were the forerunners of all the modern crustaceans (crabs, shrimps and so on), insects and arachnids (spiders, scorpions and mites), which are lumped together in the great group Arthropoda (jointed-limbed animals). Despite their common name, horseshoe crabs are much more closely related to the arachnids than to crustaceans.

Ancient armour

According to the record in the rocks, horseshoe crabs were once reasonably widespread, particularly in European waters, but today are limited both in numbers and distribution. A mere four species survive: *Limulus polyphemus*, the most studied of the four, lives along the Atlantic coast of the USA and Mexico. Adults measure some 45 cm across and weigh about 2 kg. The other three species are all residents of the warm seas of Southeast Asia.

Sometimes confusingly dubbed king crabs (a title due more correctly to a species of crustacean), the horseshoe crabs get their common name from the shape of their *carapace* – the tough outer armour covering the head end of the body. Made, like the external covering of the ancestral trilobites, from protein-impregnated chitin, the carapace is coloured like a beach pebble to camouflage the animal from predators.

Apart from the eyes, of which it has three pairs — an unusual arrangement — all the head's working parts are on the under-surface of the animal. They include a mouth ringed by 10 legs and equipped with a pair of pincers, which the horseshoe crab uses to catch its prey, a variety of small sea creatures, including worms and molluscs. It uses four of its legs to scuttle across the seabed.

A huge hinge stretches the entire width of the body, making a mobile joint between the head end and the squat, segmented abdomen. By using its hinge to the full, the animal can jack-knife rhythmically to and fro and so rapidly bury itself in the sand — an action aided by its long, sword-shaped tail. Beating the short legs on its abdomen, this versatile creature can also swim — always upside-down for maximum stability and efficiency. When it stops swimming, it settles on the seabed still inverted, then uses its long tail-spine to right itself.

Within, the body bears many resemblances to those of spiders and scorpions; the outstanding feature shared between them is the breathing apparatus which consists of a concertina-like arrangement of aptly-named 'book gills'. The 'pages' of these gills are used to trap water for the exchange of oxygen and carbon dioxide during respiration.

As if inextricably tied to an age-old way of life, whose original pattern was determined by the natural rhythms of the planet, horseshoe crabs time their sexual activities by the Moon and tides. Every year at full Moon and high tide in May and June, the adult American horseshoe crabs begin to congregate on the beach in their thousands. Their approach is relatively unsubtle: the males march up and down the shore with an eye open for an eligible female. A partnership is forged as the male grabs the female of his choice with a pair of modified limbs, then watches as she digs a hole some 15 cm deep, in which she lays up to 100 eggs.

Hazardous future

When the nest is filled, the male deposits his sperm inside to fertilize the eggs, then the pair wait for the ebb-tide to carry them back out to sea — if they miss the tide, they risk death by dehydration. As for the fertilized eggs, they too face a hazardous future. Many make ready meals for fish and shore-birds, while many more are washed out to sea and are sieved out of the water by hungry filter-feeders such as tubeworms and sea-squirts.

A less precarious existence is enjoyed by the trilobite larvae that hatch in the nest some two weeks after fertilization. They are released from the eggs with the help of the eroding action of sand-grains thrust against the eggs by the force of the waves. However, the larvae have a long way to go: they must somehow manage to avoid being eaten by predators or battered against rocks while their protective armour is slowly developing. It takes them 9-11 years

and 15 or 16 moults before they are sexually mature and ready to produce offspring of their own.

Horseshoe crabs are not popular with New England clam fishermen because they believe that the animals threaten the young softshell clams, and there is indeed evidence that they will eat quantities of shellfish. Somewhat surprisingly, however, these zoological relics have also brought important benefits to man.

Since 1928, when the American biologist H. K. Hartline (a Nobel Prizewinner) discovered that the lateral eye of the horseshoe crab was ideal for research into the physiology of vision, extensive studies have yielded fundamental understanding of visual processes in more complex animals, including Man. At New York's Rockefeller University, for instance, researchers connected an electrode to the optic nerve serving one of the animal's eyes, and recorded the responses it made to different levels of light intensity. They discovered that the nerve responds most to *changes* in light intensity, not to absolute levels.

Given the long-documented history of the horseshoe crab, it is reasonable to assume that this ability, which also happens to be crucial to the efficiency of mammalian vision, is one that was established very early in the evolution of animals. It would also help to explain, at least in part, how the crab is able to use the full Moon as a signal for its frenzied burst of mating with such precision, because the response is greatest when the boundary between light and dark is sharpest, as when the full Moon is silhouetted against a black night sky.

Recent research by biologists at the Marine Biological Laboratory at Woods Hole, Massachusetts, USA has thrown new light on the role of vision in the animals' mating behaviour. It seems that they discriminate form by analyzing information from various senses, but distinguish contrast using vision alone.

Horseshoe crab blood — like that of some arachnids, molluscs and crustaceans — is a dramatic shade of blue when oxygenated, due to a chemical change in the copper-based respiratory pigment called haemocyanin (equivalent to the iron-based haemoglobin in our bodies which gives our blood its red colour). Not only is horseshoe crab blood blue, it also helps in the fight against disease: medical researchers use a portion of the blood called Limulus Amoebocyte Lysate (LAL for short) as a test for various diseases, including spinal meningitis, Legionnaire's Disease, bubonic plague and gonorrhoea. To help conserve crab populations, the animals are returned to their home waters after being deprived of a portion of the LAL from their blood. Marine biologists are looking at improved methods of 'bleeding' to increase the animals' chances of survival after this operation. But survival is a game the crabs are good at.

Above **One of the three S.E. Asian species of horseshoe crab,** *Tachypleus gigas,* **caught in the act of righting itself in shallow water. It is using its long tail-spike as an anchor while it performs this demanding manoeuvre. Together with the single American species,** *Limulus polyphenus,* **the three S.E. Asian species are the only living representatives of this ancient group of animals.**

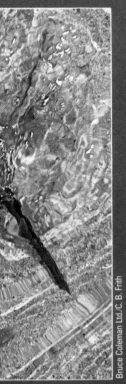

Below **Limulus** viewed from above (*left*) and below (*right*). The animal gets its common name from the horseshoe-shaped carapace, or body armour, which covers the front end. The long, sharp tail, or telson, on which it can balance, adds to the animal's bizarre appearance.

Right **Looking like strange mechanical toys, horseshoe crabs mate on the shore at Tampa, Florida, USA. Timing their breeding to coincide with the full Moon and high tide, up to several thousand come together on the beach to perform their mating rites in an age-old ritual.**

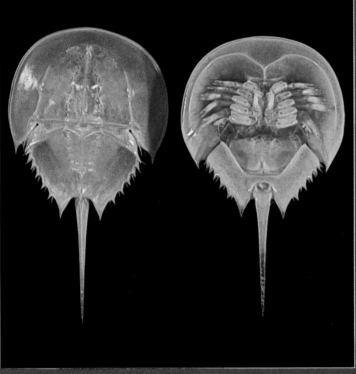

Bruce Coleman Ltd./C. B. Frith

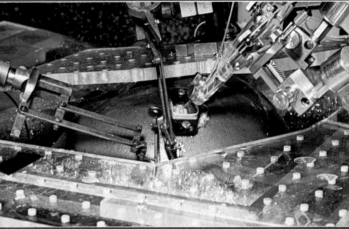

Bruce Coleman Ltd./M. P. Kahl

Below **Close up of the undersurface of Limulus. The pincers are at the top: the animal uses them to catch its food. Below them is the mouth surrounded by five pairs of legs.**

Professor Robert B. Barlow/Institute for Sensory Research

Below **At Syracuse University, New York, Prof. Robert Barlow leads research into vision by experiments on the horseshoe crab's simple eye. He isolated single active nerve fibres from the 800-1,000 in the optic nerve trunk. With the aid of tiny fibre optics light pipes he could then illuminate a single photo-receptor in the eye of a living animal and record its response.**

Bruce Coleman Ltd./G. W. Frame

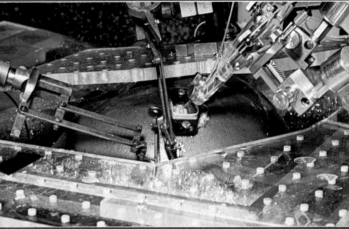

Professor Robert B. Barlow

Left **Close-up of the Syracuse University experiment. The small black chamber, attached to the animal's cell near one of its lateral eyes, contains part of the optic nerve, exposed by cutting into the shell. The research researchers used five needles to tease out single fibres.**

Professor Robert B. Barlow

ALL PUFFED UP

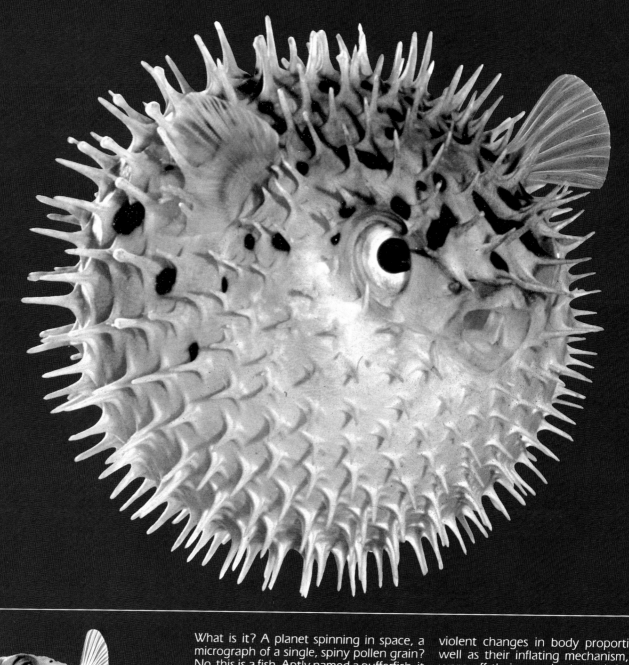

What is it? A planet spinning in space, a micrograph of a single, spiny pollen grain? No, this is a fish. Aptly named a pufferfish, it has a spectacular way of deterring predators — when danger threatens, it swallows water into its highly elastic stomach (or air if it happens to be at the ocean surface) and inflates itself to horrific proportions. Native to the world's tropical waters, pufferfish can blow themselves up like this because their bodies do not bear restrictive, spiny fins. And instead of having two rows of fins like most fish, they are equipped with a beak-like structure, split in the middle, which can mould itself to accommodate violent changes in body proportions. As well as their inflating mechanism, puffers warn off their enemies by emitting noises which are among the loudest in the piscean world. To add to their armoury, many puffers are painted in bright colours to warn predators that their bodies contain a deadly poison. Identified as the chemical tetraodontoxin, and calculated at 200,000 times more powerful than curare at blocking the passage of impulses along the nervous system, this toxin is the cause of many deaths by food poisoning in Japan where the pufferfish dish *fugu* is considered a delicacy.

MASTERS OF DECEPTION

Alwin Clements

Despite elaborate devices to ensure pollination,
some species of orchid face extinction. They are
difficult plants to cultivate, but some — like
this sun orchid — are quite easy to grow from seed

The shape, colour and texture of orchids is related to their method of pollination. Some have evolved very convincing disguises which trick insects. The actual response of the insect – amatory or aggressive – depends on the mimicry employed. *Right* **A bee orchid,** *Ophrys speculum,* **has in-** duced a bee to try to copulate with it. The bee picks up pollen during pseudo-copulation, and transfers it to another orchid during its next 'seduction'. A glance at the fly orchid, *Ophrys insectifera* (*below*) **and a bee orchid,** *Ophrys speculum* (*inset*) **shows the effective-ness of mimicry.**

Biophoto Associates

Oxford Scientific Films/David Thompson

In the wake of the dinosaurs came an equally remarkable form of life – the orchids. These often beautiful and sometimes weird flowering plants are represented by some 20,000 species throughout the world. Tropical orchids are usually *epiphytes,* living on trees, while temperate orchids stick to the ground. They get their name from a curious misconception. Medieval herbalists, noting the suggestively paired underground tubers of some European orchids, concluded that the plants promoted virility and duly called them after the Greek for testicle (*orchis*).

Orchids owe their amazing flowers to the insects which pollinate them. The three inner petals of an orchid flower are very distinctive – two are alike but the third is elaborated into a uniquely shaped and coloured lip or *labellum.* Many orchids in the genus *Ophrys* attract pollinating insects by developing hairy, suggestively coloured labella which mimic another insect.

Male bees or wasps are fooled into thinking that the orchid is a female of the species and attempt to copulate with the flower. In the process they become covered with the flower's sticky pollen which they carry to the next flower they visit. The common name of many orchids – the bee orchid, the sawfly orchid, and the spider orchid testify to their verisimilitude.

One orchid, *Oncidium bahamanse,* that grows on Grand Bahama Island, produces flowers that resemble male insects and thereby attract the wrath of territorial males. Other flowers mimic the prey of the pollinator.

Not all orchids are total cheats. Some do produce nectar, to feed the visiting insects, in a drawn-out tube or *spur* attached to the base of the lip, but the design of the flower ensures that insects cannot get at the nectar without picking up pollen. *Nigritella nigra,* with a flower known as a brush blossom, has developed a spur so narrow that it can only be drained by the fine probosces of butterflies; the pollen sticks to the base of their mouthparts.

One-way system

Cypripedium calceolus, the lady's slipper orchid, produces no nectar but has a deceptive nectar-like odour. It has a large yellow labellum so slippery that the bee slides down into the flower and can get out only by squeezing through a narrow one-way system that takes it past the pollen-laden stamen. The flower of *Listera ovata,* with its distinctive green flowers, has a spring-loaded structure, the *rostellum,* that fires pollen onto the head of the insect trying to reach its nectar.

The orchids really are masters of deception. Some species of *Ophrys,* pollinated by tiny wasps, even secrete a chemical that attracts male wasps because it is very similar to the sex pheromone of the female wasp. Males have been known to go to a flower in preference to a real female.

Each species of orchid is thus specially adapted to pollination by a particular kind of insect. Hybrids are rarely successful in Nature – not least because upsetting the balance between odour, size and stickiness of the flowers could turn them into death-traps for visiting insects.

The fascination of orchids lies as much in their mysterious life cycle as in the complex forms of mimicry which they employ. Each flower produces thousands of tiny seeds

Right This side view of a Japanese orchid *Habenaria radiata* shows its long, thin spur; its nectar can only be reached by long-tongued insects. The shape ensures that they cannot gather nectar without picking up pollen. *Below right* Unlike the Mediterranean *Ophrys speculum*, the British bee orchid, *Ophrys apifera* employs a self-fertilization mechanism, shown in cutaway. *Below* An Australian bearded ground orchid, *Calochilus paludosus.* Variety in orchids includes that of smell as well as appearance. Some give off a nectar-like smell, others mimic sex pheromones — some smell like rotting flesh!

Biophoto Associates

Alwin Clements

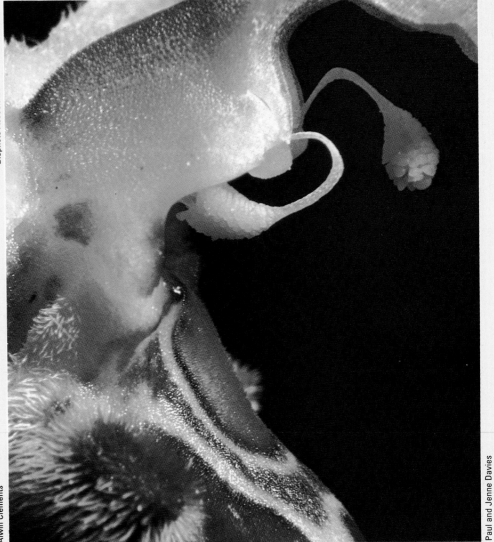

Paul and Jenne Davies

Biophoto Associates

Paul and Jenne Davies

Left Cypripedium calceolus, **the lady's slipper orchid's large labella are so slippery that visiting bees slide down into the flower, and can only escape by squeezing past the pollen-laden stamen. Despite the ingenuity of this device, only one specimen of the lady's slipper survives in Britain. Its existence is protected by a round-the-clock watch.** *Above and right* **The military orchid and the ghost orchid are also under threat.**

designed to be dispersed by the wind. The seeds contain very little nutrient for the young plant and the germinating seed has come to rely on getting help from a fungus. A fungus invades the seed and provides it with food in its early stages. Sometimes this is the beginning of a lifelong association between plant and fungus – usually a *Rhizoctonia*.

This association of plant and fungus is a form of symbiosis. The fungus breaks down organic material in the soil and incorporates the nutrients into its hyphae (filaments that form its body). The orchid then extracts the nutrients from the invading fungus.

Some species appear as small leaves above the ground only two to three months after germination. At this time, a tuber is developing under ground. If the seedling manages to produce a large enough tuber in the first growing season, it may flower the following year. However, this is very rare. Most ground orchids take at least $2\frac{1}{2}$-$3\frac{1}{2}$ years before they flower. Some species take even longer – up to 15 years. With rare exceptions, they can be seen as leaves during each growing season.

Spiranthes spiralis, autumn lady's tresses, takes several years to develop flowers. As it grows it may grow less dependent on the fungus. Some species of orchid are *saprophytic* all their lives – they never develop chlorophyll, the green pigment in plants that allows them to synthesize sugars in the presence of sunlight, but obtain nutriment from rotting vegetation via the fungus.

The ghost orchid, *Epipogium aphyllum*, is one such orchid. It has no leaves, only brownish scales covering a pinkish stem. Now very rare in Europe, the remaining specimens live in beechwoods and probably spend most of their lives – some 20 years – underground, without flowering.

Many terrestrial orchids die off above ground over winter; they live off the carbohydrates stored in the tuber, which also lies dormant in winter. Several temperate orchids, like species of *Aceras* and *Ophrys apifera*, have leaves throughout winter but they may still rely on the fungus since they probably cannot photosynthesize effectively at low temperatures. The underground fungal back-up probably helps the fragile orchids survive droughts, cold, and heavy shading in dense woods.

These weird and wonderful plants are under threat. Their habitats, in temperate and tropical regions alike, are rapidly being destroyed. In Britain and Europe agricultural pressures have wiped out the rich populations of orchids that used to thrive on calcereous (calcium carbonate containing) grasslands; orchids are highly sensitive to improved drainage, fertilizers and trampling. The tropical rainforests which are home to the exotic epiphytes are fast disappearing.

The striking beauty of the orchid's flowers also encourages overenthusiastic gardeners to pick them. Only one specimen of the lady's slipper orchid is still living in Britain – and its survival has been ensured only by the vigilance of wardens who guard the lone orchid round the clock during the month it is in flower.

T. C. E. Wells and his co-workers at Monks Wood Experimental Station in Huntingdon, England, have been monitoring populations of terrestrial orchids living in grasslands for some 20 years. The mid-1950s were a good time for orchids, it seems, because grasslands were heavily grazed by rabbits. The short turf and the

Orchids' habitats are both wide-ranging and very specific. As habitats are changing or being destroyed, many species are fast disappearing. The rare Australian *Rhizanthella gardneri*, above **and** *right*, lives only among the roots of the broom honey-myrtle. The South African *Polystachya pubescens* (*left*) is an epiphyte. Ground orchids such as autumn lady's tresses (*below*) remain below ground for at least a year – or, as in this case, for several years.

Oxford Scientific Films/J. L. Cooke

absence of competing coarse grasses let orchid seeds get a foothold. After myxomatosis was introduced to control rabbits, conditions for the orchids deteriorated.

There are a few encouraging signs on the horizon. Botanists sponsored by the World Wildlife Fund have used satellites to search for and safeguard rare orchids in Western Australia. The orchid *Rhizanthella gardneri* lives only among the roots of the broom honey-myrtle *Melaleuca uncinata;* only the orchid's flowers appear at ground level. Patches of these bushes were spotted by satellite and over 100 specimens of the orchid have since been located.

Introducing seed to fungus

Some workers, such as Mark Clements, an Australian botanist working at the Royal Botanic Gardens at Kew in England, are encouraging the recalcitrant orchid seed to germinate in the laboratory, by introducing the seed to the right fungus under carefully controlled conditions. The fungus from living plants is removed and cultured in agar. Seeds taken from the same plant are introduced to the agar in a test-tube, and the

Biophoto Associates

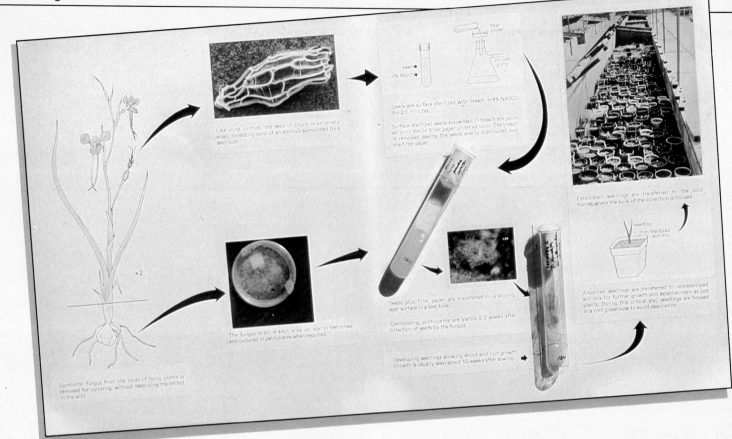

Like most orchids, the seed of *Diuris* is extremely small, consisting only of an embryo surrounded by a seed coat.

Seeds are surface sterilized with bleach (~4% NaOCl) for 2-5 minutes.

Surface sterilized seeds suspended in bleach are poured onto sterile filter paper under vacuum. The bleach is removed leaving the seeds evenly distributed over the filter paper.

Established seedlings are transferred to the cold frames where the bulk of the collection is housed.

The fungus strain is kept alive on agar in test tubes and cultured in petri-dishes when required.

Seeds plus filter paper are transferred to a sloping agar surface in a test tube.

Germinating protocorms are visible 2-3 weeks after infection of seeds by the fungus.

Advanced seedlings are transferred to non-sterilized soil mix for further growth and establishment as pot plants. During this critical step seedlings are housed in a cool glasshouse to avoid desiccation.

Symbiotic fungus from the roots of living plants is removed for culturing, without destroying the orchid in the wild.

Developing seedlings showing shoot and root growth. Growth is usually seen about 10 weeks after sowing.

Above **Orchid experts are introducing seeds to the specific fungi on which they depend under carefully controlled conditions. Epiphytic orchids – like the tropical** *Vanilla* **(right) – are easier to grow. They have been cultivated at Kew for 200 years.**

fungus grows and infects the seed, which then germinates. The temperature favours the orchid over the fungus slightly, so that the fungus does not 'take over'. This technique gives new hope to conservationists fighting to save endangered orchids, since one flower produces thousands of seeds which could be germinated and grown to maturity.

This research means that eventually a whole new range of orchids may become accessible to the public for the first time, if the technique is adopted by commercial growers and orchid enthusiasts.

Tropical epiphytic orchids have always been easier to grow and have been in continuous cultivation at Kew since the 1780s. They are grown on artificial trees – an outer layer of cork bark over a steel rod frame filled with polyurethane foam, because natural cut branches of wood decompose too rapidly in a tropical greenhouse. The *Vanilla* species can be trained to climb on wires – and they have a commercial use aside from their beauty; vanilla essence is extracted from their seed pods. While these less rare species flourish, the fight to save the ghost orchid and the lady's slipper continues. One stray step could mean the end of a species.

THE ROTTEN WORLD OF FUNGI

Were it not for a group of plants, none of which flower and many of which smell quite awful and look equally horrendous, the planet Earth would be ravaged by disease, unable to sustain life and completely uninhabitable to mankind

Not all plants can turn mere sunlight, water and air into the sugars that ultimately feed us all. Some plants are more like us: they feed on the dead, sometimes even the living.

These plants – the fungi – are parasites, scavengers or predators, gobbling up the complex molecules so cleverly constructed by green plants. The green-less plants are nevertheless clever too; fungi are an incredibly diverse group of organisms that have exploited and thrived upon every part of the globe, in every environment.

Mycologists, the scientists that specialize in fungi, have identified well over 50,000 species of these microscopic plants. It is probable, however, that some 250,000 different kinds of fungi actually exist. Most share three characteristics: they have no chlorophyll – the green pigment that traps the energy from sunlight – so they cannot manufacture their own food through photosynthesis; fungi mostly reproduce by spores, although the unicellular yeasts divide by putting out buds, and the food-procuring portion of the fungus is a series of microscopic, tubular, branched filaments, called hyphae. When the hyphae are aggregated together they form the fungal body, known as the mycelium. Hyphae grow quickly, penetrating the fungus' source of food, and digesting it by releasing enzymes that break down the substance. The fluids are then absorbed.

Above **The beginning of life for the Earth star (***Geastrum triplex***) fungi. In asexual reproduction certain hyphae grow upright, swell to form a sporangium (spore container) then burst, dispersing a cloud of microscopic spores, many of which will find a suitable place for growth.** *Left* **A photomicrograph of the fungal hyphae of powdery mildew (***Erysiphe***) on a barley leaf.** *Right* **Cerato-cystic ulmi, responsible for Dutch Elm disease.**

Biophoto Associates

Theoretically a fungal colony can grow forever and live forever. But in practice the fungus is stopped by lack of food or physical barriers to growth. Sometimes hyphal branches fuse together. Their cell walls grow thicker and coalesce to form a compact and massive structure. This tremendous surge of growth produces the reproductive structures of some fungi that we know as mushrooms and toadstools. Underground the fungi is still a mat of hyphae stretching through metres of soil.

Fungi have a great number of different lifestyles. The majority are *saprophytes*, literally 'rotten plants'. They feed on dead material like fallen trees or decaying plants and animals and extract essential organic nutrients from them. Others are parasites: they feed on living plants and animals and extract nutrients, damaging their hosts in the process. A few have become *symbiotic* with plants or animals, living with them to their mutual advantage or at least without doing serious damage.

If it wasn't for the saprophytes, we probably wouldn't be here. They, as much as the green plants, are essential to the ecosystem. For they are the great 'recyclers', breaking down the bodies of dead animals and plants and releasing the essential nutrients bound up in their tissues. They can break down fundamental structural carbohydrates with ease: the cellulose and lignin of plants, the chitin from insect exoskeletons, and the keratin from feathers and hair. Hardly any other creatures can release carbon from keratin. Only these fungi can flourish on a diet of keratin in birds' nests, the pellets of birds of prey and the quills of

Below **Toadstools, here Scarlet hood** (*Hygrocybe coccinea*), **are the prettiest fungi. They are** *saprophytes*, **feeding on organic nutrients in dead plants and animals. Their hyphae thread through a soil containing decaying humus like leaf-mould and manure.**

The familiar, umbrella-shaped part of the toadstool is actually the reproductive body or *fructification*. *Insert below* **Orange bracket fungus** (*Trametes cinnabarina*) **growing on a dead log.** *Insert far right* **The striking hallucinogenic mushroom** *Aminata muscaria*.

G. R. Roberts

Biophoto Associates

living and dead hedgehogs.

Some fungi are also *thermophilic:* they love high temperatures, anything above 50°C. Outstanding components of compost heaps; they efficiently decompose cellulose from the remains of plants, and don't mind the heat. Others are *'psychrophiles'* and can grow at temperatures below zero; one species *Cladosporium herbarum* can grow on meat stored in refrigerators at −6°C.

Unfortunately, the incredible resourcefulness of fungi often puts them in conflict with humans. They can cause decay in anything from wood to electrical insulation to the lenses of binoculars. Over a third of dwellings in the UK are estimated to be afflicted by dry rot or wet rot, caused by *Serpula lacrymans* and *Coniophora cerebella* respectively. Another fungus, *Amorphotheca resinae* can even grow in the fuel tanks of airplanes that fly on kerosene-based fuels. As long as some water is available, the fungus can use kerosene vapour (or liquid) as a source of energy. It also corrodes the sides of aluminium tanks.

Some fungi are pathogenic causing serious diseases in plants and animals — the *parasitic* fungi. A huge collection of mildews, rots, rusts, blights, and wilts attack our crop plants every year. The Irish potato famine, which led to terrible starvation in 1845-9, was caused by *Phytophthora infestans*. The fungus destroys the leaves so that potatoes do not form, or rots the tubers during storage. Even today, much agricultural loss is due to fungal infections. A pathogenic fungus can spread rapidly from one locality to another — often through the

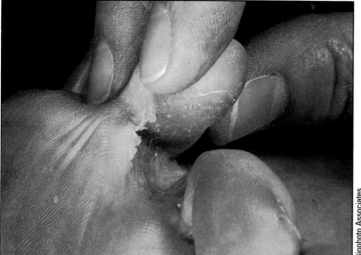

Biophoto Associates

air. Potato blight spores seem to spread in this way, sometimes covering 80 km a week!

Less dramatically, but with insidious thoroughness, Dutch elm disease has spread throughout the UK in the last decade or so. A fungus, *Ceratocystis ulmi*, spread by a beetle, was responsible. Human diseases caused by fungi include ringworm, athlete's foot and many lethal tropical diseases.

But, not all fungi are harmful. Some live in peaceful coexistence with other animals or plants. Lichens, for instance, are *symbiotic* associations of a fungus and an alga; algal cells live scattered among loosely tangled fungal mycellium. Other fungi live in the roots of higher plants, forming associations known as *mycorrhiza* or fungal root. Many of the mushrooms, such as *Amanita, Russula* and *Lactarius,* form mycorrhiza with trees. They seem to benefit the trees by increasing the uptake of nutrients. The hyphae of the fungi grow into the roots of the trees and some of the organic material broken down by the fungus probably gets transferred to the trees. The fungus does well out of the bargain too: it may extract some nutrients from the tree and get a place to a live that is secure and relatively free from competition.

Heathers

The heathers and other members of the *Ericaceae* family (cranberry, bilberry, rhododendron) can grow on poor moorland soils, largely because of the fungi associated with their roots. One member of the family seems completely dependent on the fungi: the Indian pipe, *Monotrapa uniflora,* that grows in the forests of North America. This plant is pure white or pale pink, with small scale-like leaves and a single flower. It has no chlorophyll but can live in the densely shaded forest floor thanks to the nutrients extracted from the soil by the fungal root.

Animals too have learned to love the fungi. About 100 species of ants, mostly in the Americas, actually cultivate fungal gardens. These leaf-cutting ants like *Atta,* the parasol ants, collect particular kinds of leaves, chew them up and pack them along with their own dung and dead in to a compost for the fungus to grow on. Somehow just one kind of fungus, in the genus *Agaricus,* grows, and it produces special nutrient-rich cells that are eaten by the ants.

Humans too enjoy eating many fungi. Although some, like the stinkhorn, produce a disgusting odour, like decaying meat, in order to attract pollinating carrion flies, others are very appealing to the human palate. Truffles, for instance, produce fruiting bodies beneath the ground. So attractive is their odour and flavour that the French train dogs or pigs to scent them out so they can be harvested and consumed by fungal gourmets. Fungi are used to ferment soy-

Far left Athlete's foot is caused by a fungal parasite known as *Epidermophyton*. *Left* The musty smell of *Serpula lacrymans* is unmistakable to the feckless householder as it consumes his timbers with dry rot. Lichens are strange plants that form symbiotic relationships with green algae. *Right Xanthoria parietina*, an orange lichen, is one of the most common and is often found growing on old walls and roofs everywhere.

Heather Angel

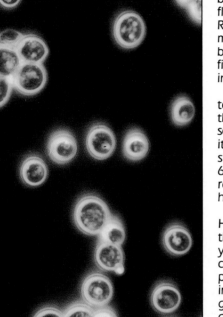

Heather Angel

beans to produce soysauce and to flavour and ripen cheeses like Roquefort and Stilton. Cultivated mushrooms, *Agariculs bisporus*, have been a thriving industry since the French first grew them in quarried caves near Paris in the 1850s.

Mushrooms are now being seen as a potentially important source of protein. While the protein content of mushrooms is low, several crops can be grown every year so it is possible to achieve high yields. For instance, cereals give annual yields of up to 6000 kg of protein per hectare but mushrooms could give up to two million kg per hectare.

Some food manufacturers, like Rank Hovis McDougall, are more interested at this stage in using microfungi, particularly yeasts, as a source of protein. This 'single-cell' protein will probably become an important food for livestock, if not for humans, in the next few decades. They could be grown in waste products from various industries, such as wood pulp sulphite liquors from the paper making industry, whey from milk processing or molasses from sugar refining. Yeast can even make protein from crude oil and natural gas.

Fungi are also, of course, the source of many useful and unusual drugs. Moulds like *Penicillium* produce a range of antibiotics: penicillin, streptomycin, aureomycin and terramycin. And, many mushrooms contain psycho-active drugs that have formed the basis of religious rituals. Two well known hallucinogenic mushrooms are *Amanita muscaria* and *Psilocybe mexicana. Amanita* is the archetypal mushroom, a bright red cap with white dots and is widespread in more northerly regions of both the old and the new world. The Lapplanders seem to have used the mushroom in rites designed to communicate with the spirits. *Psilocybe* was used by Amazonian tribes and the ancient Aztecs. Both contain chemicals which may be useful in some clinical applications or in research on how the brain works.

Heather Angel

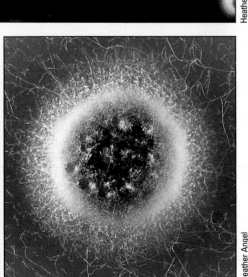

Heather Angel

The ability of yeast (*centre*) to break down sugar into carbon dioxide and ethyl alcohol makes it particularly valuable to bakers, brewers and distillers. *Bottom far left* The tawny grisette (*Amanita fulva*), one of the mushrooms that lives on trees to the benefit of its host, increasing its nutrient uptake. *Bottom left* The *Penicillium notatum* mould from which the antibiotic penicillin is produced. *Above* The egoted head of purple moor grass, infected by *Claviceps pupurea*.

THE TARDIGRADE: NATURE'S TOUGHEST BUG

Boil it, freeze it, the tardigrade still gets up to walk away. And it can switch itself off for years at a time

Science Photo Library

The tiny tardigrade (no more than a pin-head in size) has proved to be one of nature's toughest survivors. Laboratory experimenters have immersed it in liquid helium down to a savage −272°C. They have left it at −192°C for 20 months, and cooked it for a week at 92°C in ether, alcohol and other noxious chemicals. Restored to normal temperature and given water, the tardigrade strolls away. Some specimens were brought briefly back to life after 120 years in a dry and dusty museum.

Plainly the tardigrade has some talent humans lack. And scientists are intrigued.

Tardigrades dwell in mud, damp seashore sand, or on the water film surrounding the leaves of mosses, liverworts and lichens. Some varieties are entirely aquatic. Zoologically they fall somewhere between worms and insects – and can get about by wriggling, or on four pairs of stubby legs. But if success is measured by numbers, they are in the top league. There are tardigrades worldwide except in the tropics and Antarctica. And a single gram of dried moss has been known to yield 22,000 of them.

Feeding is straigh-forward. Using a piercing apparatus that forms part of its mouth, the tardigrade injects its way into the centre of plant cells and extracts the contents. Growing is not so easy. Not only does the tardigrade have to moult its outer covering before it can increase in size – it also has to grow half a new gut each time. This is because the 'skin' tucks inside the mouth to form the front half of the digestive tract. So for 12 times or more in its lifespan, the tardigrade endures a compulsory fast.

Sex is a complicated business too. No-one has ever seen two tardigrades in the act of copulating, but there is no doubt that in most of the 400 known species the eggs are fertilized while still in the female's body. Making use of the compulsory moult, a female often lays her eggs as she sheds her skin, providing eggs and newly hatched offspring with a ready-made protective wrapper. The new tardigrade measures a minute 50μ.

But how does this soft-bodied creature have the unqiue ability to switch itself off and on when times get hard – enabling it to spread a normal lifespan of 18 months over some 60 years?

It seems to have developed this talent to enable it to cope with frequent occasions when the mud or sand dries out. The creature tucks itself into a barrel shape, keeping only 15 per cent of its body water intact – carefully distributed in a thin film around each cell. In addition, the little creature turns down its control systems to the lowest possible setting, and waits for better times.

With active research continuing on ways to freeze larger organisms – and bring them back to life – the tardigrade may provide some of the answers.

Among nature's best hitch-hikers, tardigrades – in egg or dehydrated form – have travelled the world in wind currents, tucked inside bird feathers, or trouser turn ups. Their travels have taken them to the icy conditions of Northern Canada and the Baltic, while others live on algae around the hot sulphur springs of Japan – above the boiling point of water. In the vast variety of life, this armoured arthropod will probably outlast us all.

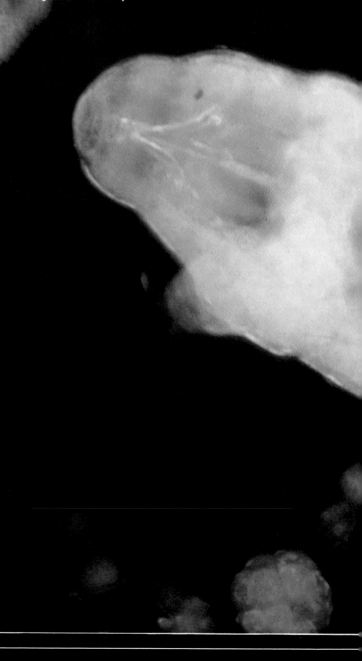

The tardigrade can survive boiling and freezing. This tiny creature which has a brain, two eye spots, a digestive tract, but no heart or lungs, shrinks as dry conditions make its tissue water evaporate – and its oxygen consumption virtually stops. Dried out specimens – 'tuns' – are blown about by the wind, reviving when they land on wet moss or any suitable, damp environment.

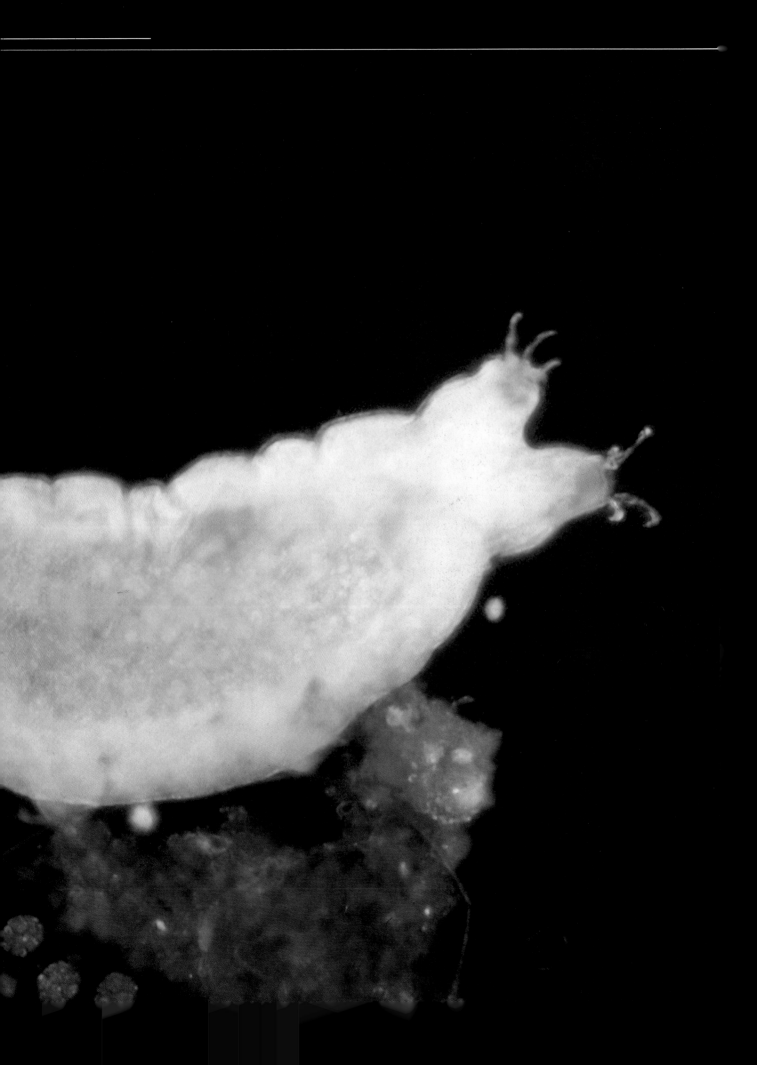

THINGS THAT GO CRUNCH IN THE NIGHT

Creeping and crawling scuttling about — the uninvited guests arrive to raid the larder . .

Bruce Coleman Ltd./Jan Taylor.

Prema Photos/K. G. Preston-Mafham

Who'd give a home to a cockroach? Ask anywhere and it's sure you'd come up with very few takers, for roaches are insects universally despised and detested by people the world over for their filthy habits.

At nightfall, they sneak out of the woodwork and scavenge on the bowls of pet-food and other remains we have conveniently left for them. In return, the roaches may leave a trail of dirt laden with potentially death-dealing micro-organisms such as those responsible for polio, typhoid, salmonella, hepatitis or even plague.

However, these undesirable qualities are the province of a few species only. Of the 3500 or so known cockroach species, only about a dozen are disease carriers. The rest live clean, peaceful lives in a range of habitats, from tropical forests to the waters of freshwater lakes and ponds.

Love them or loathe them, roaches are in fact worthy of a deal of admiration for their remarkable powers of survival. They are the only insects to have remained virtually unchanged since the Carboniferous Era, some 300 million years ago, when tree-fern forests carpeted an Earth ruled by dinosaurs. They have hitch-hiked all over the world and provide an amazing example of animal efficiency and engineering.

Though they have even been found 800 metres down a Welsh coalmine, cockroaches originated in the tropics and subtropics, and most still prefer to live in warm, damp conditions – like those found in the modern centrally-heated, draught-excluded, high-condensation house. Most cockroaches are black or brown, and all are of the same basic design. The leathery, shiny, six-legged body bears a downward-pointing head on which are two extremely long antennae. The male roach has two pairs of wings, with the larger, hind, pair folded in unique fashion against the sides of the body. Here they usually remain, for roaches rarely fly. The female is typically flightless, with tiny, vestigial wings or none at all.

Hit list

Top three on the human 'hit-list' of cosmopolitan cockroaches are representatives of three large cockroach genera. These are the German cockroach *Blatella germanica,* the American roach *Periplaneta americana,* and the oriental or common European cockroach *Blatta orientalis.* Despite its name, the German cockroach originated in Asia. Mid to pale brown and about one centimetre long, its favourite dining places are bakeries, hotels, bathrooms and kitchens. Known as the Croton bug in the US because of its high numbers round New York City's Croton Aqueduct, it is the most widespread of all the pest species of roach.

The American cockroach is the largest of this infamous trio. Originally from the tropics and subtropics of the continent whose name it bears, it is a dark reddish-brown colour and up to five centimetres long. Supermarkets, restaurants and bakeries are its usual haunts, and it is often found in homes. The oval, shiny black oriental roach measures about three centimetres in length and first came from Asia. Far from fussy in its habits, it will go wherever people go and feed on anything on offer.

With the might of human ingenuity massed against them, it would be reasonable to expect that cockroaches would be hard pressed to survive. In fact they are efficient enough to outwit us and instead play on our fallibility in letting standards of hygiene slip.

Bizarre diet

Cockroaches feed by scavenging. Glue, bones, wallpaper, photographic film, ink, emery paper, telephone cables and even the dead bodies of their own kind have been recorded as cockroach food, apart from the sorts of items you would expect, such as ingredients intended for or left over from human or animal consumption.

The cockroach eats by chewing food with its paired jaws, or *mandibles,* but before it does this it softens the food with saliva and takes an exploratory taste, using the fleshy palps found on a second pair of mouthparts, the *maxillae.* Sensitive to sweet, salt and acid flavours, these palps are studded with porous pegs which are the actual taste receptors. They also help alert the roach to the presence of any poisonous substances, which can then be avoided. In the longer term, cockroach

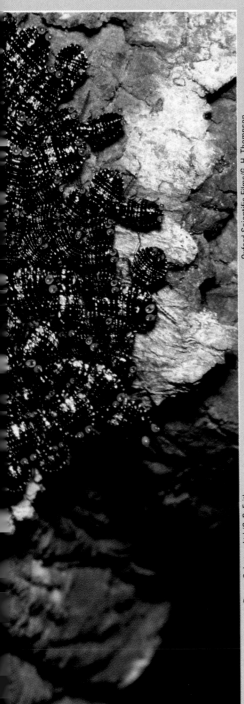

Oxford Scientific Films/G. H. Thompson

Bruce Coleman Ltd./C. B. Frith

Cockroaches are found all over the world, and they can be very good climbers (*left top*). *Left* **Sometimes cockroaches congregate in large groups like these nymphs.** *Top* **An American roach, one of the 'terrible trio' of roach species that carry diseases such as polio, typhoid and hepatitis.** *Above* **A nymph and its old skin after emerging.**

MADISON COUNTY
CANTON PUBLIC LIBRARY SYSTEM
CANTON, MISS. 39046

evolution has made the insects even more immune through the development of genetic resistance to DDT and other insecticides.

Even if food supplies break down altogether, the cockroach can survive. The American roach, for example, can live for as long as 12 weeks without any kind of food, simply by drawing on its internal food stores. And it can even survive for three weeks without water – a remarkable feat for any animal – protected by the external skeleton within which its soft, water-rich

Left Among the roach's most important sensory organs are the antennae. These long whip-like structures are tubular and have about 180 ring-like segments. The antennae taper and the segments furthest from the head are very thin and long. The antennae have tiny hairs that detect moisture and pressure; they also act as a temperature receptor telling the animal whether the surroundings are favourable or not. Roaches tend to prefer warm conditions. *Right* The roach's mouthparts are adapted for chewing food. It has paired jaws, mandibles to crush the food and maxillae that bear fleshy palps to soften and 'test' the food. The palps are sensitive to sweet, salty and acid foods and are able to distinguish between palatable (to a roach) and unpalatable substances.

body parts are housed. This *exoskeleton* is so heavily impregnated with oils and waxes that it prevents evaporation from within.

Apart from the taste hairs on the maxillae, a battery of other sensory organs help the cockroach to survive. The *cerci*, a pair of protrusions from the rear of the abdomen, bear sensory hairs which can detect vibrations in the air, such as those created by the approach of a human foot. Sensitive to vibrations ranging between 100 and 3000 hertz, each cercal organ consists of several hundred fine hairs, and it is possible that these organs may form a primitive kind of hearing mechanism.

Sprint start

Alerted to danger by messages received via the cerci, a roach will make a dash for it. With reaction times of around 54 thousandths of a second, the American roach has a racing start that any athlete would envy.

The long whip-like *antennae* are a vital part of the cockroach's sensory input. Each

Antenna

Taste hairs

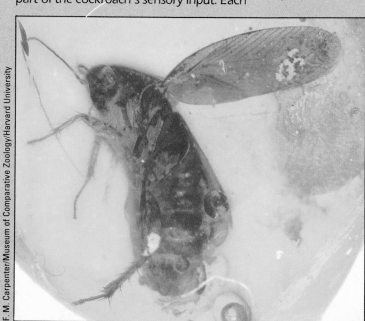

F. M. Carpenter/Museum of Comparative Zoology/Harvard University

Left Cockroaches have remained unchanged for many millions of years. This roach is preserved in amber and is 35 million years old. Amazingly these prehistoric roaches are very similar to modern day creatures that plague Man (*above*). One of the reasons the roach is so successful is its ability to diversify. It will eat almost anything, yet it is smart enough to avoid most poisons. In any case it is now resistant to a bewildering array of pesticides.

Body wall

The body wall of the cockroach is a vital part of its defence mechanism. *Above* The body is protected by an exoskeleton that is impregnated with oils and waxes. It serves two functions; it prevents the body fluids drying out and stops poisons getting in. *Below* Cerci which stick out from the rear of the animal have sensory hairs that detect vibration so the roach can flee its enemies.

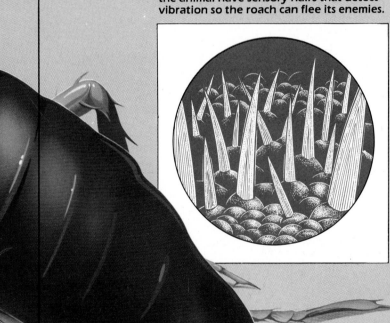

Sensory hairs

antenna is a tube made up of between 120 and 180 ring-shaped segments, which get thinner and longer the farther they are from the roach's head. As well as having hairs that detect pressure and moisture, the antennae assist the roach in finding the best possible living conditions by monitoring air temperature. The thickest of the antennal segments bear cold receptors, each composed of a hair-like sensillum surrounded at its base by a raised circular wall. At constant air temperatures, the cold receptors are continuously active, reaching a maximum frequency of discharge of electrical impulses at about 28°C. When the air temperature drops suddenly, the discharge rate speeds to around 300 per second, warning the roach that its surroundings are far from favourable. When the air temperature rises rapidly, the discharge rate falls to almost zero.

Other, similar, receptors on the roach's legs sense ground temperature while vibration sensors at the leg joints tell the cockroach when a predator is approaching. The eyes, among the least effective in this array of information-gatherers, inform the roach about the amount of light and create shadowy images of its surroundings.

Features which help cockroaches to survive include a highly efficient method of reproduction. Male cockroaches, probably attracted to the females' chemicals called *pheromones,* prefer to mate with virginal females who, it seems, send out the most potent sexual odours. At mating, the male approaches the female with wings fluttering, then deposits a bag of sperm – the *spermathaca* – within her. In most cockroaches, the eggs are laid in cases, called *ootheca,* with up to 30 eggs in each case. Covered with a protective secretion, the cases are buried in dirt or rotting rubbish.

The female may carry the egg case around with her until the eggs are just about to hatch, when the embryo roaches

Below **Roaches are adept at avoiding capture. This one is pretending to be a seed pod.**

Tony Lodge

Prema Photos/K. G. Preston-Mafham

Oxford Scientific Films/Dr. J. A. L. Cooke

Oxford Scientific Films/G. I. Bernard

display remarkable co-operation in getting themselves out. One or two of the embryo roaches within the ootheca become very active. They stimulate the other embryos, until the movements of all the embryos become synchronized. It is only then that the embryos can muster the energy to break open the egg case and escape.

Young cockroaches do not undergo a complete *metamorphosis* (change from the larval to the adult form) during their development. Like other insects of the group *Exopterygota*, such as grasshoppers, stick insects and earwigs, cockroaches develop in a series of stages, or moults, with each stage a little more like the adult than the last. Within a period that ranges from 95 to 225 days after hatching, the nymph is mature enough to reproduce itself.

The great majority of cockroaches are neither household dwellers nor pests. The North American roach *Cryptocercus punctatus,* for instance, lives in woods, where it feeds on decaying bark and branches. To aid digestion, the roach harbours in its gut protozoa which make the necessary enzymes. In return for this favour, the protozoa are supplied with an unfailing food supply.

Panesthesia, an Australian cockroach, does not live the solitary existence common to most cockroaches. Instead it forms family groups made up of an adult male, an adult female and some 10-20 offspring. The blind, wingless cockroach *Nocticola* lives in caves and relies on the ants with which it dwells to help supply it with food.

Survival mechanisms of a different kind operate in the Philippine roaches of the genus *Prosoplecta*. These cockroaches protect themselves from predators by mimicking inedible ladybirds and leaf beetles. Instead of the normal, dullish cockroach colours, these species are brightly coloured and decorated with a pattern of spots, blotches or stripes.

If some major tragedy befalls humanity, cockroaches are likely to live on. Since they are able to tolerate many times more radiation than we can, they might even survive a nuclear holocaust!

Left top **The American roach is a menace. Even the cleanest homes may harbour them.** *Left centre* **Roaches can be wingless and live amongst the litter on forest floors.** *Below* **Camouflage can be something of an art.**

POCKETS OF SURVIVAL

Isolated for millions of years in South America and Australasia, marsupials evolved into animals closely resembling deer, dogs, cats, mice and even moles

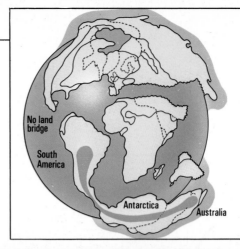

Left Marsupials probably evolved about 100 million years ago somewhere in South America, Antarctica or Australia. These land masses were at that time joined, so that the marsupials were able to disperse through all three continents.

No land bridge

South America

Antarctica

Australia

For anyone studying the evolution of mammals, Australia is like another planet, full of strange yet also very familiar creatures. The island continent became isolated by sea from the rest of the world about 45 million years ago. Not until about 50 thousand years ago, when the first Aborigines arrived from South-east Asia, was that isolation broken. For this reason, the marsupials that live there today are the result of a large-scale natural 'experiment' in evolution.

Marsupials are mammals whose young leave the uterus at a very early stage in their development. They are so immature that they must complete the rest of their development in their mother's pouch. Kangaroos are the most familiar marsupials. There are nearly 250 species – 6 per cent of all mammal species on Earth today.

All the other mammals (except for the primitive egg-laying *monotremes*) – including humans – are classified in a group called placentals. Their young spend the whole period of embryonic development in the uterus, where they are attached to the maternal tissues by a highly organized *placenta*, from which they obtain nourishment until birth.

At birth, a red kangaroo baby, or 'joey', is a mere 25 mm or so long and weighs only 1/30,000 of its mother's weight – compare that with a human newborn, which averages about one-eighteenth of its mother's weight. The baby kangaroo must crawl unaided from the mother's cloaca across her furry belly to one of the teats in the pouch. Its mother gives it no help on this difficult journey, and makes no attempt to rescue it if it drops off, but the baby's large forelimbs, well armed with claws, help it in its struggle. The journey takes about 3 minutes.

The pouch has to be tough and elastic, since it has to support a considerable weight – by the time it is ready to leave the pouch, a joey may weigh as much as 9 kg. A pair of pelvic girdle bones, the *epipubic bones*, strengthen the pouch. Not all marsupials have a forward-facing pouch like the kangaroos: in many species, such as koalas, wombats and bandicoots, its opening faces backwards. Many of the small, mouselike marsupials do not have a proper pouch, being equipped merely with a pair of fleshy flaps enclosing the nipple area, and the young have to hang on for dear life.

Australia provides the most spectacular

Tom & Pam Gardner/Frank W. Lane Agency

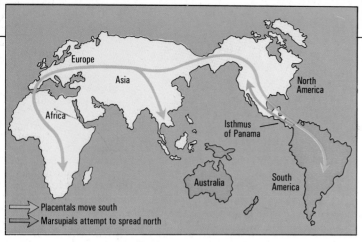

Above The joining of North and South America by the Panama Isthmus about 2 million years ago enabled the placentals to invade South America – at the expense of the marsupials.

Marsupials also moved north, but only one, the Virginia opossum, survives there (*right*, young in pouch). By contrast, they could thrive in Australia in isolation. *Below* Marsupial evolution.

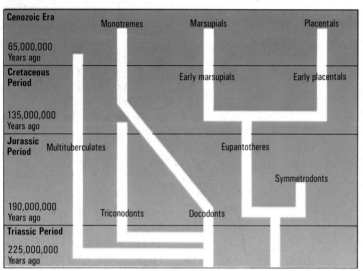

Cenozoic Era	Monotremes	Marsupials	Placentals
65,000,000 Years ago			
Cretaceous Period		Early marsupials	Early placentals
135,000,000 Years ago			
Jurassic Period	Multituberculates	Eupantotheres	
			Symmetrodonts
190,000,000 Years ago	Triconodonts	Docodonts	
Triassic Period			
225,000,000 Years ago			

living examples of what biologists call *convergent evolution*. A basic law of evolutionary theory is that life will evolve to fill all available habitats, and the marsupials have done just this in Australasia (Australia, New Zealand, New Guinea and the small adjacent islands). Although there are only six families of Australasian marsupials, they contain the counterparts of dogs and cats, deer and cattle, mice and moles, and even lemurs and flying squirrels. Yet all have evolved from ancestors basically different from the ancestors of the placentals of Europe, North America, Africa and Asia.

The marsupials were an isolated offshoot of the main mammalian tree. Primitive mammals had lived for millions of years virtually under the feet of the dinosaurs: when the giant reptiles finally died out, about 65 million years ago, the mammals took their place. Except in isolated Australia, and in South America, too, which was also cut off by sea until 3-4 million years ago, the placental mammals were more successful than the marsupials. The fossil evidence suggests that marsupials were once abundant in Europe and North America, but were wiped out there because of the competition from their placental rivals.

The oldest known marsupial fossils are

about 80 million years old. They come from late Cretaceous rocks in North and South America: the original animals probably resembled a sort of primitive opossum.

The first marsupials reached Australia about 80 million years ago. They probably came from South America via Antarctica, the three continents then being connected. Antarctica was much warmer – scientists know this from fossils discovered there – and Australia was further south.

Fortunately for the marsupials, placental mammals never reached Australia, except for bats, which were able to fly in, and a series of invasions by rats and mice, which began about 20 million years ago. Marsupials were the only predators of marsupials until the Aborigines and their dingoes arrived.

The picture was rather different in South America, however. Some placentals did manage to reach that continent before it became isolated by sea about 60 million years ago, but they evolved alongside the marsupials without ousting them. In fact, most of the newly evolving South American predators were marsupials. They preyed on the placental herbivores which, in isolation, had evolved into animals that resembled the Old World horses, rhinos and camels.

Above A Bennett's wallaby quenches its thirst. As with other marsupials, they have been persecuted in many parts of Australia by Man and introduced dogs and foxes. This species has been introduced to Germany, the Channel Isles and Derbyshire, England.

Their marsupial predators looked remarkably like Old World placental carnivores. There was a sabre-toothed marsupial 'tiger', *Thylacosmilus*, which looked very like the placental sabre-toothed tiger, *Smilodon*, which evolved independently in North America. There were also panther-like marsupials, *Borhyaenas*, and marsupial wolves, *Prothylocymus*.

Marsupials flourished in South America until 3-4 million years ago, when a land bridge – the Isthmus of Panama – formed, linking the continent to North America. Volcanic islands created earlier had enabled several kinds of mammals to 'island hop' from North to South America, but with the formation of the Panama Isthmus, larger numbers were able to move freely in both directions.

For the marsupials it was a trip north to extinction. The Virginia opossum is the sole survivor in North America today. By contrast, the placental mammals prospered in South America – at the expense of the mar-

L. N. Robinson/Frank W. Lane Agency

Jen & Des Bartlett/Survival Anglia Ltd.

Above **Grey kangaroos – also known as great greys or forester kangaroos – are important grazers of the Australian plains, equivalent to the deer and antelopes elsewhere. Males may weigh as much as 100 kg. A baby kangaroo** (*inset*) **is tiny and relatively undeveloped.**

supials. About sixty species of two marsupial families, mostly tree-dwelling types and opossums, survive there today, but the large South American marsupials are extinct.

The really large marsupials have also vanished from Australia. Giant species evolved there during the Pleistocene period, about a million years ago, when the northern continents were in the grip of ice ages, and they survived until recent times. There was a giant relative of the wombat, a vegetarian the size of a hippopotamus, called *Diprotodon*; a carnivorous possum 'lion', *Thylacoleo*; a koala as large as a real bear; and a giant kangaroo, *Sthenurus*.

Few of the marsupial fossils found in Australia are more than a million years old, but the search for fossils there is a relatively recent activity compared to its long history in Europe. Yet the living marsupials – as well as their long-dead ancestors – can tell us so much about the story of evolution.

The kangaroos and wallabies are the counterparts of deer and cattle in the rest of the world. They fill the same grazing role, and have evolved similar stomachs and methods of digestion to cope with their tough diet of grass and other plants. The group *Macropodidae* to which they belong contains more than sixty species – all herbivores. The red kangaroo, which lives in the inland plains and open bush, is perhaps the most abundant species.

The koala may not be as common, but it is certainly the most popular marsupial, made famous the world over by Qantas, the Australian airline, and the soft-toy industry. Though often called the koala bear, it is not at all related to the placental bears: being placentals ourselves, we are more closely related to bears than is the koala.

In a land full of eucalyptus trees – more than 250 different species grow in Australia – the koala has evolved to feed exclusively on their leaves. The oils which they contain would poison other mammals. The only side-effect for the koala is that it smells like a cough lozenge. Somehow, it has acquired bacteria in its gut which are able to digest the tough leaves. Strangely for a tree-dweller, the koala has lost the tail possessed by its ancestors, but it has evolved very powerful limbs and claws like grappling hooks.

Unlike the koala, which looks like a bear but follows a very different lifestyle, the Tasmanian devil looks like a hyaena and behaves like one. The thylacine, or Tasmanian wolf, was the counterpart of a wolf, a fierce predator of kangaroos, wallabies and birds. Wrongfully blamed for killing large numbers of sheep, it was exterminated by European settlers. The Tasmanian devil still survives, a marsupial 'hyaena' evolved to scavenge after a 'wolf' which no longer exists.

The marsupial 'cats' belong to the same family, the *Dasyuridae*, as the Tasmanian devil and the thylacine, and do indeed look

Edward Ashpole

Natural Science Photos

Alan Root/Survival Anglia Ltd.

Right **Once widespread in Australia but now found only in Tasmania, the Tasmanian devil hunts for small mammals, birds and lizards in the wilder parts of the island.** *Below* **A relative of the Tasmanian devil, the tiger cat is the largest of the Australian 'native cats' or dasyures. Persecuted by farmers and other settlers, they became even rarer after a mystery epidemic hit them in the early 1900s. The tiger cat, which spends much of its time in the trees, has a similar diet to the Tasmanian devil's.** *Below right* **The common, or Virginia, opossum ranges from Argentina to as far north as southern Canada.**

Top **One of the most attractive of all marsupials is the numbat, or banded anteater. About the size of a large cat, it inhabits scrub woodland in South Australia, where it feeds by day on termites.** *Above* **Kangaroos that climb: tree kangaroos of New Guinea and Queensland have rough pads and sharp claws on their feet to help keep their grip.**

very cat-like, except for their sharp noses. They prey on smaller animals and birds, although some of the smaller species eat lizards and insects, too.

The highly specialized numbat – another dasyurid – has evolved to cope with a diet of termites. Its carnivorous ancestors must have preferred a more varied diet, because the numbat has more teeth (50-52) than any other mammal. Despite their impressive number, they are now degenerate – hardly surprising, considering their mushy diet.

The possums – not to be confused with the American opossums – provide a wonderful example of convergent evolution. They have evolved to exploit the forests of Australia and New Guinea and, in consequence, some resemble the lemurs of Madagascar, which are primates like monkeys, apes and humans. It is tempting to speculate on what would have happened had Australia remained in isolation for another 50 million years. Would one of the ancestral possums have managed to evolve into a marsupial 'human'?

Some of the possums that did survive evolved in very different directions. They include the possum gliders, the counterparts of the placental flying squirrels. There is also the honey possum, one of the most extreme 'models' which millions of years of evolution has produced from the basic stock. The honey possum, the size of a mouse, feeds on nectar with its long tongue and pollinates the flowers it visits in the process.

Although the possum gliders are able to float down from the treetops, no truly flying marsupial has evolved because of the competition from the many bats which were able to reach Australia. Also there are no marsupial whales or dolphins.

There are marsupial 'mice', however, which resemble the 'real thing' so closely that it is hard to believe that we are more closely related to the latter than are these little marsupials. Yet they are really less like mice than their appearance suggests. While placental mice are mainly vegetarians, marsupial mice are ferocious predators of insects and other small animals.

The prize for evolutionary convergence, however, must go to the marsupial mole. The original marsupial stock has in this case undergone a total transformation. The marsupial mole has similar modifications for a subterranean life to the placental mole: huge front claws, a smooth cylindrical body, vestigial eyes and no external ear-flaps.

Such remarkable convergence came about through the normal process of evolution. The marsupials – and their placental counterparts – spread originally into all available habitats, where they were then subjected to natural selection. The best adapted individuals were the most likely to survive and produce more offspring. Thus, after millions of years, similar niches are occupied by animals that look surprisingly alike, even though they have evolved continents apart.

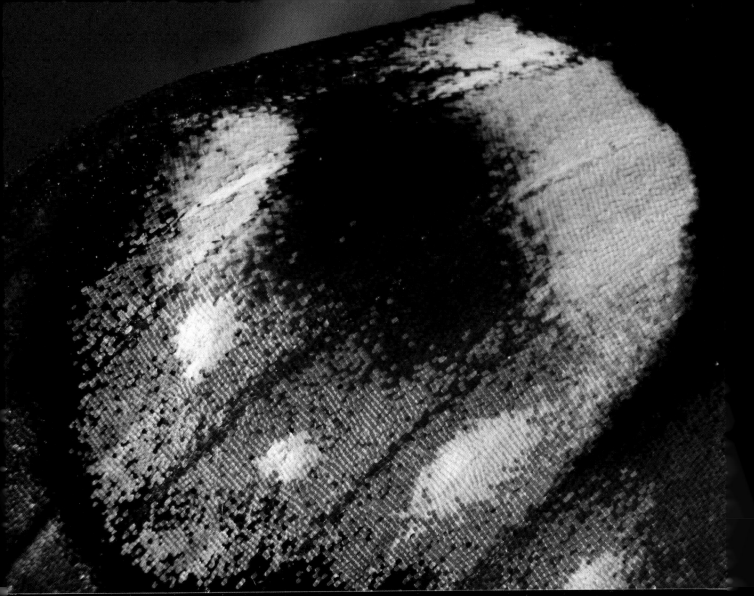

EYE SPY

In the flash of an eye a life is saved, deceiving the enemy to live another day

Butterflies are usually so brightly coloured they seem to be offering themselves up as a delicious snack to any passing bird or animal. How do such bright and relatively slow-moving animals protect themselves? One way is to frighten away the predator, and butterflies have developed a very good method of shocking an approaching animal into sudden retreat. Eyes are the answer. Large intimidating 'false eyes' on the wings are extremely good at saving butterflies from becoming instant dinners.

The wings of butterflies and moths (*Lepidoptera*) are covered with millions of small, coloured scales arranged in precise patterns. The scales actually overlap like the tiles on a roof, and are attached in rows by means of a pointed end which penetrates the wing surface like a dart. Each scale is either pigmented by chemicals, or has structural properties which break up the light as it strikes the scale, producing iridescent colours

Above **'Defenceless' butterflies and moths attract the attention of birds and animals, but with a flash of the wings the insect can frighten the predator, giving itself time to escape. The eye-spots on this Peacock butterfly can trick an animal into thinking it has come up against a bigger animal; if not, only its wings are**

wing scales can only be seen with the aid of a scanning electron microscope. Each scale is hooked onto the wing in ordered rows. When the scales are analyzed in a laboratory it has been found that the different colours are produced by a variety of different chemicals, like, for example, melanin.

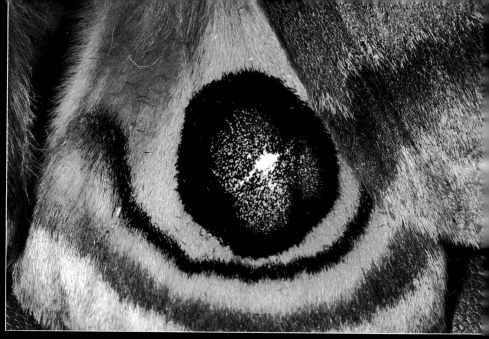

Laboratory analysis of pigmented scales shows that different colours are produced by a variety of chemicals. For example, black and brown, commonly present in eye-spots, are produced from melanin and the white and yellow colours of the Cabbage White group are formed from leucopterin and xanthopterin, derivatives of uric acid (an excretory product of Lepidoptera). Recent research suggests that the pigments are synthesized in the scales, with the enzymes for melanin production present in the scale cuticles. The bright red and orange pigments found in butterflies like the Peacock probably originate in the food eaten by the caterpillar, and are assimilated by the adult during pupation. Colours aren't always what they seem to be. 'Green' colouration can be produced by the juxtaposition of black and yellow scales.

Coloured scales are often arranged to produce eye-spots which draw attention to the insect. This might seem, at first, to be a strange way for the creature to defend itself, especially in species which are camouflaged as a means of protection.

Eye-spots can be on both fore and hind wings. Often they are not visible when the insect is resting with its wings closed or overlapping. But if the insect is disturbed by vibration or touch, it opens its wings suddenly, flashing the large, bright eye-spots at the predator. Two species which use eye-marks in this way are the Peacock butterfly and the Bull's Eye Moth. Birds and small mammals are alarmed and often frightened away by this display. In one experiment carried out with a Jay and a Peacock butterfly, the behaviour was tested. The two creatures were put in the same cage and when approached the butterfly flashed its 'eyes' and the startled Jay leapt away in fright and lost his meal. The Peacock butterfly hibernates in its adult stage during the winter and even when hibernating, it flashes its eye-spots if disturbed.

Genetic studies

Genetic studies have recently shown that the eye-spot markings in the Bull's Eye Moth are genetically protected from

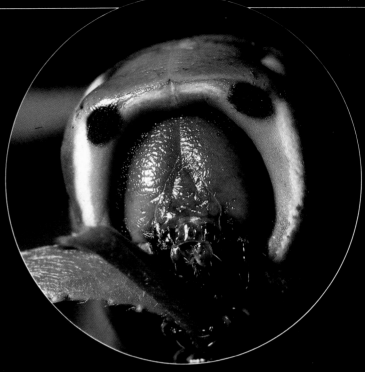

Left **For use as a 'flash' warning to predators, the Bull's Eye Moth has two enormous eye-spots on the edge of each hind wing. When at rest, only the brown forewings can be seen. If disturbed, the wings open to reveal the eye-spots, giving the insect time to make good its escape.** _Top left_ **Minute coloured scales are arranged in patterns producing a realistic 'eye'. The scales are like tiny roof tiles, attached in overlapping rows. The vivid colours can be a result of pigments made in the scales, the shape of the scale, or even what the caterpillar ate.**

Top left **Grayling butterflies will attract attention away from the head by exposing eye-spots at the top of the forewings.** _Left_ **Emperor Moths display a fine set of eye-spots on all the wings.** _Top_ **Butterflies and moths go through many stages of development all of which have their different dangers. Caterpillars are particularly vulnerable, so they exploit eye-spots. The Puss Moth caterpillar can withdraw its head leaving a false head and eye markings to scare away predators. If this doesn't work, it can squirt formic acid at the attacker.**

and strong than those with complete markings. There are many records of eye-spots being used in a different way. In some species such as the Meadow Brown, the Grayling and the Small Heath, the eye-spots are visible when the insect is resting with its wings closed above its body. These eye-spots act as a focus of attention to predators, and birds and reptiles have been observed biting at these markings. In many cases large chunks of the wing are removed, but the insect can flutter away, its body intact, still perfectly capable of breeding. Many Hairstreak butterflies take this system a stage further. As well as having bright spots of colour on the hind part of their folded wings, they also have 'tails' on their wing ends closely resembling antennae, which the insect can quiver producing a remarkable 'decoy head'. Predatory birds will peck at this exaggerated head, and the real head escapes damage.

When the adult is freshly emerged from its pupa, its wings are soft and limp. It cannot fly for some time, so is very vulnerable to attack. The Emperor Moth is a day-flying European species with

large eye-spots which are visible on the limp folds of the drying wings, presenting a frightening appearance to a predator while the moth is such an easy prey.

The life cycle of butterflies and moths consists of four stages, egg, caterpillar, chrysalis and adult. All these stages are open to attack from predators. Eggs and chrysalids are often coloured to merge in with surrounding vegetation. Caterpillars may be covered with spines and bushy hairs to make them less tasty or have bright colours to warn attackers that they are not fit to eat.

And some caterpillars such as that of the Puss Moth have eye-spots. The caterpillar can withdraw its real head into the abdomen, making the two eye marks swell, producing a frightening 'false head'. In case the eyes are not frightening enough, it also squirts formic acid at an attacker.

It seems these delicate creatures can be formidable adversaries.

ADAPTING TO THE ENVIRONMENT

Plants and animals are as much at the mercy of the elements
as they are vulnerable to other predators. How some cope
with their particular environment is fascinating . . .

THE BIG SLEEP

Internal 'clocks' that tell ground squirrels when to wake; birds that remain lifeless for months; fish that sleep buried in mud for years: these are some of the strange discoveries biologists have made investigating hibernation

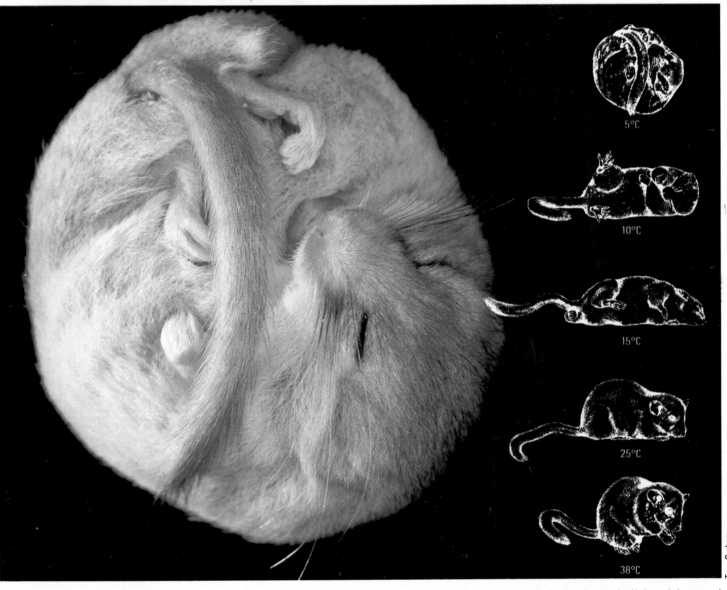

5°C

10°C

15°C

25°C

38°C

Tony Graham

The legendary ability of the dormouse of sleeping soundly, immortalized in Lewis Carroll's *Alice in Wonderland*, makes our nightly slumbers seem like wakefulness by comparison. With the approach of winter, this appealing little animal turns down its internal thermostat, lowers its heartbeat to tick-over level, slows down its breathing and switches off its brain. Curled up in a deep burrow, safe from frost, it goes into the deep, deep sleep of hibernation.

Hibernation is just one of the methods animals of temperate climates have evolved to overcome the problems posed by a food supply that is abundant only in the warmer seasons of the year. To such animals, the warmth of summer offers a life of ease and

plenty, a feast followed very soon by the lean time of winter.

Instead of hibernating, some animals, including most birds, migrate to less hostile climates for the winter. Others, such as the wolf, grow a thicker coat of fur as insulation against the cold and are able to find enough food to survive. Some, such as squirrels, hoard stores of food to help see them through winter. Yet others, such as European brown bears or North American black bears and racoons, choose sleep as their escape route from harsh conditions. Though they sleep deeply, their sleep is not the same as hibernation. If their body temperature falls below about 15°C, they die. True hibernators can survive even if their

Above left **Curled into a ball, head, legs and tail tucked snugly into its body for warmth, a European Hazel Dormouse spends winter in the deep sleep of hibernation in its nest of twigs, moss and grass. Drawings** (*above*) **show stages in a dormouse's awakening from hibernation. Temperatures shown are approximate body temperatures. Dormice hibernate for about six months.**

body temperature plunges to that of the surrounding winter air, as low as 2°C. How can they do this?

Mammals, including ourselves, are warmblooded, with a built-in thermostat that regulates body temperature. Indeed, were it not for this ability to maintain our temperature at a constant level, we would

suffer from the lethargy that affects cold-blooded animals, such as reptiles and amphibians, in both hot and cold conditions. Nevertheless, mammals pay a price for their sophisticated temperature-regulating systems. Temperature regulation involves considerable use of energy, and thus a high food intake to provide this energy.

Switching thermostats

During hibernation, small mammals, such as dormice, are able to switch their thermostats from the normal body temperature of about 40°C to a level only just above freezing. In this state of self-controlled hypothermia, the body's metabolism slows right down. The animal breathes very slowly and its heartbeat drops from a normal 300 beats to a mere 7 to 10 per minute. Natural body reflexes (like the knee-jerk in humans) cease and the electrical activity of

the brain is so low it cannot be detected. One of the dangers of inactivity during very cold weather is that tissues may freeze and even be destroyed by ice crystals. In hibernators, the fluids become bound with chemicals of large molecular weight which lower their freezing point and prevent such damage. These physiological changes are not enough, however. The animal finds or excavates a warm, snug burrow well below frost level which it lines with leaves and other material to form an insulating nest, or *hibernaculum*. Some species, such as hamsters, first collect a store of food and thus delay hibernation, while others go straight into the fully dormant, or *torpid*, state, having built up a store of body fat. This is a special form of fat called brown fat, whose primary function is to produce heat – especially important when the animal emerges from its long sleep.

Should the air temperature in the nest drop to freezing, however, the animal will wake and switch on all its body systems to raise its temperature towards normal. If it did not do so, it would die. Some American ground squirrels may wake up about once every ten days, but it is to their advantage not to do so too often, since they use up as much energy on the eleventh, wakeful, day as they did during the previous ten of hibernation. Many bats of temperate regions hibernate, though they often emerge on mild winter days to hunt their insect prey, which has also briefly taken to the wing. But, like the ground squirrels, they must not waste too much energy on these hunting flights, since the balance between the stored fat they burn up and the weight of insects they catch is precarious. For this reason, thoughtless human disturbance of hibernating bat colonies can bring disaster.

The African Lungfish (*below left*) **adopts an ingenious method of escape from drought. If the lake in which it lives dries up, the fish retreats as the water-table falls** (*diagram, below*), **then secretes a leathery cocoon**

around itself and enters a deep sleep. Breathing trapped oxygen via a ventilation tunnel to the surface, it lives on its own muscle tissue. After a year or more, it looks shrivelled, but soon revives in water.

Graph (*below*) **shows seasonal variations in weight of the European Greater Horseshoe Bat. Its average weight reaches a peak value in December, then drops off rapidly as the bat uses up its stored fat during hibernation.**

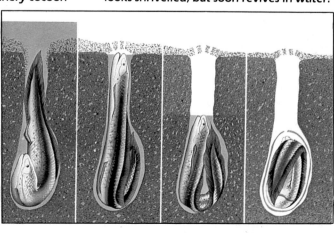

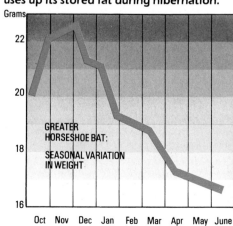

GREATER HORSESHOE BAT: SEASONAL VARIATION IN WEIGHT

Grams

22
20
18
16

Oct Nov Dec Jan Feb Mar Apr May June

Far left **A hedgehog sleeps soundly in its winter nest.**
Left **At the approach of cold weather, a group of American garter snakes prepares to sleep it out entwined beneath a rock.**

Above left **Like lungfish, earthworms escape summer droughts by sleeping underground.**
Above **An Indiana Bat hibernates in a cave in Illinois, USA, its fur beaded with droplets of dew.**

Above **Ladybirds, such as this group in North America, gather in large numbers in sheltered places, including outbuildings and houses, to spend winter in a state of suspended animation.**

Some hibernating mammals, such as the North American ground squirrels and woodchuck, have been found to have a marked annual rhythm which governs their seasonal hibernation. In the wild, ground squirrels hibernate for three or four months in winter, during which they lose weight dramatically. When they awake in spring, they make up for this loss by eating increasing amounts of food until a peak is reached just before the onset of hibernation. Even when the animals are isolated in a laboratory under uniform conditions, the annual rhythm persists for up to two years. More surprising still, if serum (the clear part of the blood) from a hibernating ground squirrel is injected into a non-hibernating individual, the recipient will go into hibernation. So it appears that hibernation is controlled by some basic physiological mechanism, driven in turn by an internal 'biological clock', which is independent of external conditions.

In fact, the situation is more complex than this, in that temperature does seem to have some effect on the basic rhythm, to a different extent in different species. On the other hand, the hibernation cycle seems to be hardly affected by light intensity or daylength, or even by the amount of available food.

A myth exploded

Until the eighteenth century, nearly all naturalists believed that birds, the only other warm-blooded animals, hibernated like mammals. The idea of swallows, for example, flying all the way to Africa was too absurd for the pre-aeroplane age to believe. During migration, swallows pass the night communally among reeds, and it did not require a great stretch of the imagination to believe that when they disappeared

into a pond on an autumn evening, they were going to hibernate in the mud at the bottom. Marking individual birds with numbered rings finally exploded this myth by proving that birds are capable of the most extraordinary journeys. Yet, as is so often the case, once exploded, the myth was soon proved.

Short-term torpor

About 30 years ago, an American ornithologist found a poor-will, a relative of the European nightjar, in a torpid state in a rock cleft in the south-western United States. Careful observation and examination showed that the poor-will hibernates, with a body temperature 22°C below normal, for up to three months. Since then, biologists have found that other birds, such as hummingbirds and swifts, frequently pass into a short-term torpid state to reduce their energy consumption when food is scarce.

Many cold-blooded animals pass the winter in a deep sleep in cold climates. Unable to alter their body temperatures independently of their environment like mammals or birds, they become more and more sluggish as the weather gets colder, finally reaching a state of 'cold anaesthesia'. Unlike the true hibernators, they cannot break the spell of sleep themselves; only a rise in temperature can do that. Snakes, lizards, frogs, toads and newts spend the winter curled up alone or entwined in groups under stones or buried in damp soil or mud.

Some fish also sleep away the winter months, as do many invertebrates, including honeybees, houseflies, ladybirds and snails.

Sleeping as a way of surviving difficult conditions is not exclusive to the colder countries. Hibernation has its counterpart

in hot, dry seasons in many tropical or subtropical regions. Such summer sleep is called *aestivation*. Some desert snails seal up their shells with a thick diaphragm during droughts, to reduce water loss. They may remain in this walled-up state for several years before rain provides the trigger to release them. Even in temperate regions, the summers may be hot and dry enough to force some moisture-loving creatures to suspend activity for a while. Some earthworms aestivate, hollowing out small chambers deep in the soil, where they curl up in intricate tangles.

Sleepy fish

The most remarkable example of aestivation is seen in the freshwater lungfishes of Australia, South America and Africa. If the rivers or lakes in which they live dry up, they burrow down into the bottom mud, secrete a watertight cocoon around the body, and sleep deeply for up to a year or more. A breathing tube through the mud supplies oxygen. African lungfish have even been transported hundreds of kilometres in cans of mud by biologists studying their bizarre lifestyle. The fish obtain energy while asleep by absorbing part of their own muscle tissue as food. This self-cannibalism may result in the fish losing as much as 3 cm in length by the time it awakens.

Whatever strange bed an animal may choose in which to sleep away difficult periods, it seems that hibernation is a time of rest and renewal — resistance to infection and parasites increases and even otherwise damaging levels of radiation seem to be withstood. If humans ever need to hibernate — as on long space-flights — we should learn much from the deep sleep of animals.

53

Sean Morris/Oxford Scientific Films

The icy waters of frozen Antarctic lowering temperatures to −80°C. *Left,* **the largest land-dweller.**

GOING TO EXTREMES: COLDEST, HOTTEST

Climate on Earth varies from numbing cold to searing heat, yet Man and beasts survive it all

In 1946 the people of Wyndham in the province of Western Australia suffered a heat wave that lasted 333 days. During this time the temperature did not drop below 32.2°C. But Wyndham had known worse. A few years earlier the same province blistered for 160 days at temperatures running to 37.8°C, hotter than normal body temperature in human beings.

Even these are not world records of high temperatures. The highest ever recorded is 59.4°C. This was at Insala in Algeria in 1973. Just how hot that actually is can be gauged by the fact that most people cannot stand putting their hand into water hotter than 48°C. Compare this to the coldest temperature recorded, which was an amazing −88.3°C. That was at Vostock in Antarctica on 24th August, 1960.

Early explorers

It wasn't until Man, in his search for valuable minerals and new lands, began to travel to the ends of the globe that the range of climates on the Earth began to be reported. Early explorers found to their cost how inhospitable some parts of the world can be. Many perished from heat stroke or froze to death simply because they did not know how to deal with the climates they found

themselves committed to conquer.

So, what gives the Earth such a wide range of climates? The Sun, our nearest star, has a surface temperature of about 5500°C. It pours out energy in the form of light and heat onto the Earth which is saved from being grilled out of existence only by distance, the atmosphere and its own radiating properties.

From the point of view of life on Earth, our relationship with that rampaging nuclear furnace in the sky is an extraordinarily delicate one. The Sun's heat would only need to drop by 13% for the Earth to be swiftly encased in a layer of ice a mile thick. Fortunately, the Sun has another 30,000 million years to run.

Light hitting the Earth is partly reflected back out into space. The total fraction reflected is called the *planetary albedo* and is about 35 per cent of the energy arriving from the Sun. But the amount reflected from different surfaces varies enormously. Fresh snow and white clouds can reflect as much as 90 per cent of the Sun's rays, while bare earth reflects as little as 10 per cent. All heat transfer works to ensure that the temperature of the Earth does not on average become cooler or hotter. But within this system there are enormous variations in temperature. If latitude were the only factor controlling temperature then a world

This little lizard (*left*) has a whole range of behavioural adaptions to help him cope with the intense heat of this shimmering desert, one of the hottest places on Earth.

Spectrum Colour Library

temperature map would be a simple map of isotherms (lines of equal temperature) lying parallel to each other. This is not the case in the world we inhabit.

The irregular distribution of land and sea masses is responsible for variations of temperature at any given latitude. Both land and sea take up and give out heat but the sea does both more slowly than the land. Sea air is relatively mild throughout the year and so acts as a moderator of severe weather as it blows over the land. Continental air, however, is very hot in summer and extremely cold in winter. Altitude and exposure are also important factors determining the temperature of a region.

Polar regions, because they are shaded by the rest of the world for about half the year, have very long nights and cool half-year 'days'. The sunshine hits the ground at a very oblique angle and the snow hardly melts even in mid-summer. Average temperatures are about −50°C, temperatures at which metal becomes brittle and motor oil freezes. Men working in such temperatures must wear layers of cellular clothing with lots of air pockets to hold the heat. The Eskimos living in the Arctic Circle have developed the igloo, an architectural marvel. Its hemispherical shape gives it a very small surface area to volume ratio so it can be easily heated. The Eskimos also wear animal skins, ideal protection against the cold and wind for fur is a perfect insulator.

Bitter cold

The cold of the polar regions does not mean they are devoid of animal life. All animals living in these conditions have an array of adaptations to help them cope. Warm blooded mammals have thick fur coats and a good layer of insulating fat. Many sleep out the worst of the winter by hibernating. Some fish living in

Antarctic waters have a substance in their blood that prevents the body fluids solidifying, a natural antifreeze.

By contrast, in the tropics, sunshine is so strong that exposed sand can be heated to 84°C, only 16°C less than the boiling point of water! To live in such extreme heat requires quite another strategy.

Human beings cope with high temperature by sweating: the sweat evaporates and cools the skin. Clothing must be light and reflective and most important, cover the body from head to toe. Houses are designed to be cool with small windows to keep the sunlight out. Animals cope with the heat mainly by the way they behave. They keep out of the sunshine during the hottest part of the day and many desert animals are nocturnal. Cold blooded animals that need the sunshine to raise their body temperature so they become active will bask in the sun for as long as possible. They then use other means to prevent the sand from burning them. One type of lizard actually hops from foot to foot so that only two feet are in contact with the burning sand at any one time. Other reptiles and insects will stay out as long as they can and then quickly bury themselves in the sand when it all gets too much for them.

Despite the small size of our planet there is a huge range of climates from the mild coastal zones to the searing heat of the tropics and the numbing cold of the poles. It is comforting to know that since the days of the first intrepid but ill-prepared explorers we have come to understand and cope better with our diverse world. It is alarming to realise how delicately balanced world climate is and how easily Man could wreck it by a nuclear holocaust.

BETWEEN THE TIDES

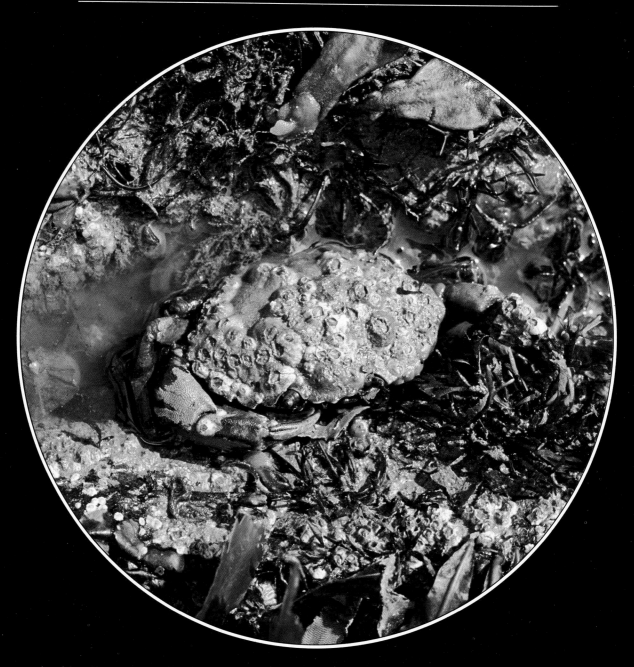

Heather Angel

Time: between the tides: Place: a rocky Northern European shore. Question: which two animals in this scene are unintentionally engaged in a programme of mutual aid? Scan the picture minutely and you will see that not all the large, dark shapes it contains are rocks. One of these shapes is the body of a shore crab whose grey-green back is, like the surrounding rocks, encrusted with a mass of acorn barnacles. The crab's gain from housing these pick-a-back riders is clear: the barnacles help it stay hidden from voracious sea birds and even from human predators in the form of children armed with buckets, spades and shrimp nets. While the barnacles run the risk of being smashed to pieces if their living, moving homestead is killed and eaten, they have the advantage of an increased mobility not afforded to their rock-bound neighbours.

During the hours of darkness, and at high tide — not low water as you might expect — the crab scuttles sideways around the shore scavenging on the dead remains of creatures killed or left stranded above the water line. The crab may also take a dip into the shallow waters of a sandy or rocky pool to catch fish with its pincer arms or *chelae*.

For the acorn barnacles, which are in fact near relations of the crabs on which they hitch a ride, the hours when the crab is eating represent a period of inactivity. To prevent themselves from losing vital body water they close down the valves at the top of the hard, chalky box in which their soft body parts are enclosed. Clinging on to the crab's carapace with a muscular sheet of tremendous strength, each barnacle stays shut down until the crab takes a dip in the water. Only then do the barnacles open their valves and flick out their feathery *cirri*. These cirri work like a kind of drag net: as they move through the water they capture the microscopic marine animals which the barnacles use for food.

EVOLUTION IN ISOLATION

Remote islands offer biologists a living laboratory in which to study the process of evolution

n the autumn of 1835 a small ship sailed into 'Las Islas Encantadas', off the coast of Ecuador, South America, with a young British scientist on board. The ship was the 'Beagle' the scientist Charles Darwin; the 'enchanted islands' were the Galapagos.

Within a few brief weeks, Darwin's theory of evolution had crystallized in his mind. Species, he realized, were not unchanging, and the Galapagos had proved it. Darwin's clear setting out of his discoveries, which followed over thirty years later, was to alter our whole concept of the world and lead to a conflict that still rages over a century later. Charles Darwin's 'On the Origin of Species' is, along with the Bible, arguably the most significant book ever published.

Yet what had happened on these enchanted islands? What had impressed the young Darwin so much? And how could five weeks ashore so radically change the course of human thinking?

The Galapagos emerged from the ocean floor about a million years ago. They were the result of immense pressures within the Earth and the intense volcanic activity that followed the release of these pressures in the form of eruptions and their associated explosions and lava flows. Quite suddenly there were islands where there had been no land before, but islands that

were separated from the nearest point of the mainland of South America by 1,000 km of open ocean. Out there in the Pacific it was like the beginning of the world – a barren landscape devoid of life and totally lacking the means of supporting it.

By the time Darwin arrived, the islands, though still partly barren as they are today, were clothed with mosses, lichens, shrubs and trees and there were seals and sealions, reptiles and birds. How had they got there? Where had they come from?

The answer to the first question was not too difficult to find. Mangrove forests along the shoreline had doubtless originated from seed-pods which had drifted over the seas from the mainland, and other plants had grown from seeds passed through the digestive systems of birds. The birds and a bat species had simply flown in: the seals and sealions had swum ashore, and the reptiles probably drifted across on natural rafts.

The second part of the question proved much more difficult to answer. Where had they come from?

Charles Darwin recognized that many of the plants, the reptiles and the birds were simply unknown to science – they were new species. Today we know that 47% of the plants, 75% of the birds, 86% of the reptiles, the only land mammals (rice rats) and even 37% of the inshore fish are *endemic*. That is they are unique to the Galapagos and found nowhere else in the world.

Darwin's finches

Just as important was the fact that some of the species, while clearly distinct one from another, were just as clearly related. Darwin was particularly taken by a group of small sparrow-like birds that could be divided by colour into black and greyish birds, but which were otherwise remark-

Inset, above **The island of Surtsey, 30 km to the south-west of Iceland, was created by volcanic eruption beneath the waves in 1963. One of the first plants to colonize the bare ash and lava was sea lyme grass (***above***), fertilized by the droppings of the great black-backed gulls that began to breed there.**

ably similar. In fact, they differed significantly only in the shape of their bills. Bill shape and size is related to food, and it did not take Darwin very long to work out that here was a group of species that had descended from a common ancestor. This must have flown over from the South American mainland, since when it had become extinct there. Now these drab birds rejoice in the name 'Darwin's finches', and to this day offer the student of biology a superb example of the process of radiating evolution – by which a single common ancestor gives rise to a diverse group of species.

After colonizing the various islands,

Inset Icelandic Photo & Press Service

Right A young great black-backed gull surveys its new home on Surtsey Island: to date, over 60 bird species have been seen on the new island and several have stayed to breed. In contrast to Surtsey, the Galapagos Islands off the coast of Ecuador contain a great variety of different habitats for animals to exploit. These range from bleak outcrops of sulphur deposits (*below left*) to lush tropical forests (*below right*).

Dr. Sturla Fridriksson, Reykjavik, Iceland

the finches' common ancestor gradually changed by adapting to life on the different islands. Those individuals best able to cope bred more successfully and became progressively adapted to major food supplies on the particular island they inhabited. Over a long period of time, they became quite distinct from birds that had adapted to a different life on a different island. At some later time birds from one island colonized another, but by then they had become sufficiently distinct as to neither compete with nor interbreed with those birds already present. In this way two species had evolved from a single ancestor and so on. Today there are thirteen distinct species.

Man-made problems

Though the finches have become separate species, the giant tortoises that formerly inhabited many of the islands have been slower to evolve and are recognized only as subspecies. Nevertheless, they have become quite clearly distinct in many ways. Their success in surviving, while such giant reptiles have been eliminated virtually everywhere else in the world, has been due

Dr. Sturla Fridriksson, Reykjavik, Iceland

to the lack of competition from herbivorous mammals. Today, however, they face such competition from introduced goats, cattle and donkeys, and already some populations have disappeared. Only sound conservation measures will ensure the survival of the Galapagos giant tortoises – a supreme example of how a delicate natural system can be destroyed by Man's unthinking interference. Adapted to less vigorous competition than that found on a mainland environment, the plants and animals of the Galapagos have all suffered from introduced competitors. Other forces have been even more direct.

The islands have been settled for four hundred years, during which time areas have been cleared for settlements and farming. Animals have been killed for food, sport, oil and skins. A hundred and fifty years ago, ships would call in and load their holds with tortoises stacked three or four deep to ensure a supply of fresh meat for months to come. Captain David Parker of the *USS Essex* loaded fourteen tons of tortoises in four days in 1815. Today the Galapagos are an Ecuadorian national

Heather Angel

Heather Angel

park, and the ships bring tourists instead. But even they unthinkingly buy souvenirs that degrade the islands and destroy their wildlife. Zoos and museums, functioning in the name of science, take their toll of wildlife as well. So a fauna and flora that took a million years to evolve may easily be destroyed within five hundred years of their discovery.

Islands like the Galapagos are to be found in other parts of the world, though, for various reasons, none are as rich or as exciting to the biologist. The Solomon Islands, for example, extend over 965 km of ocean though in the south only 95 km of water separates Guadalcanal and San Cristobal. Yet these 95 km have been sufficient to enable quite distinct species of pigeons, babblers, flycatchers and sunbirds to evolve. Overall, some 25% of the birds of these islands are represented by distinct forms. The isolation offered by islands enables the whole process of evolution to be speeded up because there is little chance of mixing with other elements of the original population. They can indeed be regarded as 'evolutionary hothouses'.

A dream come true

To have seen the earliest days of the Galapagos and have documented their colonization and the subsequent adaption of life to new circumstances would have been a biologist's dream. Yet for some this dream has come true, albeit in a much smaller way, at Surtsey to the south-west of Iceland.

On 14th November, 1963, a volcanic eruption occurred 120 metres beneath the sea some 30 km to the south-west of Iceland beyond the Westmann Islands. Within days a cone had emerged to form the island of Surtsey. Before the volcanic activity had ceased, life had started to colonize this new world, and gulls were seen perched on the lava flows before they were even cold. Over the intervening years scientists have recorded in great detail the process of colonization.

At first the island was just bare ash and lava, but immediately the wave action of the Atlantic Ocean started taking its toll, and soon 30-metre-high cliffs lined the southern shore. The broken-down material was washed to the north and east, where it formed beaches and promontories. When the eruption stopped in 1967 Surtsey was 280 hectares in area. Since then it has lost 7.5 hectares a year to the ocean.

The pioneers

Though seabirds were probably the first life form ashore, it was not long before various micro-organisms were detected on the island. Some were doubtless carried by birds, but others were borne by wind and ocean. Bacteria and moulds were followed by algae, while the first lichens appeared in 1970. Mosses arrived earlier, the first being noted in 1967, and by 1972 no less than 63 distinct species had been found and identified.

Hans D. Dossenbach/Ardea London

Top **Family group of marine iguanas. Also exclusive to the Galapagos are the 13 species of Darwin's finches that have evolved different sized bills on the different islands of the group. At one extreme is the large ground finch** (*above*) **which can crack large seeds, while at the other is the warbler finch** (*above right*), **whose narrow bill enables it to exploit small insect food.** *Right* **In heraldic pose, a Galapagos flightless cormorant dries its wings in the sun: with no natural enemies, many island birds have become flightless.**

Sea rocket was discovered in the second summer of Surtsey's existence, and it remained the only species of higher plant until 1967 when sea sandwort arrived. The latter had been the most successful colonizer of the 19 higher plant species that have been so far recorded. By plotting every plant (there were 50,000 sea sandwort in 1981) botanists have shown that seeds carried by the sea have been the major colonists in the north and east of the island. Plants such as scurvy grass and chickweed, found in the interior of the island, are more likely to have been carried there by birds. The botanists have also found feathery seeded plants and spore-producing species that were blown in on the wind.

Insects, too, came by both air and ocean. Flies and midges were noted as early as 1964, and by 1970 over a hundred species of insects had been recorded. Butterflies and moths came unaided, some insects hitched a ride on birds, and at least two species were brought in with scientists' stores, despite the strict regulations aimed at preventing just such occurrences. Spiders have floated to the islands on their silken threads: eight species now breed there.

Early birds

From the earliest days birds started coming ashore, and to date over 60 species have been recorded. The first to nest, in 1970, were the fulmar and the black guillemot, both abundant breeders on the nearby Westmann Islands. Since those early days, kittiwakes and great black-backed gulls have joined them as regular breeders, while the Arctic tern has done so at least once. The effect of the birds' droppings and food remains on Surtsey is to speed up the process of soil growth and thus increase the opportunities for colonizing plants.

Studies at Surtsey have shown just what it must have been like in the early days of the Galapagos. A whole host of organisms have had the opportunity of colonizing, but in the hard struggle for existence only the most durable have survived the difficulties of transportation and the inhospitable environment that awaited them. Yet already a parasitic wasp that is endemic to the Westmann Islands has been recorded.

Mammals are, so far, represented solely by the seals that come ashore and lie on the beaches. Female common seals and their young are more or less permanent residents.

Soon there will be ledges of soil ready to receive crowberry and dwarf willow and then perhaps will come the first small land-bird colonists. These may never develop into Darwin's finches, but in the thousands of years that Surtsey will exist they will probably adapt and change in some way to differentiate them from their nearby cousins, providing biologists of the future with the spectacle of evolution in action.

Top **Galapagos giant tortoises caught in the act of mating. Sadly, their survival on many islands is threatened by competition for food from goats, donkeys and cattle introduced by Man.** *Above* **Adult and baby giant tortoises on Santa Cruz island. As well as problems from introduced animals, Galapagos wildlife is threatened by tourists, who disturb them and cause soil erosion** (*left*).

New Guinea

10°S

DEATH ON THE REEF

Beneath the blue waters of the Pacific, the Great Barrier Reef is being eaten to death

GREAT BARRIER REEF

N

Cairns Green Island

Howie Reef

QUEENSLAND

Rib Reef

Townsville

Broadhurst Reef

20°S

In the 1960s, off the coast of Queensland, Australia (*above*), a plague of starfish destroyed most of the hard coral cover of the central portion of the Great Barrier Reef. The culprit was the crown-of-thorns, *Acanthaster planci.* For some reason, there was a population explosion of these multi-limbed, spiny starfish. Millions of them swept across the coral, leaving bleached skeletons, covered in dull green algae, where once the living coral had been both a source of beauty and the home for an immense variety of species. Renewed out-breaks now threaten the reef.

Chris Lyon

Walter Deas/Seaphot Ltd.: Planet Earth Pictures

Swain Reefs

In the early 1960s, articles appeared in the press with headlines such as 'Doomsday for coral?' and 'Voracious march of the crown-of-thorns'. They told of sudden, unexpected and devastating attacks on coral reefs by a starfish with the dramatic name of the 'crown-of-thorns'. The attacks paralleled a plague of locusts: they were unexpected, and they almost totally destroyed the environment. In some places 80 per cent or more of the coral reef had been destroyed. This represented an environmental disaster of the highest magnitude.

A coral reef is an intricate structure. Living coral is a carpet of tiny sea-anemone-like animals, each sitting on its own tube of lime. Countless generations of coral animals have left their tubes as foundations for succeeding generations and they have piled up to form reefs. A host of other animals — fishes, crustaceans, worms and seashells — find shelter among the coral growths and they feed either on the living coral, the floating plankton or on each other, to form a complex, interconnected web of life.

The immense variety of species and their often gaudy colouration and bizarre life styles make coral reefs, which grow only in shallow, clear and warm water, a fascinating place for both naturalists and holidaymakers. The reefs are of considerable economic importance as they support fishing industries and encourage tourism. But in the 1960s the crown-of-thorns starfish stripped the colourful living surface of the reefs, leaving bare, bleached skeletons. Eventually the reefs became covered with a carpet of dull green algae, the surreal forms of the coral heads crumbled away and the colourful reef fish departed.

The first 'plague' of crown-of-thorns was discovered on the Great Barrier Reef of Australia in 1962, at a place called Green Island — a favourite sight-seeing area. By 1966, about four-fifths of the coral in that

Until the outbreaks, virtually nothing was known about the crown-of-thorns. Now thousands of pounds have been spent on research. Under normal circumstances, there are about six adult specimens per sq km — on infested reefs, population density increased over 2000-fold. The starfish creeps along on tube-feet topped with suckers (below). **It feeds by everting its stomach, which can be seen** below right. Below left **A starfish has just been removed from this slime-covered coral. The damaged coral releases chemicals which attract other starfish to the scene. The coral's skeleton is exposed after the crown-of-thorns has eaten,** left **and** right**.**

Christian Petron/Seaphot Ltd.: Planet Earth Pictures

Christian Petron/Seaphot Ltd.: Planet Earth Pictures

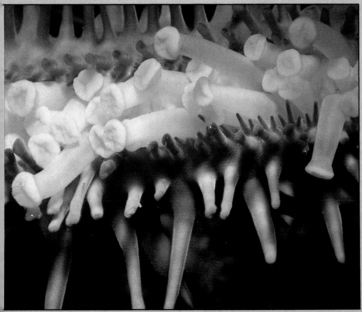

Bill Wood/Bruce Coleman Ltd.

Carl Rofessler/Seaphot Ltd.: Planet Earth Pictures

Rod Salm/Seaphot Ltd.: Planet Earth Pictures

G. R. Roberts

G. R. Roberts

area had been killed, and the starfish became a part of Australian politics. Biologists, conservationists and the public demanded action for protection of the reefs, while the tourist industry tried to play down the problem.

At the time of the first outbreak, virtually nothing was known about the crown-of-thorns. It had been assumed to be a rare animal, because it was hardly ever seen or collected by marine zoologists. Only in 1961 was its habit of feeding on coral discovered. Two decades later, the vast amount of money which has been spent on research make it the best known member of a rather obscure animal group.

A starfish is a radial animal; it has no head, and any limb can lead the way. There is a simple nervous system and the starfish reacts to light intensity, touch and water-borne chemicals.

It creeps forward on its rows of tube-feet which are topped with suckers. The tube-feet are also used for pulling open shellfish. Feeding is accomplished by everting the stomach out of the mouth and applying it to the prey, so that digestion takes place outside the body. Sex is simple: eggs and sperms are shed into the sea where fertilization takes place, and the larvae float around until settling down and becoming adult. (Some species keep the eggs in the body and the baby starfish develop inside their mothers.)

The crown-of-thorns starfish, *Acanthaster planci*, differs from the standard starfish in the number of arms. This ranges from 9 to 21, the average number varying in different geographical locations. Fully grown individuals span about 60 centimetres. The En-

glish name, as well as the scientific name (*Acanthaster* – 'spiny star' in Greek), refers to the covering of 1.5 to 4.5 centimetre spines on the upper side of the body. They give the starfish a rather sinister appearance, which is compounded by the poison in the spines.

Under 'normal' circumstances there are only a few *Acanthaster* starfish in every square kilometre of coral reef. During the day the starfish lie up in nooks and crannies in the reef, coming out at night to browse on the coral. Such is their aversion to light that a crown-of-thorns placed on white coral sand heads at full speed, 20 metres per hour, for the relative darkness of the reef.

These and other facets of *Acanthaster* behaviour came to light when intensive study of the species started after the first

Left **Looking like a marine tarantula, a crown-of-thorns sets about its prey, while some reef inhabitants swim past, blissfully ignorant of the fact that their home is being destroyed. The colourful forms of the reef could disappear, as could the anenome fish** (*below left*) **and other species living on the reef** (*below, far left*) **unless scientists discover how to stop the starfish plagues.** *Right* **A starfish succumbs to attack from a giant triton. One theory is that harvesting of predators such as the triton and the sergeant-major fish** (*below*) **leads to the population outbreaks.**

Richard Chester/Seaphot Ltd.: Planet Earth Pictures

wealth of coral reefs for centuries, but there is no account in any islander's folklore of reefs being devastated like this.

However, it was discovered that *Acanthaster* could migrate. 'Herds' of starfish could sweep across reefs at a rate of 3 kilometres a month, and travel from reef to reef. Where one was feeding, chemicals liberated from the damaged coral attracted others. These observations would explain the clustering of starfish, but not the enormous increase in total numbers.

Destroying the balance

The alternative view is that, around 1960, an abnormal event occurred which altered the natural stability of *Acanthaster* populations. Human interference is an obvious target for blame, and an attractive theory is that the removal of predators has favoured the survival of young starfish. Crown-of-thorns are eaten by fish such as wrasses and the sergeant-major, and by shellfish like the trochus and giant triton. These animals have been harvested heavily in recent years by commercial fishermen and scuba divers.

Yet there is no evidence that the survival pattern of young *Acanthaster* has changed, or that there is a difference in survival between exploited and unexploited reefs. Neither is the evidence convincing that plagues are centred on areas of high human activity, where predators have been removed, or, perhaps, pollution and disturbance have upset the natural balance.

Attempts to halt the plague have had as little success as the quest for the cause. Numerous proposals have been made, and two methods have been tried extensively. Starfish have been collected by hand and left to die in the air, or they have been in-

plague' was reported. The Australians and the Americans at Guam and neighbouring islands have investigated the plague areas, while a Cambridge University group has studied the starfish in the Red Sea to assess its biology under conditions of low population density. The twin aims of the investigations were to find out why *Acanthaster* had suddenly become a menace, and what could be done about it.

The fear was that if the plague of starfish continued unabated, two oceans could be affected. The crown-of-thorns is found wherever there are coral reefs in the Indian and Pacific Oceans. One authority has stated that we are witnessing the beginning of the extinction of the stony or reef-building corals — and of all the animals which live among them.

Such statements have caused feelings to

run high among the general public and politicians, as well as those more directly involved with coral reefs, and it became difficult to find out the true facts of the matter.

Suggestions for the cause of starfish plagues fall into two categories: normal and abnormal events. Normal events would include the possibility of natural fluctuation in the population. Each female *Acanthaster* produces millions of eggs; there is a massive mortality rate, and only a minute fraction become adult starfish. Perhaps the plagues have been caused by the mortality rate being reduced by a rise in water temperature or some other environmental factor. However, this does not explain why there should be a plague on one reef and not a neighbouring one, nor why plagues never happened in the past.

People have been exploiting the natural

jected with formalin by divers. The nocturnal habits of the species reduces the effectiveness of such measures and, although a significant reduction of some populations has been reported, no permanent solution has been reached.

Return to attack

Hopes were raised at one time by reports that the reefs were recovering from devastation more rapidly than expected. The starfish do not destroy systematically, and remnants of living corals are left behind to 'seed' a recovery. Growth is, nevertheless, very slow and other marine organisms sometimes take over and prevent the coral from spreading. Moreover, the crown-of-thorns return to renew the attack.

In 1979, a party from the University of Queensland investigated a reported attack on the Green Island reef. It was estimated that about 60 per cent of the reef's hard coral cover had recently been destroyed by *Acanthaster*. A follow-up survey in 1981 revealed that an estimated 90 per cent of Green Island's hard coral cover had been killed, and that the rest of the coral was due to suffer the same fate.

Unless there is radical development in either the course of the crown-of-thorns plagues or our understanding of them, then all we can do is hope that Nature will find a balance between coral and starfish before the reefs finally disappear.

Apart from the harvesting aspect, another important human factor involved in the threat to the reef has been the breaching of the reef to allow easy access for the rapidly multiplying numbers of tourist boats (*above*). At low tide, water drains from the reef flats, and the exposed coral dies, never to be renewed (*below*).

G. R. Roberts

TROPICAL
HIDEAWAY

Heather Angel

The intricate maze of pathways within a tropical coral reef provides a welcome hiding place for many a vulnerable marine creature. But what is concealed here? Camouflaged in delicate coral pink, a perfect match to the shade of their surroundings, are a sea slug (Tritonia plebia), plus a sticky string of egg-containing spawn, coiled like knitting wool around a handily projecting horny coral branch. Secret of the sea slug's superfine colour matching technique is its diet. By eating the coloured coral, the slug can absorb the coral's colour and so make itself invisible to all but the most keen sighted of voracious ocean predators, and once

eaten, this colour can be used by the sea slug to protect its eggs by secreting it in the sticky mucus that strings the eggs together before they hatch. Not only does it adopt the colour of its food – the sea slug also manages to take on board the coral's effective form of defence mechanism, in the form of hypodermic-like stinging cells. When it eats these cells, the sea slug does not digest them. Instead, it stores them in special outgrowths ready for defence against attackers. So what happens when the sea slug moves on to a coral of a different colour? It simply gorges itself and changes shade to match its meal.

MASTERMIND OF THE SEA

Biologists have found that these strange relatives of the snails have big brains and can learn quickly. Despite their cleverness, however, their basic design has always restricted them to the oceans, where eight limbs are better than four

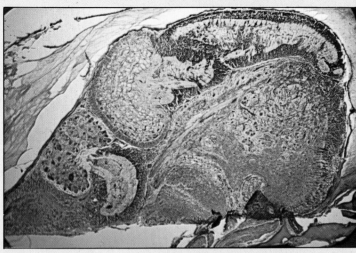

Although the octopus is a mollusc, like a snail or an oyster, it is as intelligent as many birds or mammals. Even so, it inhabits an alien world, in which it can taste by using its highly developed sense of touch, but cannot tell what its arms are doing unless it looks at them.

A carnivore, the octopus actively hunts crustaceans (especially crabs), fish and other molluscs in the open sea, mostly at night. It has abandoned the security of the typical molluscan shell in favour of speed, manoeuvrabilty and – most important of all – a quick, adaptable brain.

Compared with those of other invertebrates, the brain of an octopus is enormous – as big as that of a fish or a reptile. And the animal has even more nerve cells spread about its body – its eight arms alone contain three times as many nerve cells as the centralized brain.

Professor J. Z. Young of University College London, UK, and Dr. Martin Wells of Cambridge University, UK, have tracked down the part of the brain which changes as the animal learns: the crucial bit is a cubic millimetre of brain tissue in the subfrontal lobe. One hundred thousand nerve cells are at the core of the octopus's remarkable intelligence. 'The result', says Dr. Wells, 'is a mollusc that a primate can recognize as a fellow creature.'

A meeting with an octopus – even one safely ensconced in a laboratory tank – can

be unnerving. They watch you. They follow your movements with every appearance of interest and curiosity. Staring out from behind a pair of very human-like eyes is an uncannily 'human' creature. An octopus in a lab will approach familiar humans and take food out of their hands; it will develop idiosyncratic and sometimes irritating habits – like squirting water at people or climbing out of its tank as a human friend arrives. Can we regard the octopus as a sort of aquatic cat or dog then?

Inner world

All the evidence is to the contrary. Its inner world, extensive research suggests, is very different from ours. The octopus is a cold-blooded, basically solitary creature, with no family ties and little social life. If it knows hunger, its reaction is strange to us – an octopus deprived of food is less, not more, likely to emerge from its den and try to feed. It indulges in sex but remains calm about it – during copulation the heartbeat of an octopus never changes. During its elaborate sexual displays the octopus seems most concerned with establishing the sex of the other individual. True, the octopus, like us, is a learning animal – but what it learns is often very different from the knowledge a mammal would acquire.

The perceptual world of the octopus has been explored by several British zoologists and psychologists – notably J. Z. Young and

Above **Photomicrograph of a section through an octopus's brain reveals the key to its remarkable intelligence: the crescent-shaped structure at** *bottom left* **is the subfrontal lobe containing nerve tissue which the animal uses for learning.**
Right **The intelligent eye: octopuses have large, efficient eyes comparable to Man's.**

Brian Boycott at University College London, Martin and Joyce Wells at Cambridge University, and Stuart Sutherland, now of Sussex University. Many of them worked for a time in a zoological station in Naples, Italy, close to the haunts of *Octopus vulgaris*, the common European octopus. Together, they've found out a great deal about the brain and behaviour of this clever creature.

The octopus of cartoons is all arms – with some justification, for the sense of touch is clearly very important to the real animal. Using its eight arms, each covered with over 200 very sensitive and mobile suckers, the octopus can move about, collect food, defend itself and explore its environment. It readily learns to distinguish between objects – for instance, a rough and a smooth sphere – by touch alone.

But the touch world of the octopus is strangely different from our own. The octopus's sensitive 'touch-taste' system can detect sugar, acid or quinine in solutions up to a thousand times more dilute than we can taste. Yet it cannot judge weights or shapes by holding objects. An octopus can't make these distinctions – a simple task for a mammal – simply because it lacks the sense receptors which all vertebrates possess; strategically located in the joints of man or mouse, these sensors send the brain information about pressure and movement.

Each of the octopus's arms can bend, extend or contract anywhere along its length – and it is equipped with its array of independently movable suckers. Keeping track of such a complex unit would be too much for even the most sophisticated brain – simply because the octopus has no joints to provide easy points of reference.

So the octopus's brain just isn't wired up to receive any feedback from its arms. By contrast, insects, crabs and vertebrates – all

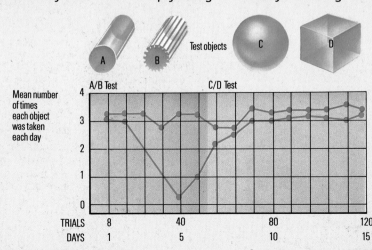

Right **Dr. Wells trained blinded octopuses to discriminate by touch between a smooth cylinder (*A*) and a rough one (*B*), then between a cube (*C*) and sphere (*D*). They were rewarded by food for taking the 'right' object and punished by electric shocks for taking the 'wrong' one. They soon distinguished the textures of *A* and *B*, but could not tell *C* from *D*.**

Artworks Chris Lyon

Test objects A B C D

Mean number of times each object was taken each day

A/B Test   C/D Test

4

3

2

1

0

TRIALS   8   40   80   120
DAYS   1   5   10   15

Above **Experiments have shown that octopuses can distinguish this impressive range of shapes by sight.**

Dr. M. J. Wells

Left **A view of the laboratory in Naples, Italy, where J. Z. Young and other zoologists did their pioneering work on octopus behaviour. The tanks contain the animals used for training.** *Above* **The octopus is equipped with arms very different from ours. It uses its highly mobile limbs to pull itself across the seabed, to anchor itself to the rocks, for seizing prey and also during reproduction.**

the jointed creatures of the world – know exactly where their bodies are; they have a sense of bodily position. This sense makes it possible for rats, cockroaches and humans to learn mazes and develop manipulative skills. But the vast majority of animals – the soft-bodied invertebrates, including the octopus – are forever debarred from such activities.

We can perform skilled movements, turning a screwdriver for instance, because we know exactly how far we have moved it. The same precise knowledge of bodily position allows bees to build honeycombs and spiders to construct webs. But an octopus never learns a maze that even an ant could conquer, nor can it manipulate tools with its flexible tentacles. Despite the octopus's phenomenal intelligence, it can never acquire complex motor skills.

The octopus must be roughly in the position of a man with no sense of balance driving a car – he gets very little feedback from the moving system he is controlling, since he can't directly feel the tyres on the road. He can only crudely judge where they are by noticing where the car is headed.

The eyes of the octopus, that stare back at us so strangely, are extraordinarily like our own; they possess all the major features of the vertebrate eye – cornea, iris, lens and retina. These prominent eyes can focus and compensate for changes in light, just like ours. And, Young and his co-workers have discovered, the beasts can rapidly learn to discriminate visually between different geometric patterns, shapes and sizes.

But striking differences between our visual world and that of the octopus lie under the surface. Octopuses are apparently colour blind. They never learn to distinguish between different wavelengths of light in the laboratory. Yet octopuses are amazingly colourful beasts which use their ability to change the size of pigment cells in their skin to striking advantage in social displays. They can also perfectly match their skin hue to the background, as they lie cryptically waiting for prey; how they manage to do this without colour vision is a mystery. Octopus eyes can also detect the plane of vibration of light falling on the retina – which is

Right **Dr. Wells used this apparatus to examine intelligence in the octopus. The results showed that octopuses could learn to make detours to reach prey not directly accessible to them. The animal lived in a pile of bricks in a 'home' compartment. It was usually kept there between trials by lowering the door. Then the door was opened and the octopus shown a crab in one of the two feeding compartments. To get it, the octopus had to make a detour through the central corridor out of sight of the crab. When it left the corridor at the far end it entered a 'choice' compartment, with open doorways leading to the two feeding compartments. The best performers took only 10 seconds to make the detour.**

Chris Lyon/Dr. M. J. Wells

DETOUR EXPERIMENT APPARATUS

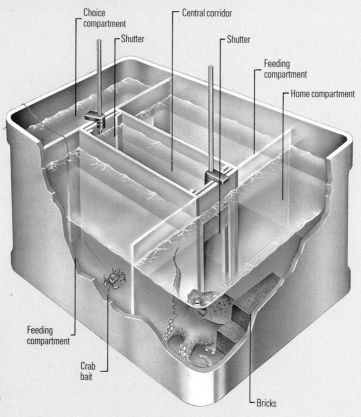

Choice compartment

Shutter

Central corridor

Shutter

Feeding compartment

Home compartment

Feeding compartment

Crab bait

Bricks

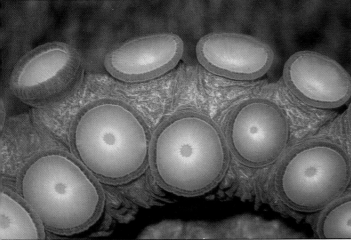

Valeria Taylor/Ardea

Oxford Scientific Films/Waina Cheng

invisible to us. This ability to see polarized light could enable them to see the Sun or Moon behind clouds, and use them to find their way about — just as bees do on cloudy days.

A creature living the life of an octopus needs to see well. It relies upon its sharp eyes as it swims round a complex marine environment, hunting its prey. Octopuses also engage in elaborate social displays and find their way home to shelters built in the rocks. A small, young octopus, one which has just left its life as a tiny member of the drifting clouds of plankton to settle on the seabed, has to be able to tell friend from foe in an instant. Newly-settled octopuses must avoid carnivorous fish at all costs. Life probably gets a bit easier as the octopus grows to an armspan of a metre or more, but the octopus doesn't grow foolhardy. It quickly retreats deep into its home at the first sign of danger.

Why has a soft-bodied invertebrate become so bright? Its intelligence probably evolved in a world that had suddenly become dangerous for it. Our own ancestors, the mammals, were also born in an inhospitable world. There are haunting similarities in the history of the octopus and our own.

The intelligent octopus probably began to evolve when a group of serious competitors, the bony fish, appeared on the scene. These fish, which evolved in freshwater and then rather suddenly moved into the sea, were quick, efficient predators. They could easily consume the tiny young octopuses, only a few centimetres long. Two options were open to the octopus's ancestors: either grow armour and move to a less fish-infested part of the sea, or become smarter than the enemy fish.

Some of the advanced, mobile molluscs took the first path; they responded to the fish menace by retreating into deeper waters and developing heavy gas-filled shells. But the plan wasn't a success; today, the unwieldy chambered nautilus and its relatives are sole survivors from that era.

But another group of molluscs, the ancestors of the modern shell-less octopus, followed the second road to survival. They

Above **Close-up of a few of the 200 or so powerful yet sensitive suckers on one of the octopus's eight arms.** *Above right* **An octopus hides by pretending to be a clump of seaweed. Despite an ability to change colour almost instantly for camouflage or display, it is colour-blind.** *Right* **This young octopus is highly vulnerable to predators and needs its superior intelligence to help it escape from them.**

stayed on in the warm and productive coastal waters and held their own against the new powerful carnivorous fish by going through a tremendous burst of adaptive change — they developed remarkable eyes and brains.

With this new equipment, the octopus could stay out of trouble but still efficiently hunt 'safe' prey, such as crabs. The octopus had developed vision acute enough to make fine distinctions and a brain capable of learning from past mistakes.

Our ancestors, the first mammals, evolved their substantial brainpower under similarly harrowing circumstances — in the shadow of the great reptiles, the dinosaurs. Agility of mind is far more important than armour to a tiny furry mammal living with scaly reptilian giants. Man and the octopus have both emerged from the wilderness as unspecialized but highly successful exploiters of some of the world's most complex ecosystems.

Why are the intelligent, successful cephalopods — the octopuses and their relatives, the squids — entirely confined to the sea? Nearly every other group of animals has at least a few species amongst its members which have left the sea and taken up life on the land or in freshwater instead. Even the more primitive shelled molluscs have managed to evolve land snails and freshwater clams as well as sea-dwelling molluscs. Why have the cephalopods alone been so conservative?

Dr. Wells thinks the answer lies in the cephalopods' physiology. These large, active animals have, he believes, pushed the rather primitive and inefficient molluscan design as far as it will go; they live so close to the limits set by their own physiology that they are probably unable to adapt it to withstand the rigours of a totally new life style.

A digestive system which needs 24 hours to deal with a crab can't be very helpful to a fast-moving efficient predator. Its kidneys too are slow; they filter the blood at very low pressure. And although the octopus has done its best to evolve an efficient heart, its circulation is still barely adequate for such an active beast: its blood can carry relatively little oxygen because its blood pigment, haemocyanin, is inferior to the vertebrate's haemoglobin as an oxygen-carrier.

The hundred or so species of octopus alive today are some of the most powerful predatory animals in the sea. But these remarkable creatures, found in temperate and tropical seas from the Mediterranean to Japan, are trapped in the ocean. All the intelligence in the world, it seems, can't overcome a basically unadaptable design.

SPECIALISED STRUCTURES

From great soaring vultures to microscopic 'wheeling' rotifers, every animal has evolved some special feature well-tailored to its own survival needs . . .

THE FLYING START

Was it leaping up to catch insects, or gliding down from trees that led to the evolution of flight? Several fossilized birds have raised this and other questions to fascinate and tantalize leading palaeontologists

Museum für Naturkunde/Humboldt University

The first recorded fatal flying accident happened in southern Germany. The corpse was called *Archaeopteryx* and the inquest was held 150 million years later. Its findings supported Darwin's new theory of evolution, and are still being debated by palaeontologists.

The accident couldn't have happened in a better place, for the crow-sized body sank to the bottom of a lagoon and was soon covered by layer upon layer of fine sediment. These not only encased the bones of *Archaeopteryx*, but also preserved detailed impressions of its body covering. So, when the fossilized skeleton was discovered in 1861, it was found to be surrounded by clear outlines of feathers. The earliest

Above **Pefectly preserved by many layers of fine sediment, fossilized remains of the earliest known bird with feathers,** *Archaeopteryx*, **saw the light of day again in modern Germany.** *Right* **A particularly well-defined fossilized wing feather.**

known bird had been discovered.

The discovery came only two years after Darwin had suggested that living things could evolve from one another by gradual change caused by natural selection. One criticism of evolutionary theories had been that the fossil record showed no good examples of intermediates between one type of creature and another. *Archaeopteryx* was therefore an important and powerful piece of evidence for evolution, for it is a perfect half-way house between reptiles and birds.

The feathers alone are enough to show that *Archaeopteryx* was a bird. It also had a wishbone, a structure that is found only in birds. But, not surprisingly, it also shows features that later birds had lost. For example, the normal reptilian teeth had not yet been replaced by a horny beak, and its fingers still ended in sharp little claws. Reptile-like, too, was its long tail – though this had borne a row of feathers on either side in quite unreptilian fashion.

As we might expect, *Archaeopteryx* also lacks some of the adaptations for powerful flight that can be seen in its descendants today, or shows only transitional stages in their evolution. For example, it had not yet evolved the deep-keeled breastbone that provides attachment for the strong flight muscles to the wings. Its forelimbs, too, had not yet evolved very far towards the compactly folding wing skeleton of later birds.

Though all those palaeontologists who have recently studied *Archaeopteryx* agree that it was an early bird, intermediate between reptiles and later birds, they have hotly disputed two questions. Firstly, what was its mode of life and how had this evolved? Secondly, from what type of reptile had *Archaeopteryx* evolved?

Scientists at first assumed that it was rather a clumsy flier, perhaps only able to glide from branch to branch. The existence of its long feathery tail supported that idea, for this would have provided an extra area of lift for gliding. Many animals that live in tropical forests today have developed an ability to glide from tree to tree – it's quicker, safer and less tiring than a journey down one tree-trunk, across the ground and up the next.

But an American palaeontologist, John Ostrom of the Peabody Museum at Yale University, recently put forward a contrary view. He believes that many features of *Archaeopteryx* suggest that it lived on the ground. He points out that modern perching birds, like crows or sparrows, have long, curved claws on their toes, especially on the backwardly-directed inner toe, so that the foot can grasp the branch that the bird is resting on. *Archaeopteryx*, by contrast, has shorter, less curved claws, especially on the inner toe, similar to those of modern birds, such as pheasants and chickens, that live mainly on the ground. Ostrom also argues that, in the proportions of both its forelimbs and its hindlimbs, *Archaeopteryx* is very similar to some of the small dinosaurs that used their hindlimbs to run rapidly and their forelimbs to grasp their prey.

But, if it lived on the ground, what did *Archaeopteryx* use its wings for? It is generally agreed that it used its tiny sharp teeth to feed on insects, and Ostrom's answer is that it used its wings as a sort of insect-swat. He visualizes *Archaeopteryx* as running after insects and then making flapping

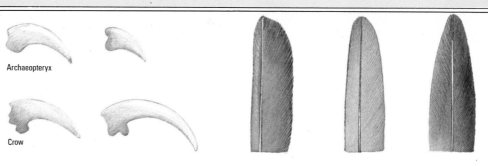

Archaeopteryx

Crow

Above **Archaeopteryx** has claws that are shorter and straighter than those of a perching bird like the crow, especially the backward-pointing inner claw (*right of drawing*). This suggests that *Archaeopteryx* lived mainly on the ground, like a chicken.

Above **Wing feathers from a flying rail,** *left,* **and** *Archaeopteryx,* **centre, show similar asymmetrical design and thickened leading edges, suggesting the primitive bird could fly. The symmetrical feather is from a flightless rail.**

Peter Hayman

Left Archaeopteryx **as it might have looked having launched itself from a tree on a typical hunting flight. The wings and spreading, feathered tail clearly present a considerable gliding surface.**

Left **The reconstructed skeleton of** Archaeopteryx **shows the elongation of its hind leg, a feature shared with modern birds, for example the pigeon,** *far left*. **Such limbs would have given it a long stride on the ground and been a lever to assist launches from trees. Claws on the wings enabled it to climb up.**

Right **A suggestion is that** Archaeopteryx **fed at ground level by running fast and swatting insects with its wings.**

leaps after those that were trying to fly out of its reach. Perhaps, he hypothesizes, such flapping leaps gradually became more powerful and led to the beginning of active flight.

Ostrom's novel views have not yet gained wide acceptance. Palaeontologists are happier if, when suggesting ways of life for extinct animals, they can point to living creatures that have similar habits — and there are no animals today that live on a diet of swatted insects. The long, feathery tail of *Archaeopteryx* is also easily explained if it was an arboreal glider, but has no obvious function if it was a terrestrial runner. Nevertheless, Ostrom's ideas have made scientists look again at the evidence.

The first comment came from American biologists Alan Feduccia and Harrison Tordoff, who examined the shapes of the wing feathers of various living birds. The largest part of the wing surface is formed by the strong feathers known as primaries. Feduccia and Tordoff found that these feathers are very asymmetric in fast-flying birds such as swifts and falcons. Asymmetry in the feathers shows as a thickened axis which lies closer to the leading edge of the feather than to the trailing edge.

Tiny wing

As a result, each feather acts like a tiny wing, directing air more quickly over its upper surface and providing extra lift to the wing as a whole. Slower-flying and flightless birds show less asymmetry in their primary feathers. Significantly, the impressions of the primary feathers of *Archaeopteryx* clearly show that they were very asymmetrical. Feduccia and Tordoff regard this as evidence that these feathers had an aerodynamic function and that *Archaeopteryx* could fly.

But if so, why did *Archaeopteryx* not have the deep keel or *carina* on its breastbone that in modern birds provides an attachment area for the powerful wing muscles? Together with another colleague, Storrs Olson, Alan Feduccia provided a possible answer to this problem. The main power for the downward stroke of the wing, which both lifts the bird up and also propels it forwards, is provided by the great breast muscle called the *pectoralis*. Olson and Feduccia pointed out that most of the muscle is not attached to the carina, but is instead attached to the area of the wishbone. Since *Archaeopteryx* does have this bone, which is found only in birds, it is reasonable to guess that it also had a *pectoralis* muscle.

What, then, *is* attached to the *carina* in living birds? Olson and Feduccia found that it is mainly connected to another muscle, called the *supracoracoideus* — and it is this muscle that proves to be significant in interpreting the mode of life of *Archaeopteryx*. Though it is attached to the carina far below the shoulder joint, its function is nevertheless to raise the wing. It can do this because the tendon of the supracoracoideus runs through a hole near the shoulder and is fixed to the upper surface of the wing bone. It's not surprising to find, then, that *Archaeopteryx* lacks this pulley arrangement as well as the carina – suggesting that it had not yet evolved this elegant method of raising its wings.

But would this mean that *Archaeopteryx* could not fly? No, say Olson and Feduccia, pointing out that birds in which this pulley tendon has been damaged are still able to raise their wings by using other muscles that run from the wing to the shoulder blades. What these birds cannot do, though, is to take off from the ground. All this suggests, then, is that *Archaeopteryx* could fly, but that it would have had to commence each flight by launching itself from the branch of a tree.

So, it looks as though we should think of *Archaeopteryx* as an early bird that could not only glide, using its wings and long feathered tail to prolong its flight, but could also actively flap along, even if not as powerfully as modern birds. Though its flights had to begin with an aerial launch from a tree, some of its flights must have ended on the ground.

So how did it get back into the trees? The clue here may be an unbirdlike feature of *Archaeopteryx* – the sharp hooked claws on its wings. These could have been used to grasp the trunk of the tree as *Archae-opteryx* climbed up for the next launch.

As well as trying to work out the mode of life of *Archaeopteryx*, palaeontologists have also been trying to establish what type of reptile it evolved from. One of the most useful pieces of evidence here is its hind limbs which, like those of living birds, are elongated. These longer hind limbs would have provided a longer stride when running on the ground, and a better lever for propelling *Archaeopteryx* into the air at the start of each flight.

This type of hind limb is also found in a major group of reptiles that includes dinosaurs and crocodiles. However, modern crocodiles, at least, are very specialized for their semi-aquatic way of life, and most workers decided that some kind of little dinosaur was the most likely ancestor. John Ostrom, who had earlier worked on the fast-running types of dinosaur called coelurosaurs, believes that these show many similarities to *Archaeopteryx*. For example, he points out that the hands of both coelurosaurs and birds have lost two of their fingers, or digits, and that the inner toes of both point backwards.

But, here again, other ideas are now being put forward. The evolutionary record seems to show that the coelurosaurian dinosaurs had lost the fourth and fifth digits on their hands, but the embryology of birds suggests instead that they have lost the first and fifth digits. And re-investigation of the hind feet of the dinosaurs has led the American palaeontologists Samuel Tarsitano and Max Hecht to question the view that their inner toes were turned backwards. They conclude that there is little firm evidence of close similarity between *Archaeopteryx* and the dinosaurs. Instead, they suggest that birds, dinosaurs and crocodiles all evolved from a group of reptiles called thecodonts.

The crucial character that identifies *Archaeopteryx* as a bird is its possession of feathers. Though in living birds some of these are elongated and used for flight, the remainder are mainly used to insulate the body. But how did feathers themselves evolve? The most recent suggestion is that of Philip Regal of the University of Minnesota. He believes that they may have originated as elongated scales that protected the body from overheating.

So, though *Archaeopteryx* remains important evidence of the evolution of birds, the little creature is still provoking lively controversy of its exact mode of life and ancestry, over 150 million years after it fell out of the sky and into the warm waters of a subtropical lagoon.

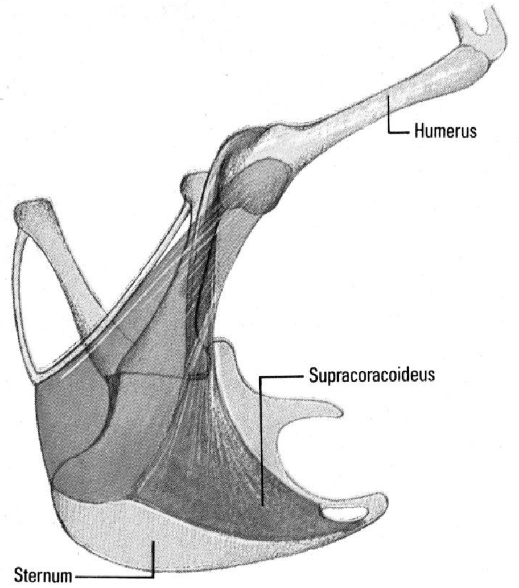

Left On modern flying birds the *supracoracoideus* muscle, attached to the large keel of the **sternum** well below the shoulder joint, is used to raise the wing. Its tendon runs up through the smooth, pulley-like holes of the shoulder joint to attach to the *humerus* or main wing bone. Because *Archaeopteryx* seems to have lacked this arrangement, one observer suggested, probably wrongly, that it was incapable of flight: other muscles can raise the wing, if not as efficiently. The downward stroke is achieved by the massive **pectoralis** muscle, not shown here.

Humerus
Supracoracoideus
Sternum

Below right Skeleton of a small dinosaur compared with *Archaeopteryx*, below left. Minor elements of the drawing are reconstructions, but the basic similarities – especially the long legs used for running, or later, flapping flight – are central to the modern view that birds evolved from a group of reptiles called thecodonts.

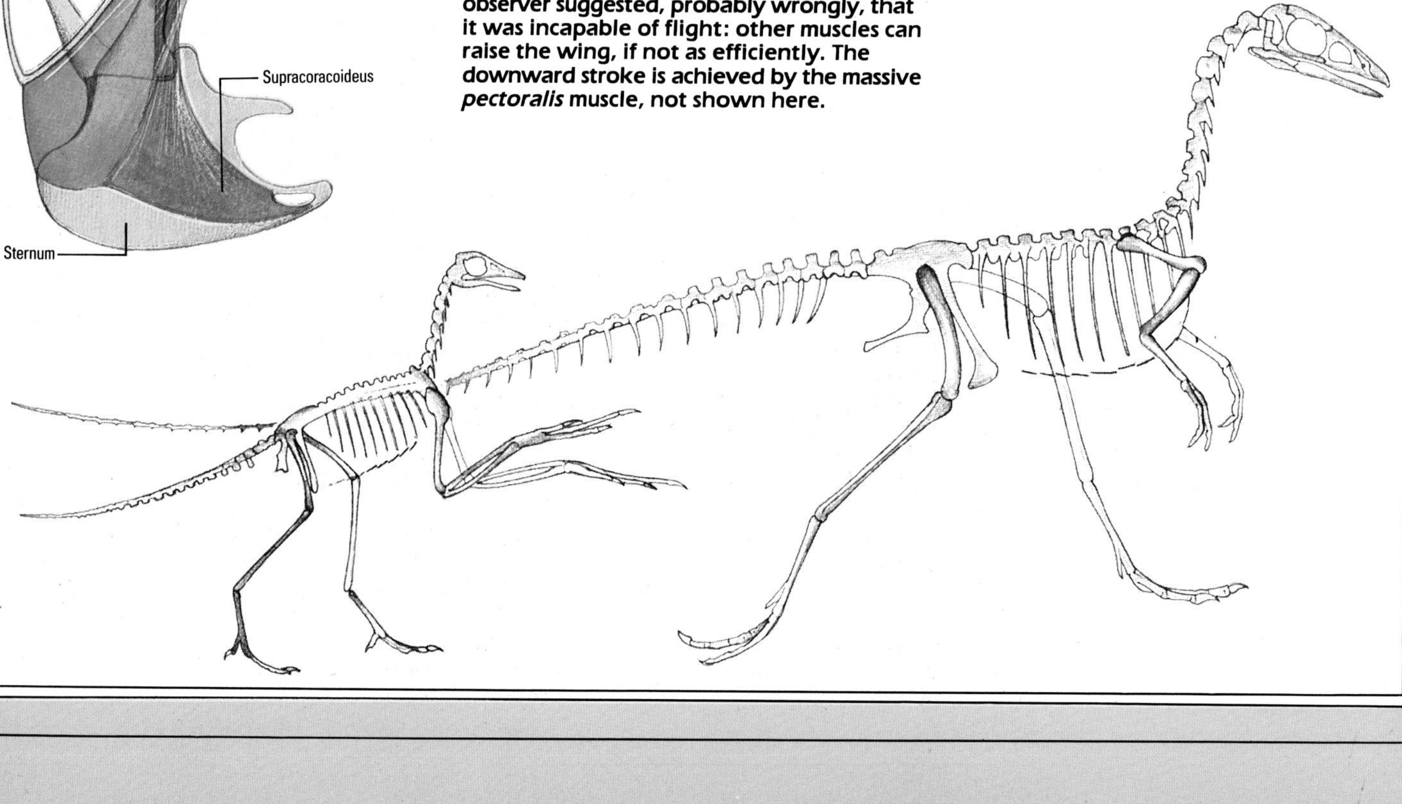

Peter Hayman

EASY FLIERS

Birds use various ingenious methods to hitch a ride on the wind, from albatrosses skimming the waves to vultures using 'thermals' of rising air

Flying is an energy-demanding business for a bird, To keep airborne, it requires massive chest muscles, a large heart and an overall lightening of the skeleton and other parts of the body. It has been suggested that if angels were not supernatural beings they would need 2-metre chests to supply enough power to fly.

Flight gives a bird many obvious advantages over earthbound animals. The rewards are worth the huge energy demands; hummingbirds, for instance, hover with wings beating more than 50 times per second because this gives them the manoeuvrability to tap supplies of energy-rich nectar. Nevertheless, many birds have sought ways of reducing the energy demands of flight.

The kestrel is a familiar bird of prey in Europe, Asia and Africa that is well known for its habit of hovering as it looks for prey, with wings rapidly beating, or held outstretched as if dangling from a wire. This method of catching prey is called *flight-hunting*. This is not the only method of hunting, however: kestrels frequently hunt by watching from a perch on a tree or fence post, then flying down onto their prey: a method known as *perch-hunting*.

The hunting behaviour of kestrels has been the subject of detailed research to assess its efficiency. A Dutch study has shown that flight-hunting yields three-quarters of a kestrel's prey. It catches voles and mice at a rate of 2.7 per hour, compared with 0.14 mammals per hour from perch-hunting. The advantage of flight-hunting is that the kestrel can survey a much broader expanse of ground than if it were confined to perches.

The Dutch ornithologists showed with the aid of cine film that, as the kestrel is buffeted by the wind, its body moves around its head, which is kept completely motionless in space, as if held in an invisible clamp. This gives the kestrel the best chance of picking out a tiny animal far below, and recalls the way that a gyroscope in a warship keeps a gun trained on the target despite pitching and rolling in a high sea.

The drawback to flight-hunting is that it uses up large amounts of energy. Ornithologists have shown that this is so in the black-shouldered kite of North America, which hunts partly by hovering, although not so frequently as the kestrel. The kite spends only $2\frac{1}{2}$ hours out of every 24 flight-hunting, but this requires six times the energy expended in perch-hunting, and accounts for 50 per cent of the day's energy budget.

Studies in both Britain and the Netherlands have revealed that kestrels flight-hunt only when it is worthwhile. During the winter, perch-hunting is preferred, because it supplies enough prey to keep the kestrels in good health, but in summer the demands of rearing a family require a much higher capture rate. This can be supplied only by flight-hunting.

The birds regulate the timing of flight-hunting to achieve the maximum return. The main prey of the kestrel are voles which

Top **The kestrel, one of the commonest birds of prey in Europe, Asia and Africa, is able to hover like a helicopter in search of food.**

This 'flight-hunting' technique enables it to catch nearly 20 times as many voles and mice as it can by hunting from a perch.

P. A. Hinchliffe/Bruce Coleman Limited.

Ron Cartmell/Bruce Coleman Limited.

live in burrows but come out to feed on grass. Their lives are monotonously regular and they have feeding bouts every two hours. The kestrels' flight-hunting is timed to coincide with the voles' appearance above ground. Kestrels also have the habit of catching prey during the day and returning to eat it at dusk. This effectively reduces the weight of the kestrel during the day and the amount of energy it needs to keep airborne. Catching one vole in the morning and eating it in the evening will save 7 per cent of the kestrel's subsistence energy requirement.

Hovering in the wind

The kestrel further reduces the energy expended during flight-hunting by making use of the wind. It habitually hovers into the wind, so as to increase the flow of air over its wings, and if the wind is strong enough, the kestrel can get sufficient lift to 'hang' with wings outstretched. By hunting over ground that slopes into the wind, the bird will get extra help as the airflow is directed upward.

The technique of extracting energy from air movements to assist flight is called *soaring*. The kestrel is only one of many birds to use the trick of soaring as an energy-saving device. Soaring ability is a mark of these species' mastery of the air. They must pos-

sess extremely sensitive methods, such as the kestrel's 'gyro-stabilized' head, for detecting the air flow around them and controlling the flight mechanism.

The sight of birds soaring effortlessly and acrobatically in the wind has always excited envy in earthbound human beings. Dr. Colin Pennycuick of Bristol University, England, has for many years combined glider flying with ornithology, studying the soaring flight of both birds and gliders in an attempt to understand its methods and advantages. Soaring conveys two benefits. It reduces the energy cost of staying airborne while searching for food, patrolling territories and so on, and thus it increases the range of long distance movements. By gliding, a gull saves 70 per cent of the energy it expends in flapping flight.

Energy from air movements

There are six ways by which a bird can extract energy from air movements. A kestrel hanging above a hillside and a gull gliding along a cliff face are *slope-soaring*, using the draught created as the wind is deflected upwards. When a strong wind flows over a hill, it is thrown into standing waves, and birds can be seen *wave-soaring* some distance behind it. Gannets and other seabirds use the standing waves created by an island. Rarely, the turbulence set up by

T. L. G. Grande/Bruce Coleman Limited.

Wayne Lankinen

Bruce Coleman

Top left **The gannet is a large seabird which can soar for hours on end around the cliffs where it breeds in huge colonies. This type of soaring, called** *slope-soaring,* **is made possible by the updraught of wind as it hits the cliff. Gulls, too, are adept at slope soaring, as these kittiwakes (***top centre***) demonstrate. Pelicans, like the white pelican (***top***), are expert soarers. Flocks of these birds on migration spread out to search for thermals that will give them a free ride.** *Above* **White storks, too, rely on careful co-ordination to save energy on their long annual migration between Northern Europe and Africa.** *Left* **Vultures, such as this griffon, soar for huge distances in search of carrion.**

smaller obstacles can be used for *gust-soaring,* as when gulls hover around the stern of a ship. Updraughts are also created at a weather front – the boundary between two air masses – and birds indulge in *front-soaring.* Sea-breeze fronts along the coastline were discovered only when radar showed flocks of swifts soaring in them. The two remaining types – *thermal-soaring* and *wind gradient-soaring* – have been particularly investigated by Dr. Pennycuick.

Thermal-soaring is used by birds in the warmer parts of the world, especially in the interior of continents. When the ground is warmed by the Sun, the air next to it heats up, becomes lighter and rises through the atmosphere as a *thermal,* in the form of a rising column, often known as a dust devil, or a spinning doughnut-shaped *vortex* of hot air.

Vultures

Although the vultures of Europe, Africa and Asia and those of the New World (such as the condors) are not closely related, they have independently evolved methods of using thermals to carry them aloft and provide a vantage point where they can survey the ground, like a kestrel flight-hunting. By gliding from thermal to thermal, a vulture can cover an enormous area in a day.

When the Sun rises in the morning, ther-

Bottom **Diagrams illustrate four methods birds employ in soaring.** *Slope-soaring (1)* **depends on uphill air movement.** *Wave-soaring (2)* **occurs on the leeward side of a slope.** *Thermal-soaring (3)* **is mainly restricted to hot areas, while** *front-soaring (4)* **occurs where two air masses converge and produce lift. Albatrosses** *(right)* **are specialist slope-soarers, using the lift from wave crests.**

mals begin to rise. The smallest vultures take off first, in the weakest thermals. They are followed by larger species as the air warms up. The vultures float within the updraught and, as the fastest moving air is in the centre of the thermal, they circle so as to balance the pull of gravity against the lifting effect of the rising air. If they want to climb, they move nearer the centre of the thermal and are carried up.

Thermals are also used by other birds of prey, as well as members of the stork family, especially for migration. The white stork, which nests in central Europe, migrates about 7,000 kilometres to spend the winter in Africa. If it travelled all the way using flapping flight, it would need to stop and feed four times. By gliding between thermals for six or seven hours a day, the journey takes three weeks and leaves plenty of energy, in the form of stored fat, in reserve.

Thermals do not form over the sea, because water is slow to warm, so soaring migrants must avoid lengthy sea crossings. Large birds of prey and storks heading for Africa are funnelled through the Iberian Peninsula and the Balkans to leave Europe by the Straits of Gibraltar and the Bosphorus.

Thermal-soaring is usually limited to the warmer part of the day, but white storks have learned to make use of gas flares in the Algerian oilfields. They fly at night, swooping to within 5 metres above the flames, then spiral upwards and glide to the next flare, some 5 kilometres away.

Albatrosses and other seabirds, including petrels (relatives of the albatrosses), gannets and gulls, employ wind gradient-soaring and slope-soaring. A wave has the same effect as a hill or cliff in deflecting air upwards, so the seabirds can gain lift by flying along the crest of a wave. Even in a flat calm, slope-soaring is possible because the movement of large swells produces updraughts.

At intervals in gliding along a wave, an albatross will turn sharply into the wind and climb rapidly. When it is 10-15 metres above the waves it turns again and glides away across the wind. The bird is using the wind gradient to gain energy. The wind is slowed by contact with the water surface, so as the albatross rises, it meets increasingly faster wind, which will counteract the loss of groundspeed. When minimum gliding speed is reached, the bird turns and gains speed by descending.

With a strong wind and a little help from flapping, smaller seabirds, such as petrels, may also employ this technique of soaring over the waves, but long-winged albatrosses fly with hardly a wingbeat for kilometres at a stretch.

They are virtually 'freewheeling', with very little expenditure of energy. They have a special tendon to lock their wings in place and save the effort of keeping them outstretched. The amount of energy used in gliding is probably only twice that needed when the bird is resting, and Pennycuick has calculated that a 9-kilogram wandering albatross will use 1 per cent (90 grams) of its body weight on a 1,000-kilometre flight lasting 29 hours. Albatrosses, and other seabirds, are known to bring food to their chicks from foraging grounds hundreds of kilometres away. They could not do so without economical, energy-saving flight.

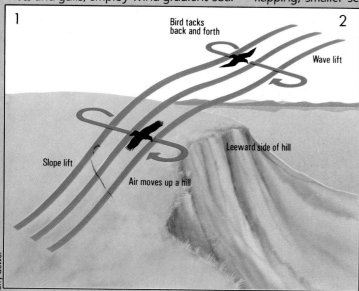

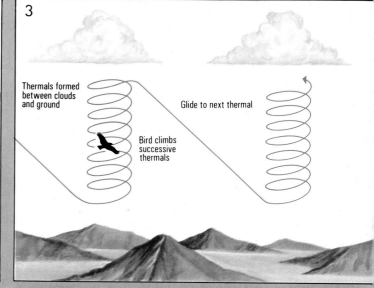

Right Thanks to their remarkable prowess at soaring, vultures can usually be sure of reaching food before mammal rivals, such as hyenas. In this case, a griffon vulture coming in to feed on a corpse attracts the attention of a distant lappet-faced vulture and a formidable competitor, a spotted hyena. The hyena, even though it runs at 40 km/h, loses out, since it takes 4.25 mins to cover the 3.5 km to the food, compared to the vulture, which, soaring in at a speed of 70 km/h, gets there in just 3 mins. *Bottom right* A New World vulture, the Andean condor.

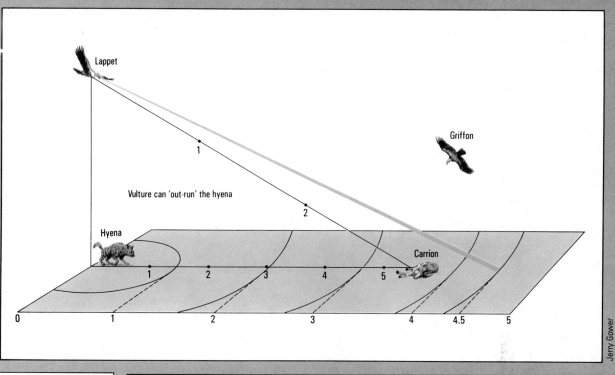

Lappet

1

Griffon

Vulture can 'out-run' the hyena

2

Hyena

Carrion

1   2   3   4   5

0   1   2   3   4   4.5   5

Jerry Gower

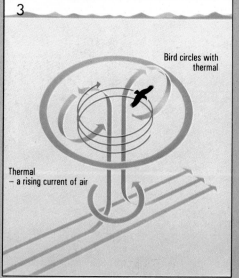

3

Bird circles with thermal

Thermal
– a rising current of air

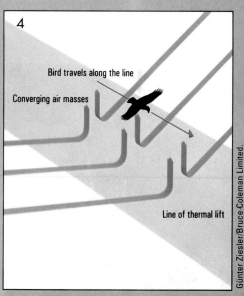

4

Bird travels along the line

Converging air masses

Line of thermal lift

Günter Ziesler/Bruce Coleman Limited.

DEATH IN THE DARK

Often heard but seldom seen, owls the world over are beautifully adapted to their night life

Below An uncompromising stare from one of the world's most enigmatic owls, the Papuan hawk owl. It lives in the lowland forests of Papua New Guinea, where it feeds on insects as well as small mammals. As with many other species of owl, much remains to be discovered about its life history.

Eric Lindgren/Ardea London

A tawny owl can seek out, catch and kill a vole in complete silence in what we would regard as total darkness. How is such a feat possible, and how are owls adapted as the ultimate nocturnal hunters?

There are about 130 different species of owl distributed throughout the world. They vary in size from the huge eagle owls to the minute pygmy and elf owls, which are little larger than a sparrow. All share specific adaptations to nocturnal hunting, though in the course of evolution some have abandoned the cloak of darkness and become daytime predators.

A range of lifestyles

Inevitably, with such a successful family, the various members specialize in hunting different types of prey and occupy different ecological niches – distinctive local environments which go with distinctive lifestyles. For example, the short-eared owl hunts voles by day over moors and marshes, whereas its close relative the long-eared owl specializes in catching the same creatures in conifer woods at night. The eagle owls are capable of killing a small deer or antelope, while the little owl satisfies itself mainly with moths and worms. In the tropics there are even owls that plunge, osprey-like, at night into water for fish. In such a diverse and large group of birds there are, of necessity, a wide range of specific anatomical differences – but the basic adaptations to a nocturnal existence are shared.

Like ourselves, and like other birds of prey, owls have their eyes set at the front of the head, giving up to 70 degrees of overlap, and enabling them to estimate distances very accurately. Such depth of vision is essential to any predator, though few are

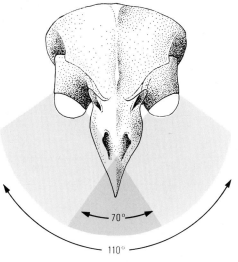

as well equipped in this respect as the owls. Most birds have 'all-round' vision which serves them perfectly well, since they do not need a highly tuned stereoscopic sense of distance to obtain their food. In their case it is better to have an all-round view so that predators can be spotted, no matter from which direction they approach.

To compensate for the inevitably restricted field of view, as little as 110 degrees in some species, owls have the ability to turn their heads through at least 180 degrees and thus see directly behind them. Such a facility is not only a guard against predators, but also helps them to locate prey in all directions.

Perhaps the most extraordinary feature of owls, however, is not the position but the size of their eyes. These are so big that they occupy a large part of the front of the head, and are separated from each other by only a thin layer of bone. As a result they fit

THE KEENEST EARS

Top left **The forward-facing eyes of owls give them a greater range of binocular vision than any other birds (70° out of a total field of view of 110°).** *Top* **A white-faced scops owl shows off one of its pale blue nictitating membranes, which protect the eyes from bright light as well as from mechanical damage.** *Above* **The large ear openings of an owl (in this case a tawny owl) are hidden beneath its head feathers.** *Far left* **A scops owl camouflages itself as a dead tree branch.** *Left* **A ferruginous pygmy owl confuses predators and prey by showing a false 'face' at the rear of its head.**

TAWNY OWL: Adaptations to night hunting

Large sensitive eyes with binocular vision.

Highly sensitive ears.

Broad wings for high manoeuvrability through dense woodlands: wing feathers have fine fringes and velvety pile to deaden noise of flight.

Camouflaged plumage conceals owl from daytime predators.

Powerful hooked bill for holding and tearing prey.

Widely spread talons for striking and gripping prey.

Top **Barn owl hunting methods. In almost pitch darkness (***1***) the owl relies on its hearing alone. Once it has located its prey, it flaps its wings, with legs swinging from side to side, and keeps its head in line with the victim until the last moment. Then it throws back its head and extends its talons. With more light (***2***) the owl can see well enough to home in on its meal in a sure glide.** *Far right* **Coming in for the kill: a barn owl spells sudden death for a vole.**

Left **The little owl is one of the most familiar Eurasian owls, often seen during the day, especially at dawn or dusk. This fierce-looking bird eats large amounts of insects as well as rodents. In Britain, where it was introduced in the 1870s, it was accused of taking gamebird chicks until a study of its pellets (indigestible prey remains ejected via the beak) exonerated it from blame.**
Overleaf top **The shorteared owl lives in open country in Eurasia and America and hunts, mainly for voles, by day.**
Overleaf bottom **Blood on the snow: a pygmy owl in British Columbia, Canada, crouches over a starling which it has just killed.**
Overleaf **The burrowing owl is a unique species which lives in open country in western North America and South America, with isolated populations in Florida and the Caribbean. It often nests in old mammal burrows.**

very tightly into the optical cavity, leaving virtually no room for controlling muscles. The eyes of many owls simply cannot be moved, and the birds rely on their highly flexible necks to look in different directions and at different angles.

Tubular eyes

Owls have tubular eyes, that is, eyes which are deeper than they are wide. The cornea is huge and the iris capable of an extraordinary range of expansion and contraction. In bright sunlight the birds not only try to find a dark hiding place, but also close down the iris to a tiny opening. At night they can open the iris wide to make use of every bit of available light.

The retina of all vertebrates consists of a series of rod cells and cone cells. Rods are associated with sensitivity to poor light, while cones are concerned with good resolution of colour and detail. Not surprisingly, the eyes of owls have a very high percentage of rods and they might be expected, therefore, to live in a mainly black-and-white world and to be rather poor at observing detail. Nevertheless, experiments have shown that some owls are capable of spotting and reacting to a predator, such as a flying eagle, long before the human eye can distinguish it.

Acute hearing

Owls do then have the power to see in the dark, but this may not be the primary means by which they locate their prey. Small mammals are generally skulking creatures that, even at night, keep well hidden among vegetation. To locate them, a predator needs a highly developed sense of hearing, as well as good sight. Owls have excellent hearing, with a wide outer ear tube. Their response to a range of frequencies is good and probably equals ours.

In some owls the ears are located asymmetrically on the head, giving them a sort of 3-D sense of hearing that parallels their binocular vision. The hearing parts of the ears, located behind the external openings to the ears, help the owl detect sounds coming from behind it. Many species, such as the long-eared owl and the eagle owls have 'ear tufts' that can be held erect, but these have absolutely nothing to do with hearing — they are used in threat and courtship displays, and may also help the owl recognize other members of its own species by their distinctive profile.

Using their well developed senses of sight and hearing together, owls can locate their prey in conditions of very poor light, though not — as experiments have shown — in total darkness. Once the owl has pinpointed its prey, it must pounce on it as silently as possible. However, most birds make a noise as they fly. The whistling wings of the swan can be heard at considerable distances as they beat through the air, and many others, particularly large birds, are also noisy fliers.

Noisy wings would be an obvious disadvantage to a nocturnal predator, serving to alert prey to an impending attack. Here, too, evolution has equipped owls with the perfect mechanism. Their feathers are soft, and the strong wing feathers that propel the bird through the air have a soft fringe to the barbs and a velvety surface that effectively deaden their sound. In this way, even nocturnal mammals with their acute sense of hearing are unaware of the approach of

Tom Willock/Ardea London

Ardea London

an owl until it is too late. By contrast, the huge eagle owls that are predominantly daytime hunters produce a good deal of wing noise as they come in to land or pounce on their prey.

Like the daytime birds of prey, such as eagles, hawks and falcons, owls are superbly equipped to kill and eat the animals they catch. Although not closely related to the daytime hunters, they have evolved many similar adaptations to suit their predatory life. They have powerful feet, equipped with long, mobile toes and needle-sharp, grasping talons. Normally, three toes point forwards and the other one backwards for perching as in most other birds. When the owl homes in for the kill, however, it reverses the outer toe so that two toes point forwards and two backwards, giving these powerful weapons the widest spread possible and the prey the smallest chance of escape.

The owl's bill varies in size according to the species and to the size of prey taken. As in daytime birds of prey, it is hooked and often large, though the greater part is hidden beneath the feathers of the face. The bill is a tearing weapon, designed to dismember the prey into bite-sized chunks. As with all predatory birds, though, it is the feet, with their razor-sharp talons, that one should be wary of — not the hooked bill.

Clever camouflage

Many animals are camouflaged to protect themselves from predators. In their turn, predators — from the tiger and leopard to eagles and hawks — are camouflaged so that they can avoid being seen by their prey. Hunting as they do under a cloak of darkness, there would seem little need for owls to be camouflaged at all. Yet most of them are.

Their camouflage serves to protect them against even more powerful predators during the day (including other owls) and also against the attentions of other birds. All predators suffer from the *mobbing* of smaller birds. An eagle soaring high in the sky may be attacked by a group of crows, or a hunting kestrel by a flock of tits or finches. This instinctive and often noisy reaction to a predator presumably alerts other small birds to its presence and location. As a re-

sult, the nocturnal owls tend to spend the hours of daylight well hidden in a hole or amongst dense vegetation tight against the trunk of a tree. In such situations, camouflaged plumage helps them to hide away and avoid the nuisance of small birds.

This mobbing behaviour has been well known for many years and has even been developed into a so-called sport in Mediterranean countries. In France, for example, a captive eagle owl was tethered on a post in daylight to attract the mobbing behaviour of diurnal birds of prey, which were then shot. Fortunately, both the owl and the diurnal birds of prey are now fully protected by law, though the practice may still continue illegally in some places.

Owls are highly efficient night-time hunters. Their adaptations are for a single purpose and based on one simple fact — the vast majority of small mammals throughout the world are largely nocturnal. Owls have evolved the means to break through this cloak of darkness and exploit a rich supply of food.

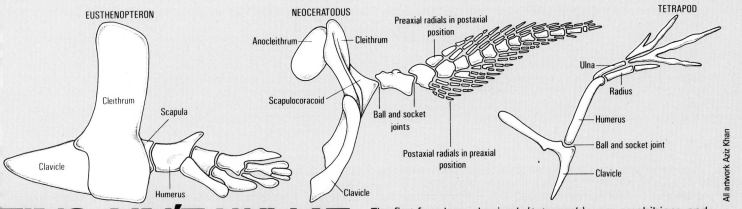

EUSTHENOPTERON
Cleithrum
Scapula
Clavicle
Humerus

NEOCERATODUS
Anocleithrum
Cleithrum
Scapulocoracoid
Ball and socket joints
Clavicle

Preaxial radials in postaxial position
Postaxial radials in preaxial position

TETRAPOD
Ulna
Radius
Humerus
Ball and socket joint
Clavicle

All artwork Aziz Khan

FINS AIN'T WHAT THEY USED TO BE

Over 400 million years ago fish began to drag themselves out of the water and on to dry land to evolve into the great diversity of four-limbed vertebrates

The first four-legged animals (*tetrapods*) were amphibians, and they evolved from a group of lobed-fin fish which, apart from one member, a bizzare living fossil – the coelacanth, are extinct. Well at least, this has been the accepted theory for the last century; but now a group of scientists has come up with a new idea, based on new information: that lungfishes and not lobed-fin fishes are the closest relatives of tetrapods.

Until about 120 years ago, lungfish were thought to be extinct. Then, three species were found alive and flourishing in South Africa and Australia. The first two species have two lungs and can survive well when out of water, while the Australian lungfish has only a single lung and cannot survive in a totally dry habitat. Back in the Devonian era, 345 to 395 million years ago, there were many species of lungfishes living at the same time as their lobed-fin cousins. In many ways today's lungfishes are like primitive land animals. Their eggs look like frog spawn, and their early stages of development are similar to that of frogs.

Grinding plates

It seems the main reason lungfishes were never considered to be the most closely related fish to the tetrapods is because today's species, as well as most fossilized lungfishes, don't have jaw bones or teeth. Tetrapods and lobed-fin fishes do. Instead, lungfishes have odd-shaped grinding plates, so it seemed that the leap from fish to land-living tetrapods was too great for lungfishes to make. Lobed-fin fishes were the obvious candidates. Now recent work has uncovered fossilized lungfishes that had jaws and teeth.

Whichever fish did give rise to tetrapods, biologists agree that about 350 million years ago there must have been a major change in the vertebrate way of life. This is because it was at this time, towards the end of the Devonian period, that vertebrates dragged themselves out of the water and began to colonize land.

Fossil and geological evidence shows that some fresh water habitats during the Devonian era were prone to drying up. The same thing happens in arid and semi-arid regions of the world

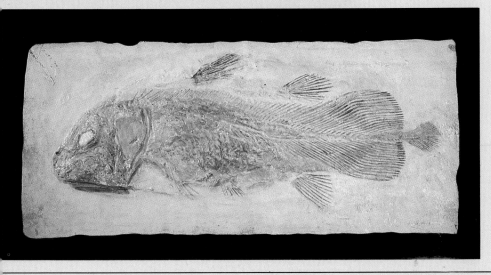

Until 1938 this fish (*left*) **was thought to be extinct. It is a coelacanth, the last remaining member of a group of lobed-fin fish palaeontologists believed to be the ancestors of land living tetrapods. Now new work, using a different method of classification, has shown that it is very unlikely that this fossil amphibian** (*above left*) **evolved from lobed-fin fish. It seems the coelacanth is a primitive fish.**

A wonderful example of fins being used as limbs for climbing is seen in the mudskipper. It uses its front fins rather like hands. It shows just how fins could have evolved into a normal tetrapod limb. Despite its ability to 'walk' on land and breathe atmospheric oxygen, the mudskipper is a true fish. Instead of lungs the fish has specialized vascular sacs. It isn't on the same evolutionary line as tetrapods.

today, and then conditions become pretty nasty for the animals. Some creatures die and decay causing the oxygen level in the water to drop rapidly, so any animal with lungs and the ability to pull itself out of the mud is at an obvious advantage.

At the time then, the evolution of air-breathing primitive lungs actually made some fish more successful as fish in their unstable watery world. The banks of Devonian waterways were certainly heavily colonized by plants and invertebrates which could provide food for any fish venturing onto land.

Cluster together

Some palaeontologists believe that lungs and limb-like fins would have enabled fish to drag themselves across the mud to waterways that had not dried up. This theory, however, is contradictory to the behaviour of living fish in a pool that is drying up. The fish actually cluster together as the water evaporates. There is even fossil evidence of this behaviour from the Devonian period, so it does seem quite likely that the transition from fish to amphibian was made in a somewhat less exhausting way.

Fins, of course had to continue to function in water as fins, even while they were evolving into limbs. It is possible that most fish fins have the potential for evolving into limbs, but the fin bones of lungfishes do seem to have evolved features found in tetrapod limbs but not in the fins of *Eusthenopteron* (the group of lobed-fin fishes that are thought to be the forerunners of tetrapods). For example the muscles of lungfish limbs extend to the extremities, but this is not the case with coelacanth fins. There are also ball and socket joints in lungfish fins which

correspond to shoulder and hip joints; elbow and knee joints are also represented.

Limbs are not the only important part of vertebrate anatomy, and palaeontologists have made extensive studies of the snout region and breathing apparatus of fishes thought to be close relatives to the first amphibians. They wanted to see if internal nostrils (*choanae*) existed. All tetrapods have choanae, so any fish possessing them is likely to be closely related, but all fish other than lungfish have external nostrils only. These end in a cul-de-sac and are used to provide a sense of smell. They are not used for breathing.

The main difference between fish and amphibians is their dependence on air breathing. Although some fish have lungs and breathe atmospheric oxygen, the lungs remain a secondary means of respiration. In most amphibians the situation is reversed, and gills are usually used only during the immature stage of the life cycle.

Ancient amphibians

Fossils of the most ancient amphibians, the *Ichthyostegas*, were first discovered in 1929 by the Danish East Greenland Expedition. The creatures were very close to fish, and even had a tail fin. All in all a few thousand fossils were found, some of which were in the larval stage and showed gills. Palaeontologists believe it must have been from *Ichthyostegas*, or a very similar creature of the Devonian period, that all land vertebrates evolved.

It seems unlikely that there were several starting points for the evolution of a vertebrate limb, because while limbs vary greatly in

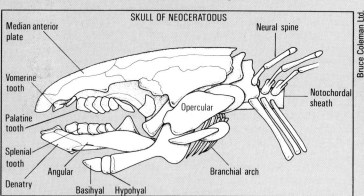

SKULL OF NEOCERATODUS

Median anterior plate
Neural spine
Vomerine tooth
Notochordal sheath
Opercular
Palatine tooth
Splenial tooth
Angular
Branchial arch
Denatry
Basihyal Hypohyal

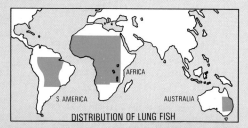

AFRICA
S. AMERICA
AUSTRALIA
DISTRIBUTION OF LUNG FISH

Above **The skull of a lungfish** *Neoceratoda* **showing grinding plates instead of teeth.** *Right* **The distribution of modern lungfishes.** *Below* **A lungfish is chipped out of its self-made mud prison.**

Bruce Coleman Ltd.

Oxford Scientific Films/Fran Allan

Bruce Coleman Ltd./Hans Reinhard

Below **The Australian lungfish** *Neoceratodus foresteri*. **This species appears more primitive than the other modern lungfish. These are found in South America** (*below left*) **and Africa** (*below right*)**. These creatures do not have jaw bones or teeth – a fact that led palaeontologists to believe they could not be related to tetrapods. However, they do have internal nostrils and the musculature of the fins is like that of tetrapod limbs.**

Above **and** *Right* **These mudskippers look much more like primitive tetrapods – scuttling about in the mud, chasing insects and small crustacea. But mudskippers are fish that have evolved locomotion on land.**

their adaptations there is a basic limb 'plan' common to all. Vertebrate limbs are all *pentadactyl* limbs, in other words they all have five digits (fingers or toes). In some vertebrates the limbs have become modified and digits have become reduced and sometimes completely lost, and these changes can be traced from the fossil record.

The coelacanth is the only surviving lobed-fin fish, and is closely related to *Eusthenopteron*. It therefore gives us a good idea of what lobed-fin fish of the Devonian period were like. When the first coelacanth was discovered in the Indian Ocean in 1938, scientists were very excited because until then it had only been known as a fossil. Since biologists had assumed that it had become extinct 40 to 50 million years ago, it was rather like finding a living dinosaur.

Since that first find, many coelacanths have been caught and examined by specialists all over the world. It was hoped that by studying the 'modern' species, palaeontologists would be able to understand the anatomy of the Devonian fish better, particularly *Eustenopteron*, and indeed the coelacanth turned out to be something of an eye opener.

Old four legs

'Old four legs' as the coelacanth was often referred to, is no more than a primitive bony fish with well-developed gills and a normal fish circulatory system, and there is no sign of choanae (internal nostrils). It is apparently not very closely related to any animal with legs. After this was discovered it seemed obvious that lungfish were indeed the nearest relatives to tetrapods, and lobed-fin fish including *Eusthenopteron* are, according to the team who have come up with the new theory, rather more distantly related.

The conclusions that have been arrived at after years of hard work owe much to the method of classification used. The *cladistic* method of grouping animals relies solely on arranging species on the basis of observable anatomical features. This new method has not only come up with a different answer to the question, 'from what did tetrapods evolve?', it is also making possible important advances in the classification of many animals.

Bruce Coleman Ltd./Jane Burton

Oxford Scientific Films/Z. Leszczynski

GROW YOUR OWN

The process by which some creatures can regrow limbs lost as a result of an accident or deliberate sacrifice to a predator reveals new secrets

Starfish have prodigious powers of regeneration, enabling them to regrow lost arms within the space of a year or less.
Below **Early days for a new arm of the starfish** *Luidia ciliaris.*
Right **The starfish** *Marthasterias glacialis* **copes with the demanding task of regenerating three lost arms; the new ones are visible as three tiny stumps, two on one side and one on the other. The animal's central mouth-containing disk must be present for regeneration to succeed. This individual has been stranded on the shore by the outgoing tide.**
Far right **Close inspection of the starfish** *Aolaster lincki,* **from the Indo-Pacific region, regenerating a lost arm shows that the tip, complete with delicate tube-feet, has already begun to grow.**

D. P. Wilson/Eric and David Hosking

Should they accidentally lose one or more of their five arms, most starfish can not only survive the trauma of injury but put matters to rights by growing – within a year – a perfectly good replacement. Even when a starfish is ripped to pieces, a severed arm that still has a piece of the animal's central mouth-containing disk still attached can grow enough new arms to transform it back to its correct size and shape.

Most efficient at this process of regrowth or regeneration are those starfish endowed with long, slender arms and small central disks. These same species are among those that use arm rejection

as a kind of defence mechanism. When subjected to potentially harmful stimuli, such as the adverse chemical conditions in stagnant water, or the mechanical stress caused by being attacked by a predator, these starfish will break off one or more arms at a predetermined point near the arm base. Usually, the arm rejected in this process of *autotomy* makes a few desultory movements before being abandoned on the seabed to decay, but in some starfish, the lost arm is employed and grows into a whole new starfish.

Whether an arm has been lost or deliberately cast off, the

starfish body reacts first to close the wound and so prevent the loss of vital body fluids. Next, a bud of tissue develops at the site, and in this bud are formed all the parts of the limb tip, including muscles and the numerous tube feet, projections which stud the undersurface of the starfish arms and are used in vital activities such as moving and feeding. Finally, body structures essential to the working of the arm as a part of the whole animal are formed. These include nerves, a system of hydraulic, water-conducting tubes which provide the force for operating the tube feet and branches of the blood and digestive systems. If more than one

arm has gone, then the same complicated processes are repeated simultaneously in each one.

Growing into a new starfish from a rejected arm is rather a different business. A new four-armed star, with its own central disk, first forms at the base of the single arm. This structure is aptly described as a 'comet' form. Where the tissues of the single arm were wounded, a new mouth forms, and once this is operational, the comet grows apace until the four new arms match their 'parent' in size. Other animals, too, share the starfishes' knack of regeneration. Sponges often form colonies of

Jen and Des Bartlett/Bruce Coleman Ltd.

Lizards can shed their tails at will, in an attempt to evade a predator: the latter is duped by the violent writhing of the tail into thinking that it has caught the whole animal, while the lizard flees to a safe hideout. Zoologists call this process autotomy, literally, 'self cutting'.
Left **Close-up of a lizard** *Phelsuma madagascarensis* **shows where body ends and new tail begins.** The mechanism of autotomy involves a weak plane of cleavage across one of the tail vertebrae; when muscles on each side of the tail contract, the tail breaks off.
Below **Two tails! One of the lizards popularly known as skinks, this** *Ablepharus boutonii* **lost only part of its original tail, and grew a replacement as well as the first one.**
Right **A slow-worm** *Anguis fragilis* **and the tail it has just shed. Slow-worms are neither worms nor snakes, but legless lizards.**
Crabs, too, are experts at autotomy. *Bottom right* **A shore crab** *Carcinus maenas* **regenerating its second claw (tiny object on left of picture).** Accidental autotomy during normal walking is prevented by a 'safety clip' mechanism. Fatal bleeding is prevented by a membrane that seals off blood vessels – and nerves – when these are torn asunder.

Jan Taylor/Bruce Coleman Ltd.

new individuals in this way; a suspension of cells from a sponge that has been passed through a fine mesh in the laboratory to break it up throughly will soon produce complete sponges. Sea anemones, corals, flatworms and earthworms are all expert in the art of growing new from old, while crabs and newts are able to sacrifice a limb and lizards their tails when caught by a predator.

Powers of regeneration

Anyone who has ever watched their own skin regrow after they have cut or burnt themselves is witness to the impressive powers of regeneration of some human body cells. And, amazingly, medical science now boasts cases where fingertips amputated in accidents have grown back, including the nails and the unique pattern of fingerprints. Even so, the idea of being able to grow a whole new human limb remains a dream. So what is it

the animals have that we don't, and how do they manage to be so versatile in adversity?

Recent research has focused on starfish. They are much simpler in construction than humans, but despite this they do show a considerable degree of differentiation of their cells into nerves, muscles, spines, tube feet, skeletal cells and so on. Genetic evidence seems to confirm that in starfish and humans alike, all the cells of the body, however specialized they have become, contain the complete complement of genetic information – which is the same for every cell. Equally, in any cell, about 10 per cent of the genetic information is used at any one time to confer on that cell its particular characteristics and behaviour.

It is the cells in which this genetic information is contained, and the way in which it is translated or transcribed, that appear to hold the key to the starfish's remarkable regenerative capacity.

Heather Angel

Below The ability to lose a limb voluntarily without losing life is known as autotomy. Shore crabs show this specialised structure when attacked by predators like large seabirds or fish, or when confronting other aggressive crabs, or when trapped between shoreline boulders or rocks. The limb is shed by a reflex action at a weak fracture point where the limb segments meet. For most animals the sudden loss of a limb would lead to massive bleeding and death, but not for creatures — like shore crabs — that can regrow them.

When the starfish arm is wounded or cast off it seems that an array of unspecialized reserve, or 'hobo', cells, with which the starfish is especially well endowed, have their crucial 10 per cent of genes activated by the chemicals released during the wounding. Particularly potent among these chemical triggers are thought to be nucleic acids liberated from destroyed cells, and calcium ions from the cell substance, or cytoplasm. Evidence comes from studies of starfish development, in which calcium ions play a vital role in the transition from one larval stage to the next, and experiments on the reactions of unspecialized cells to the injection of nucleic acids from broken-down cells.

Specialization

In theory, there is no reason why human cells should not react

their genetic makeup but the fact that they have progressed too far down the road to specialization. So instead of being hobos — footloose and fancy-free — the least specialized human reserve cells are already confined to the cellular city and can only develop into connective tissues — such as the skin.

While we may regret our lack of regenerative ability, we can console ourselves with the fact that the very existence of such an ability in the starfish and other animals is a measure of their vulnerability — a vulnerability that we would find unacceptable. As a compromise we can accept regeneration sufficient to satisfy our everyday needs, and this includes the constant renewal of nearly all body cells as they wear out.

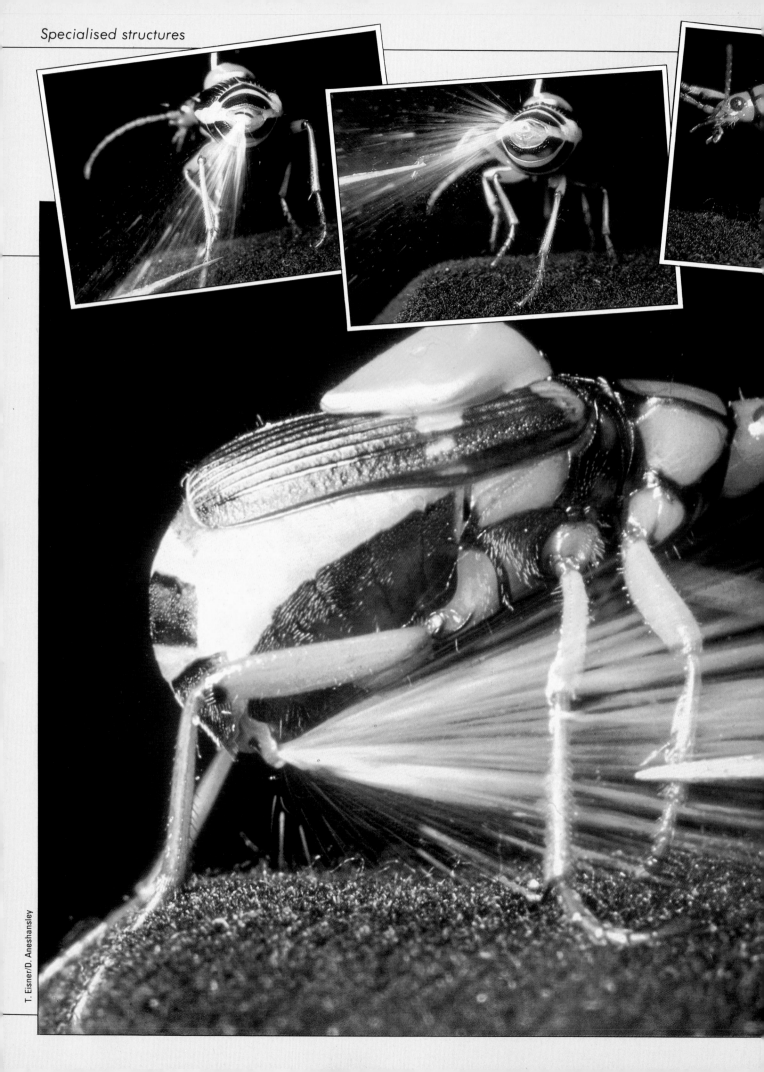

T. Eisner/D. Aneshansley

BANG GOES THE BEETLE

Far left **Fire! Anchored by a hook fixed into a wax blob on its back, a bombardier blasts off a salvo of boiling hot caustic liquid in the name of science. These studies, by Dan Aneshansley and Thomas Eisner at Cornell University, New York, involved measuring the temperature of the liquid in each blast – a constant 100°C. The beetle aims its spray very accurately in different directions. Its actual body length is about 10 mm.**

Bombardier beetles defend themselves by aiming a boiling hot caustic spray at their enemies

The members of one successful group of ground-beetles have developed an extraordinary defence mechanism. They ward off potential predators by bombarding them with a burning, distasteful chemical cocktail – a habit that has earned them the name 'bombardier beetles'.

Bombardiers are found almost the world over: in Britain and Northern Europe, the species *Brachinus crepitans* is widespread, while in the USA *Brachinus americanus* is very common from the central states westwards. Bombardiers range in length from about 5 cm to 15 cm; those found in Africa and the Far East tend to be larger than their European relatives – and their bombardments are correspondingly more ferocious.

Most bombardiers are a mixture of yellowish orange and black, but some African *Aptinus* species are plain black or reddish in colour. The large *Pheropsophus* bombardiers from the tropics and subtropics of Africa and the Far East, as far north as Japan and northern China, have a typical warning colouration – yellow with black markings, not unlike those of a wasp.

There is a considerable number of species of bombardier beetles worldwide – in the United States alone, for instance, there are some 40 species. In Europe, they tend to become more numerous further south. Although only one species occurs in Britain, half a dozen different kinds live in the south of France.

The bombardier's firepower is created by paired *pygidial glands* situated in the insect's abdomen. Secretory cells produce two hydroquinone compounds and hydrogen peroxide at a concentration of 23 per cent. These chemicals are secreted via a duct into a pair of reservoirs, where they are stored until needed. When a bombardier is alarmed or attacked, the two chemicals pass into a combustion chamber, surrounded by thick, chemical- and heat-resistant walls. The muscular valve between reservoir and combustion chamber opens to allow the chemicals to pass through. Simultaneously, catalase and peroxidase enzymes are released into the combustion chamber, and these cause the two chemicals to combine in a violent reaction, producing a small explosion.

The chemical reaction produces water, caustic quinones and oxygen – the latter provides the gas pressure necessary to expel the caustic liquid from two apertures at either side of the beetle's anus. The pressure heats the quinones so that they are blasted out in the form of a very hot corrosive spray – enough to deter any enemy. Biologists have estimated that the heat content of this secretion is 0.9 calories per mg – enough to raise the temperature of

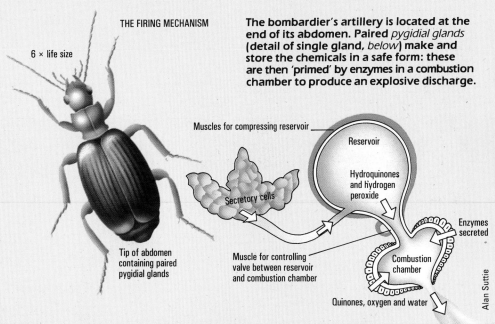

THE FIRING MECHANISM

6 × life size

The bombardier's artillery is located at the end of its abdomen. Paired *pygidial glands* (detail of single gland, *below*) make and store the chemicals in a safe form: these are then 'primed' by enzymes in a combustion chamber to produce an explosive discharge.

Muscles for compressing reservoir

Reservoir

Hydroquinones and hydrogen peroxide

Secretory cells

Enzymes secreted

Tip of abdomen containing paired pygidial glands

Muscle for controlling valve between reservoir and combustion chamber

Combustion chamber

Quinones, oxygen and water

Alan Suttie

Akinori Yoshitani/Dr. Shun-Ichi Véno

the solution to 100°C!

The beetles are able to bombard anything in sight with a series of discharges and can aim their fire extremely accurately in different directions (some relatives of the bombardier beetles even have separate 'gun turrets' which they can aim independently. When the storage chambers are fully charged, there are enough chemicals to produce between 10 and 20 discharges. Some species of bombardier puff out tiny clouds of mist at the same time as the caustic substance is released – these confuse and deter the enemy still further. Some of the larger bombardiers produce a clearly audible discharge, rather like the noise of a person spitting.

Most predators will give up the attack once they are sprayed with the caustic secretion. Even a large predator, such as a bird or a reptile, spits out the bombardier as soon as the offensive substance hits its mouth.

Reassuringly, bombardiers do not pose much of a threat to humans. They are likely to discharge their defence glands if handled, but the quinone produces a warm sensation on the fingers, rather than a painful burn. The secretion does stain skin, however, and this stain – similar to the tobacco stains of the heavy smoker – can last for up to three weeks.

Parasitic larvae

A less widely known but equally unusual feature of bombardier beetles is the behaviour of their larvae. The immature stages of most ground-beetles are active predators. Their mouthparts, well-developed eyes and longs legs suit them for a life of seeking out and capturing their prey, mostly other insects. Not so bombardiers: the life-histories of only a few have been worked out in any detail, but that of the North American *Brachinus pallidus* is likely to prove typical. Like many other bombardiers, *B. pallidus* lives near rivers, streams and ponds, and it is here that the female de-

Above **Sharpshooter on the move: this is one of the larger species,** *Pheropsophus jessoensis,* **from Japan. Its black and yellow body warns predators to keep their distance.**
Bottom **A first-stage** *Brachinus pallidus* **bombardier larva is dwarfed by its host, the pupa of the water beetle** *Tropiesternus,* **on which it feeds itself until ready to pupate.**

posits her eggs, each encased in a small ball of wet mud.

The newly hatched larva differs little in appearance from that of other ground-beetles. However, its behaviour is very different. Instead of being attracted by passing springtails or other potential prey, it seeks out the pupae of hydrophilid water beetles. Both larval and adult water beetles are aquatic, but the final larval stages leave the water in order to pupate. The first stage *Brachinus* larva enters the pupal chamber of its future host, excavated in wet mud or sand, and begins to feed on the water-bee-

tle pupa, which soon dies. After four moults (most ground-beetle larvae moult only twice), having completely consumed the water-beetle pupa, the *Brachinus* larva is itself ready to pupate.

The bombardier spends most of its larval life ensconced within its host's pupal chamber. Indeed, it is ill equipped to venture into the outside world during its larval stages, having lost many of its more typical ground-beetle features. The second to fifth stage larvae are unpigmented and soft-bodied, lack definite eyes, and have very short, stumpy legs.

Entomologists have identified the exact species of water-beetle hosts of four North American species of *Brachinus*. The several hundred other species of bombardier probably have a similar life-history. The most important clue that this is so is the fact that adult bombardiers of a particular species vary greatly in size. This is a common consequence of a life-style in which a parasite depends for food solely on a single host which varies in size itself.

Not all bombardier beetle larvae parasitize water beetle pupae, however. The larvae of the tropical *Pheropsophus* bombardiers, for instance, feed on clusters of mole-cricket eggs which are, like the bombardier's eggs, laid in mud-lined chambers. *Brachinus crepitans*, locally common in southern Britain and elsewhere in northern Europe, is found far from water in dry, chalky or sandy areas. It was the first bombardier beetle to be described – by Carl von Linné (Linnaeus), the great Swedish naturalist and 'father of biological classification', in 1758. Well over 200 years later, a vital feature of its life-history – what the larvae feed on – remains unknown.

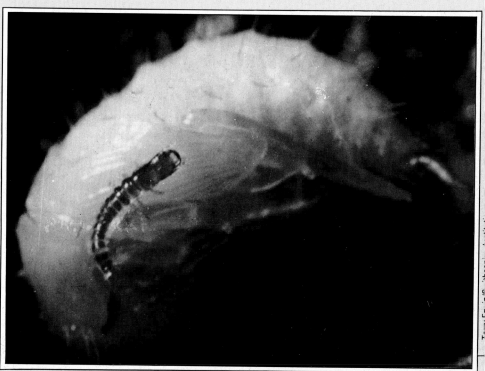

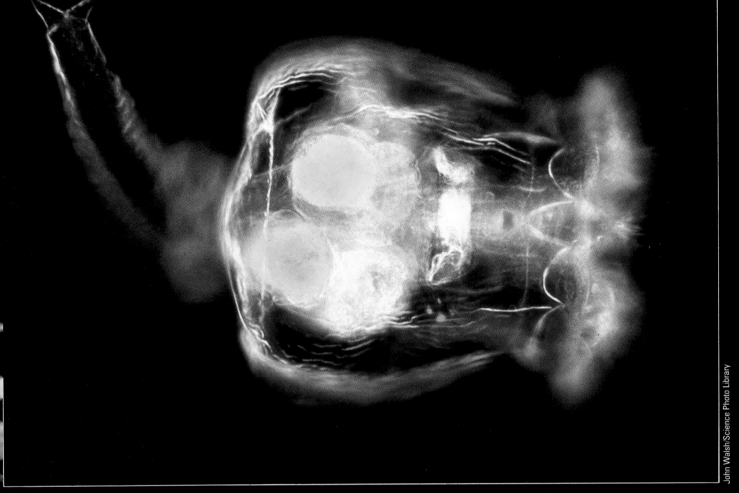

John Walsh/Science Photo Library

LITTLE ROTIFERS

The female rotifer can survive most extremes, but the male must make the most of his short life

Brachionus – **a common rotifer which usually feeds on unicellular algae – is seen here with its corona of cilia extended. Its single red eye and pointed white jaws are clearly visible. The two yellow shapes are developing eggs. At the end of its trunk-like foot are two 'toes' which secrete the cement that anchors it during feeding.**

Imagine yourself seated in complete darkness before a circular observation window so large you have to move your head to take it all in. Just beyond the window, the violently chewing jaws of some huge transparent creature are visible, reducing the brilliant green spheres which are its food to a thin porridge of suspended particles which rotates slowly in its transparent stomach. The crystalline jaws catch the light as they grind together like two sets of glass knuckles. Above the jaws is the creature's single eye, an unblinking corpuscle of the purest red. Suddenly the vision is gone – only a swirling galaxy of glittering particles can be seen against the black depths of water beyond the glass.

No – you are not exploring the depths of some ocean, but seated at the controls of a high-power dark-field microscope, and the creature you saw was a rotifer, fully half a millimetre long.

The first man to see and describe rotifers was the Dutch microscopist Anton van Leeuwenhoek, in the early 18th century. He called them wheel animals because of the vivid illusion of rotation created by the beating of their crown of cilia – fine hairs which produce a vortex by which the creatures draw food particles to the mouth.

Leeuwenhoek found his specimens in the canal which flowed outside his house in Delft, but thriving populations of rotifers can occur in almost any body of fresh water. They live amongst the decaying leaves in the roof guttering of houses, in bird baths and puddles, in freezing mountain lakes, mineral springs and even in thermal wells, enduring temperatures of 45°C and more. Many rotifers are able to resist both freezing and drying for long periods. Rotifers indigenous to the Antarctic may remain frozen solid for years at a time, only to resume normal activities within an hour or so of a thaw. Others will go into a dormant state when their watery environment dries up, and their desiccated bodies are spread to distant parts of the world by winds and migratory birds.

Organ systems

Having a brain and nervous system, digestive, reproductive and excretory systems, the rotifers are amongst the smallest of the *Metazoa* – the biological group which includes Man and all the animals whose bodies are made up of cells organized into systems of organs. But while a mammal's body is composed of many billions of cells, these same basic organ systems are distilled

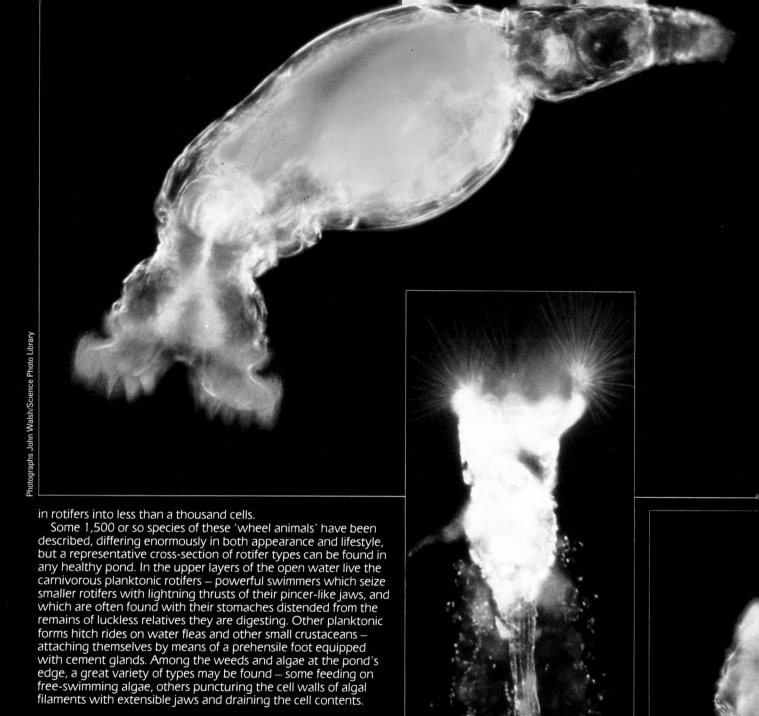

Photographs John Walsh/Science Photo Library

in rotifers into less than a thousand cells.

Some 1,500 or so species of these 'wheel animals' have been described, differing enormously in both appearance and lifestyle, but a representative cross-section of rotifer types can be found in any healthy pond. In the upper layers of the open water live the carnivorous planktonic rotifers – powerful swimmers which seize smaller rotifers with lightning thrusts of their pincer-like jaws, and which are often found with their stomachs distended from the remains of luckless relatives they are digesting. Other planktonic forms hitch rides on water fleas and other small crustaceans – attaching themselves by means of a prehensile foot equipped with cement glands. Among the weeds and algae at the pond's edge, a great variety of types may be found – some feeding on free-swimming algae, others puncturing the cell walls of algal filaments with extensible jaws and draining the cell contents.

Fixed rotifers

Other species browse amongst the debris which settles in the mud of the pond's bottom. Attached to pond weeds and tree rootlets live the *sessile* or fixed rotifers, which have developed a variety of ways of trapping passing food organisms. Some rely upon the powerful currents generated by a large corona of cilia. Others trap unwary single-celled organisms by enmeshing them in a forest of fine, rigid filaments. Most of them construct tubes of one kind or another to give themselves some protection from marauders such as worms and insect larvae.

The *Collotheca*, for example, secretes a transparent mucous tube into which it retreats in the face of possible danger. Some species, such as the *Testudinella* and *Mytilina* have evolved a

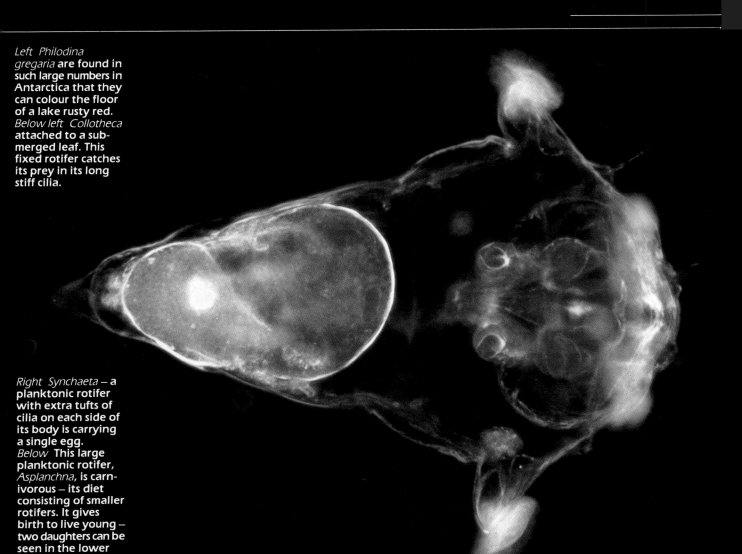

Left Philodina gregaria are found in such large numbers in Antarctica that they can colour the floor of a lake rusty red.
Below left Collotheca attached to a submerged leaf. This fixed rotifer catches its prey in its long stiff cilia.

Right Synchaeta – a planktonic rotifer with extra tufts of cilia on each side of its body is carrying a single egg.
Below This large planktonic rotifer, Asplanchna, is carnivorous – its diet consisting of smaller rotifers. It gives birth to live young – two daughters can be seen in the lower portion of its body.

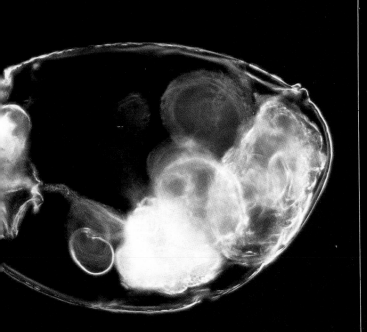

tortoise-like habit of withdrawing their head and 'tail' into their shell if disturbed. Others, such as the *Filinia*, will get themselves out of trouble in a more energetic manner – by performing a sudden backward flip.

Reproduction in rotifers is for the most part asexual, females producing eggs which hatch – without fertilization – into females. The eggs may be carried round by the parent or attached to rocks or weeds, but in many cases the young reach maturity within the parent's body and are born live.

Short-lived males

In those relatively few species for which males are known, the story is quite different. The males usually appear briefly, but in large numbers, towards the end of the summer season. They hatch from special eggs produced by the females, and have at most a day or so to seek out a mate. This time limit is set because most rotifer males have no digestive system, and after a few hours or a day of frenetic activity they will have exhausted their meagre energy reserves and die of starvation. This makes rotifer mating an urgent and violent business.

The female is suddenly set upon by an animated bag of sperms which thrusts its ciliated penis through her body wall, releasing sperms which find their way to the eggs through the walls of her reproductive system. Fertilized eggs develop hard shells and are capable of surviving winter, to hatch the following spring into females whose eggs require no fertilization – and so the parthenogenetic cycle continues. The wheel has come full circle.

THE BENIGN PRISON

Biologists are beginning to crack the secrets hidden within the shells of birds' eggs

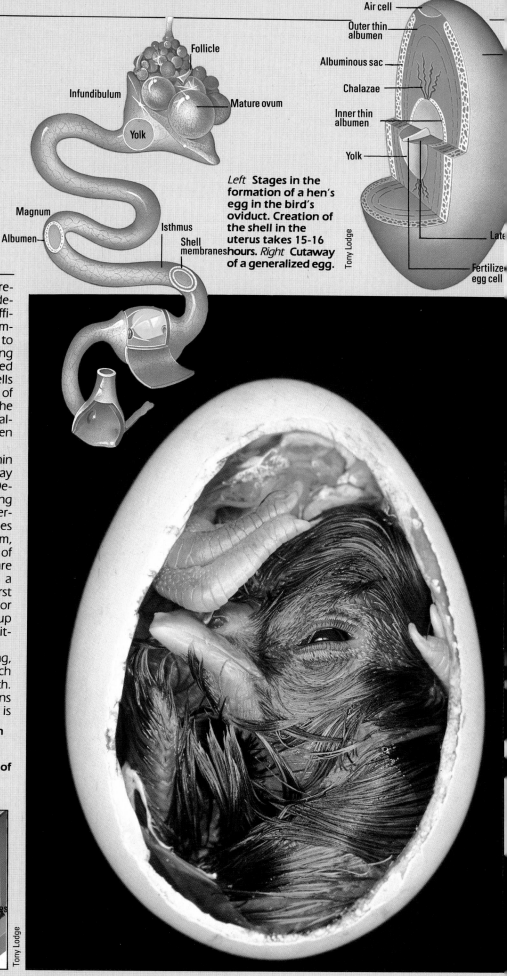

Left **Stages in the formation of a hen's egg in the bird's oviduct. Creation of the shell in the uterus takes 15-16 hours.** *Right* **Cutaway of a generalized egg.**

Tony Lodge

Next time you crack the breakfast egg, reflect on the fact that you are about to destroy an extraordinarily complex and efficient natural structure. The seemingly simple eggshell of a hen turns out, in fact, to contain as many as 15,000 tiny breathing pores, each shaped like a golf-tee, plugged by minute protein balls. And the eggshells of many small birds have the appearance of sponge rubber when viewed under the electron microscope. Such a structure allows them to bend rather than break when treated roughly.

This remarkable barrier is created within the female bird as the egg makes its way down the looped egg-tube, or oviduct. Despite the shortness of the route along which it passes from the ovary to the external opening, or cloaca, the egg undergoes various changes along the way. The ovum, or egg cell, is fertilized in the upper part of the oviduct before the egg membranes are formed. The lining of the oviduct bears a wealth of glands of various sorts: the first group of glands secretes the albumen, or egg-white, around the yolk, the next group the egg membranes and the last the shell itself.

An egg is a miracle of natural packaging, containing all the food and water which the developing chick will need for growth. The yolk contains proteins, fats, vitamins and trace elements, while the egg-white is

Right **After 20 days of incubation, the hen chick is almost ready to break its way out of the shell that has helped keep it alive so far. Diagram** *below* **shows the structure of an eggshell: mamillary cores act as nuclei for the formation of the calcite columns.**

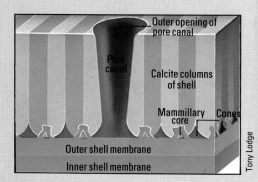

Tony Lodge

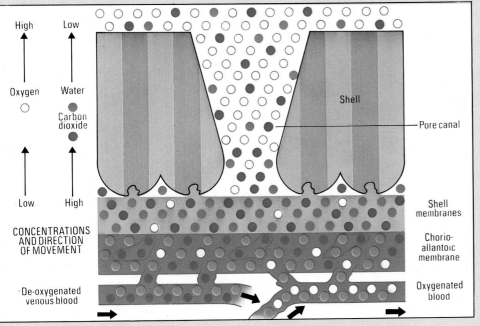

High   Low

Oxygen   Water
○   ●
         Carbon
         dioxide
         ●

Low   High

CONCENTRATIONS
AND DIRECTION
OF MOVEMENT

Shell

Pore canal

Shell membranes

Chorio-allantoic membrane

Oxygenated blood

De-oxygenated venous blood

fact, a bird's egg will not develop at atmospheric temperature, so the parents must operate a shift system of sitting on the eggs or cover them with feathers or plant material as insulation if they leave them for a while.

One extraordinary exception to the usual state of affairs is seen in the *megapodes*, or mound-builders, of Australasia. The male Mallee fowl of south Australia builds an impressive mound 5 m across and over 1 m high from plants, soil and sand. His mate then lays her eggs via a hole in the top of this ingenious artificial incubator. As the vegatation decomposes, the heat produced incubates the eggs. The female takes no further interest in the eggs, but the male stays near the mound for up to eight weeks, checking its temperature by touching it with his sensitive mouth lining or tongue; if necessary, he adjusts the thickness of the mound by adding or removing material, thus controlling the incubation temperature so that it does not vary by more than 1°C. On hatching, the chicks, which are the most advanced of all newly emerged birds, dig their way out of the mound unaided: within hours they are able to fly. Other mound-builders use sun-baked sand, rock or soil heated by volcanic springs to incubate their eggs.

Shell structure

An eggshell is made up mainly of columns of chalky calcite (a crystalline form of

a built-in water reservoir.

Both yolk and white are contained within a pliable net-like bag formed by the two membranes, which are made up of a central thread of elastic protein and a mantle of proteins and sugars. Surrounding and protecting these delicate membranes is the hard shell.

As well as food and water, the developing embryo needs a supply of oxygen, a means of getting rid of carbon dioxide, a source of heat, a source of calcium for bone formation, a system of water conservation, and protection from bacterial infection and mechnical damage. All these needs are taken care of by the eggshell. The develop-

ing chick absorbs oxygen and discharges waste carbon dioxide via the layer known as the choriallantois, which lines the inner surface of the shell membranes and is richly supplied with blood vessels. The rigid eggshell prevents the chick from pumping these gases in and out as an adult bird would do using its lungs. Instead they are exchanged by the simple process of diffusion through the tiny pores in the shell.

Though surprisingly strong, eggshells are also remarkably thin, so that it is no problem for heat from an incubating parent bird to penetrate the inside by conduction. Unlike most reptiles, almost all birds incubate their eggs by the heat of their bodies: in

Eggshells with pores protected by a layer of tiny inorganic spheres (*right*) are made by birds like the little grebe (*below*), which lay their eggs in nests of wet, muddy vegetation. The spheres prevent the pores clogging, so the chick does not suffocate.

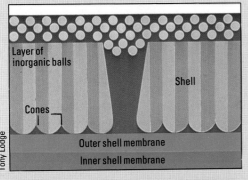

Layer of inorganic balls

Shell

Cones

Outer shell membrane

Inner shell membrane

Tony Lodge

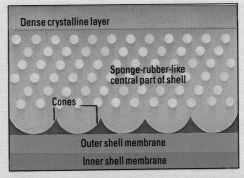

Dense crystalline layer

Sponge-rubber-like central part of shell

Cones

Outer shell membrane

Inner shell membrane

Another type of shell (*left*) has its tough, flexible centre protected by a layer of dense crystals. This type is found in birds like the ringed plover, which lays its perfectly camouflaged eggs on pebbly beaches. The crystals stop the shell being scratched as the eggs are turned.

R. Tidman/Bruce Coleman Ltd.

calcium carbonate), arranged radially from the shell membranes. Gaps between the columns form pores, which are kept open by a flow of liquid from the shell gland into the albumen.

Like that of the domestic hen, the shells of many birds' eggs contain thousands of golf-tee-shaped pores. In some species, including pigeons, the egg is laid as soon as the shell is formed and the outer opening of the pore canal remains open. In the hen's eggshell, a layer of glycoprotein spheres is laid down on the outer surface. These minute balls not only cover the openings of the pore canals, but they also protrude into the canals, forming crude plugs.

The tropical lily-trotters, or jacanas, and the tinamous of South America have golf-tee pores plugged by organic matter. In the eggshells of emus, cassowaries, storks and some birds of prey, the pore canal does not remain a recognizable structure across the entire width of the shell. Instead, the orderly growth of the columns of crystals stops. The outer part of the shell is covered with a layer of irregularly shaped crystals that fuse with one another. The spaces in between are interconnected to form a complex network surrounding the outer part of the shell and penetrating its surface, so that the pore canals are connected to the outside by a tortuous network of passages.

Evidence is slowly accumulating that links the covered pore systems with birds that lay eggs in nests that are often wet and muddy, supporting the theory that the layer of balls on the surface of their shells keeps the pores open. As each pore opening is only a fraction of a square millimetre in diameter, the pores would soon become blocked if the balls were not there. Should

Hans Reinhard/Bruce Coleman Ltd.

Left The little owl lays its white eggs in a dark hole: they do not need to be coloured and patterned for camouflage. Their almost spherical shape helps them fit into the cramped confines of the nest-hole.
Below The guillemot has pear-shaped eggs. Their shape helps them cope with being laid on precipitous sea-cliff ledges: if knocked, they roll around in circles instead of falling off the edge.

this happen, the embryo would suffocate. Similarly, the partly plugged pores of the lily trotters' eggshells appear to be an adaptation for incubation in a nest of floating vegetation where there is an obvious need for water-proofing. Laboratory studies of pore flooding have proved that the layer of balls over a pore confers considerable resistance to the inward flow of water. Not only would flooded pores hamper gas diffusion, but they would also allow bacteria to penetrate the defences of the shell.

The material from which the balls are made is related to the need to cope with humidity. The organic glycoproteins that make up the balls of a hen's eggshell would

be useless in an egg laid in a humid situation, since they soon become covered with mould. Instead, such eggs have their shells covered with balls of inorganic salts – vaterite, an uncommon crystal form of calcium carbonate, in the shells of gannets and shags, which make their nests from a shallow layer of rotting seaweed, and non-crystalline calcium phosphate in those of grebes, flamingoes and megapodes. Grebes lay their eggs on a platform of decaying vegetation and flamingoes on a pile of mud, while megapode eggs have the most humid environment of all to contend with.

The total pore area of an eggshell is one of the factors that influence the rate of diffusion of oxygen into the shell and waste carbon dioxide out of it. Other factors are the relative densities of the two gases on either side of the shell and the shell's actual thickness.

A necessary loss

Biologists once thought that the high level of water loss during incubation – about 16% on average – was an unavoidable penalty that the embryo has to suffer because of its need to have a porous shell for gas diffusion. Recent research, however, has shown that this water loss is essential for hatching in the vast majority of birds. The initial phase of hatching, in which the chick hammers a hole through the shell using the egg tooth on its beak, calls for the baby bird to move its head as well as having a supply of oxygen greater than that which can be supplied from the chorioallantois alone. As the loss of volume of the egg contents resulting from the 16% water loss is compensated for by growth in volume of the air cavity, both the necessary space and

Dr. J. A. L. Cooke/Oxford Scientific Films

Left The smallest and thinnest-shelled eggs are, not surprisingly, laid by the smallest birds, the hummingbirds of the New World. The tiny eggs of the emerald hummingbird weigh less than a gram each.

the increased oxygen for breathing are available to the chick.

Researchers have also found that the shell's ability to conduct water vapour is nicely tuned to the nesting conditions, so that the required 16% water loss is achieved. Grebe eggshells, for instance, have a water vapour conductance three times that of eggs of equal mass incubated under drier conditions. High water conductance values have also been found in the eggshells of birds such as puffins that nest in humid burrows.

Saturated atmosphere

The eggshells of the mound-nesting megapodes also have very high water conductances, but this is an adaptation to the low levels of oxygen and high levels of carbon dioxide in the mound. In fact, megapode eggs lose very little water during incubation because of the saturated atmosphere of the mound. The highly developed chick can cope with this because it is able to smash its way to freedom without first having to peck a hole in the shell. Indeed, it is so well developed that it can force its way out of the mound and fly within hours of hatching.

Low water conductances have been measured for those of species, such as the ocean-ranging albatrosses, that have very long incubation periods, and also for those of birds that nest at high altitudes. In the latter, water loss is increased by the low barometric pressure at great heights.

Interestingly, none of the many studies of water loss from eggs has shown that it is influenced by the type of pore found in the eggshell.

As well as providing a finely tuned system of gas, water and heat transfer, an eggshell must be strong. It must protect the developing chick by resisting fracture when compressed. A recent study showed that the eggshell has just the right strength to resist the weight of the incubating parent bird – and no more.

Sandy soil
Egg chamber
Fermenting vegetation

Bruce Coleman Ltd.

Nearly all birds incubate their eggs: the *megapodes* of Australasia are an exception to the rule. One species, the mallee fowl, lays up to 35 eggs in a huge mound of fermenting vegetation built by the male (*above*).

Hens lay eggs with hard, brittle shells that will not crack if they roll into each other in the nest – this type of shell is found in all large eggs. Its robustness helps to make it harder for predators to force an entry. If small eggs had hard, brittle shells they would be as delicate as bone china. Recent research has shown that the relatively thin shells of small eggs are tough and flexible instead, so that they dissipate any applied force by flexing. These eggs have many very small hollow spheres in their shells, though the exact way in which these make the shell flexible is not yet known. The main part of the eggshells of many songbirds looks like sponge rubber when examined with an electron microscope, while the shell surface bears many hemispherical depressions.

Easily scratched

Such a shell would be easily scratched if turned in a nest containing sand or other abrasive materials, and the pore canals would quickly become blocked with dust.

The nests of birds such as ringed plovers and oystercatchers – mere scrapes in the sand containing small pebbles – offer just such a hostile environment, and the 'sponge-rubber' portion of the eggshells of these birds is therefore capped by a protective layer of dense crystals.

The brittleness or otherwise of the shell not only helps cocoon the chick from damage, but also determines the way in which it emerges into the world. A chick in a hard, brittle shell needs to peck only a few holes in its broader end before thrusting down with its legs and up with its head. This makes cracks in the shell that link the holes, and then the chick can remove a cap of shell at the end.

If a chick in a tough, flexible type shell used such a strategy, it would be up against the same problem you would face trying to break an uninflated party balloon merely by pushing your finger into its rubber wall. Instead, the chick pecks lots of holes around a complete circumference of the shell before pushing the cap off. In both cases, the chick instinctively follows behaviour patterns that have evolved to work with a structure that is itself a marvel of evolution.

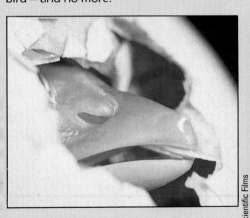

Above **The first moments of hatching, as a hen chick uses the egg-tooth on its beak to chip holes in the shell before pushing out a door to freedom.**
Right **Eggs come in a wide range of sizes.**
Left to *right*, **eggs of a hummingbird, hen, ostrich and extinct elephant bird.**

Stephen Dalton/Oxford Scientific Films

HOW WOODPECKERS PACK A PUNCH

Investigation of the woodpecker's prodigious capacity for withstanding a battering reveals a built-in shock absorber far superior to any made by Man

After a brief career of fighting fifteen or less three-minute rounds a few times a year, many professional boxers retire with a degree of punch drunkenness that could leave them destined for the human scrapheap. Yet they have taken only a few serious blows to the head over a period of, say, five hours of competitive boxing a year.

Compare this with the gruelling punishment that woodpeckers seem to suffer as a matter of routine. In excavating its nest-hole, a woodpecker may hammer away continuously for five or six hours a day. Add to this impressive performance up to five hundred periods each day of banging away at tree trunks to produce its unique 'song' during the courtship season, and also regular hacking at bark for food, and the wonder is not that all woodpeckers aren't punch-drunk, but that they have survived at all.

Hammering with its bill against a dead tree-trunk or branch, a woodpecker produces a far-carrying hollow sound, or 'drumming', that acts as a substitute for song and makes it one of the very few accomplished non-human instrumentalists. Watching a woodpecker's performance in close-up reveals the extraordinary speed of its blows. The Great Spotted Woodpecker

Hans Reinhard/Bruce Coleman Ltd.

M. P. Kahl/Bruce Coleman Ltd.

Right **Poised high up on the lofty trunk of a corkscrew pine in Florida, USA, a handsome Pileated Woodpecker pauses in its search for woodboring insects. The equivalent large woodpecker species in Europe is the crow-sized Black Woodpecker** (*above*), **seen here hacking out its nest-hole.**

Zoologists have studied the action of a woodpecker's upper bill. When it strikes a tree, the force A exerted against the bill tip is opposed by a larger force B resulting from the action of its protractor muscle. The forward pull C at the base of the rear of the skull results in an opposite, backward, movement D of the skull away from the bill.

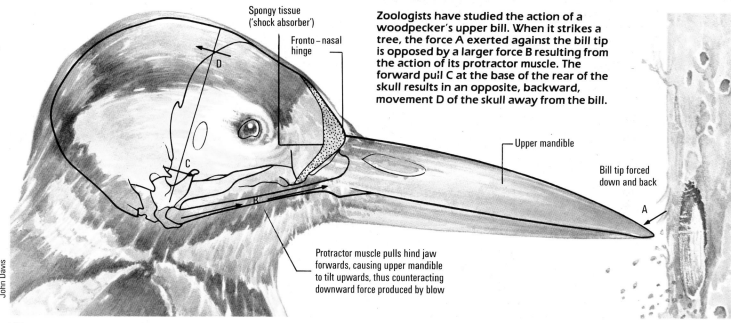

Spongy tissue
('shock absorber')

Fronto – nasal
hinge

Upper mandible

Bill tip forced
down and back

Protractor muscle pulls hind jaw
forwards, causing upper mandible
to tilt upwards, thus counteracting
downward force produced by blow

John Davis

of Eurasia drums at the rate of eight or ten beats a second, smaller woodpeckers even faster. How, one wonders, can the bird, and particularly its brain, survive without serious damage? And the bursts of courtship drumming are not the only occasions on which the woodpecker subjects its head to apparent punishment. Woodpeckers typically feed by hacking away tree-bark to reach insects and their larvae hidden beneath; and, with a carpenter's skill, they hollow out nesting chambers ten or more times their own bulk deep within solid, living trees. Clearly, a close look at woodpecker anatomy is needed to reveal their secret.

If a labourer excavating a hole in the road switched on his pneumatic drill and put his head where his hands should have been, we would be surprised if he lasted more than a few seconds. The workman uses his arms as a buffer between the drill and his brain. Similarly, a car would be shaken to pieces over rough roads if it did not have an adequate suspension system to absorb shocks. So it is with the woodpecker. And by looking in detail at the anatomy of a woodpecker's head and bill, scientists might gain knowledge that could lead to major technological advances.

In the vast majority of birds, the bones of the skull are fused together and the bill is opened and closed by movements of the jaw. Woodpeckers, however, have their bill and cranium separated by a sponge-like tissue that absorbs the shock each time they strike a blow. This elastic tissue is far more efficient than a car's shock absorbers, for it is able to cope with a huge number of impacts over a very short space of time. When the bird drums out its courtship song on a

dead branch, the tissue is able to absorb the impact of each strike and return to stability, ready to deal with the next blow, ten or more times a second. That this material is way ahead of anything developed by modern technology is patently an understatement. A second shock-absorbing effect results from the unusual arrangement of the bird's upper bill and skull, allowing the brain-case to be pulled away from the bill each time the bird strikes home.

Head bashing on concrete

The erection of nestboxes in woodland and gardens has eased the housing shortage for hole-nesting birds in many part of the world. Mostly, these boxes are built of wood. Great Spotted Woodpeckers soon found that they could easily hack their way into wooden boxes, and they are not averse to a free meal of eggs or nestlings of some smaller bird. Even concrete boxes have sometimes failed to deter these persistent birds. Armed with their own built-in drills, Great Spotted Woodpeckers have hacked away to enlarge the entrance hole and thus gain entry into the so-called 'woodpecker-proof' boxes. Finally, naturalists found that the only solution to the problem was to fit a piece of rubber around the nestbox entrance hole. The rubber absorbs the blows of the bird's bill in the same way as the sponge-like cartilage absorbs them to protect the woodpecker's brain.

Woodpeckers more than compensate for destroying nestboxes and their inhabitants by saving trees from being devoured from within by wood-boring insects. Unfortunately, felling of large tracts of woodland and improved forestry management have

led to a sharp decline in suitable soft-wooded old dead trees for woodpecker nests.

So important are woodpeckers in pest control that a research team of zoologists at Ohio State University, USA, has set about trying to lure them back into heavily pest-infested areas of woodland which they have deserted because of a shortage of suitable nest-sites. The researchers decided to tempt the birds back with plastic 'trees'. These are made of a soft foam-like plastic, painted brown. Unfortunately, this ambitious and imaginative scheme was not a success; although the woodpeckers did peck out some large cavities, there was no evidence of nesting. This was probably because when the birds tried to drum out their love songs on the artificial trees, the plastic did not resonate like dead wood, and so the birds were unable to attract mates. The Ohio researchers aim to get around this problem by covering parts of the plastic trees with a resonant material, such as plywood. Hopefully, woodpeckers will return to resume their hard-hitting lifestyle, and help forests to grow in the process – with less competition from pests.

Although modern technology is to some extent able to mimic the woodpeckers' amazing natural ability to cope with their hard-hitting lifestyle, there is no doubt that a thorough investigation of their cartilage-like shock-absorbing material would reveal new secrets. A man-made imitation might prove invaluable in all sorts of applications, and at the very least should make the life of a pneumatic-drill operator much more comfortable.

Far right **The scene of the crime: the lower hole in this nestbox was hacked out by a hungry Great Spotted Woodpecker, which made short work of the young birds inside. Even concrete nestboxes are not immune from woodpecker attack** (*below*). *Right* **Plastic 'tree' with Downy Woodpecker.**

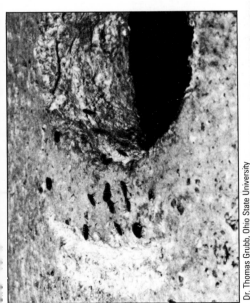

Dr. Thomas Grubb, Ohio State University

Dr. C. M. Perrins

SEXUAL AND SOCIAL BEHAVIOUR

Courtship, mating, rearing young, finding food,
building homes and killing prey reveal some of the
strangest sights seen in nature's secret world . . .

Wardene Weisser/Ardea London

THE SEXUAL TRAP

Males in the battle for mates could drive entire species to extinction

Joseph Van Wormer/Bruce Coleman Ltd.

Leonard Lee Rue III/Bruce Coleman Ltd.

What suicidal tendency could be at work to produce characteristics as bizarre as the iridescent plummage of birds of paradise or the fantastically long tails of Lyre Birds? These characteristics are obviously a disadvantage to the survival of the animal. What is more, they are only found in males. Why should some male animals hinder themselves with monstrous antlers or colours that mark them out for any passing predator? If the females of the species survive without such detrimental characteristics why do the males need them?

Charles Darwin was puzzled by these differences (or *dimorphisms*) and decided that a process that was *not* natural selection must be at work. He called this process

sexual selection. Recent research allows us to understand sexual selection using genetic models (the science of genetics was unknown in Darwin's day) and uses evidence from the wild to support these models.

Mating advantage

Sexual selection leads to the evolution of traits that give their bearers *mating* rather than a *survival* advantage. Male deer use antlers to fight other males in an attempt to win a large harem of females. Males with deformed or damaged antlers are prevented from mating because they fail to win fights and therefore mates. Weaponry has envolved time and time again among male animals and, among several verte-

The glorious fan tail of the Peacock (*top*) **contrasts vividly with the dull brown hen.** *Above* **A male Cardinal is an obvious target to predators while the female is a study in protective camouflage.**

brate groups at least, it is most pronounced in animals where the winner of a fight can mate with most females. For examples, deer with the largest antlers and primates with the largest canine teeth for their body size have the largest harems. These fierce weapons probably hinder survival – one reason why many deer species lose their antlers after the breeding season – but their cost is more than offset by the mating advantage they can confer.

This explains the possession of detrimen-

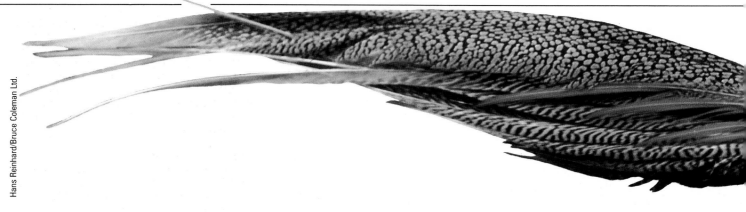

tal characteristics that are used as weapons to win females but it does not explain why male peacocks have such long brightly coloured tails, or why birds of paradise have such glorious displays. A more colourful male isn't more likely to be able to damage his opponent.

By looking at different species Darwin uncovered a vital clue: exaggerated plumage is most often found in so-called *lek* (display ground) species. These are animals where the males display for the females who pick the most 'desirable'. Darwin thought that females might have an eye for beauty and pick the most colourful males but couldn't explain how such a power to charm might have evolved.

The answers began to be found back in 1915, when R. A. Fisher, a leader in the field, used the newly-emerging science of population genetics to suggest a model for the evolution of female choice. The model had a surprising conclusion – female choice and male characteristics could evolve together to the point that the male characteristic becomes detrimental to survival.

Long tail preference

Imagine a species that has hereditable variation for a plumage character, say, tail size. If the environment changes so that males with long tails are favoured by natural selection then females who mate with such males will have young who will be at a selective advantage. It stands to reason that in the next generation the males with long tails will have also inherited their mothers' gene for long tail preference, so both genes will be found in the same animal. This linkage is called *genetic covariance* and ensures that the preference genes also increase in the population, by being passed on to the daughters.

Fisher went on to say that this runaway selection would lead to tail size increasing beyond that favoured by natural selection. Sexual selection operating through female choice would see to that.

Recently, a series of population genetic models have examined the conditions under which runaway selection operates. The simplest model is based on two genetic areas, one of which does for female preferences and the other for male characteristics. This system has been investigated by Peter O'Donald at Cambridge, UK, and Mark

Kirkpatrick at Seattle, USA. The results are very similar but the Kirkpatrick treatment reveals a fascinating finding.

It shows that there is always an equilibrium between the males with the preferred character and the number of females who prefer that character. Even if it means the males have a short life expectancy this is catered for by an increase in the number of females preferring the detrimental characteristics. If all females chose to mate with long-tailed males then even if such males had a very high death rate, the few that survived might be sufficient to service all the females. Fitter but short-tailed males are unable to find a mate.

These simple models give some insights in to the problem but lack properties that characterize more realistic systems. Most characteristics are known to be influenced by many genes. In the case of sexual selec-

tion it is possible that one gene could code for the presence or absence of a colour but not something as complicated as length of tail. Fortunately, a multi-gene system has been examined by Russel Lande of Chicago, USA. Lande says that the models show an enormous amount of hereditable variation that cannot be removed from a population quickly even if there is a strong selection pressure.

Multi-gene control

In his model Lande assumed that both male and female traits were under multi-gene control. Genetic variation is maintained when there is an equilibrium between male characteristic and female preference. However, in Lande's system the equilibrium could be either stable or unstable. If unstable and the population evolves away from this equilibrium then the species

Male animals often acquire bizarre and detrimental characteristics in the battle to win the attentions of sexually receptive females. The huge antlers (*left*) of the red deer are grown only for the mating season. The extraordinary long tail of the Golden Pheasant (*above*) might impede flight but is a very important asset to the male in finding mates. Black grouse (*right*) go in for strange communal dances, on exposed areas of moorland. And male walrus (*far right*) grow immense tusks to protect large harems from any challenge. Less well endowed males don't find mates. All these characteristics and behaviour patterns have evolved because of *sexual selection*, through female preference.

could progressively be driven to extinction! Obviously at some time genetic variation could run out but not necessarily in time to prevent extinction. The stable equilibrium model is much the same as the more simple models. Any drift away from equilibrium results in selection back to it, though not always back to the same point. A new equilibrium can be established.

Bizarre experiment

But all this would be of no use if we could not identify female mate preferences. One study of animals in the wild has made an impressive start. Malte Andersson has investigated tail size variation in the African Widow Bird. In this species only the males have very long tails, about 50 cm. Males defend territories on which one can find the nests of several females. It was thought that females chose their mates on the basis of tail size. To investigate this Andersson cut off one half of the tails of some of the males and used these feathers to artificially extend the tails of other males. Before the experiment both groups of males had about equal numbers of females nesting in their territories. Afterwards more new nests were found in the territories of the males with the extended tails. To check how valid the experiment was there were also two control groups: some males were unharmed and others had their tails cut off and then stuck on again. There was no difference in the numbers of females attracted by the two groups of males. So it seems in this species at least that females do prefer males with longer tails. Additional work by Andersson showed that tail length is not important for inter-male combat in the Widow Bird case.

It has been many years since Darwin first thought of characteristics evolving as a consequence of female choice, and only now has field and genetic modelling expertise conspired to reveal a process whereby entire populations could be driven to extinction by the exercise of female choice.

BLACK COCK DISPLAY POSES AT LEK

Side view of male, body held rigid.

Wings are drooped and combs expanded, head is lowered.

Rear view of displaying cock, head and tail held up.

Robert T. Smith/Ardea London

Leonard Lee Rue III/Animals Animals/Oxford Scientific Films

WHEN THE CUCKOO COMES CALLING

Cuckoos have evolved various adaptations for deceiving other birds into accepting their young as their own. These reveal basic rules of bird behaviour

Right **On the look-out for a suitable nest: the female European cuckoo uses over 120 species of small bird to foster its eggs and young, though each cuckoo tends to 'specialize' in one species. A common fosterer is the meadow pipit (*below*). This cuckoo chick is so big that the pipit can stand on its back to drop food into its huge, wide-open gape.**

Wayne Ford

Dennis Green/Survival Anglia

Left **Caught in the act! A cuckoo removes an egg from the host's nest just before laying one of her own. With her long tail pressed against the side of the nest for support, she is ready to use her protrusible cloaca to place the egg more neatly into the small nest than any other bird of her size could do. Even so, she must drop the egg into deep or domed nests; it is protected by an unusually thick shell. Most cuckoo eggs bear a striking resemblance to those of the host (*right*), though some, like that laid in a dunnock's nest, look different: but it may still be accepted. Though larger than the host eggs, the cuckoo's are very small for a bird of its size. Most cuckoos are 'host specific', their eggs closely matching the egg colour of one host.**

All eggs life-size

Cuckoo

Great reed warbler

Cuckoo

Meadow pipit

Cuckoo

Dunnock

Naturalis/Trötschel

David Lawrence

Arguably the best known of all bird calls, the resonant, far-carrying 'cuc-oo' of the European cuckoo has been the subject of folklore and mystery since Man first had the time to think about his environment. Although its arrival throughout Europe traditionally heralds the coming of spring for millions of people, many of the intimacies of the cuckoo's life remained secret until surprisingly recently.

The habit of laying eggs in other birds' nests, known to biologists as brood parasitism, is not restricted to the European cuckoo. Indeed, most of the other 126 species of cuckoo, spread widely throughout the world, are parasitic to a certain degree, although none has perfected the technique as well as the European species. Five or six other bird families, too, have members that are brood parasites: for instance, the South American black duck and the African pin-tailed and paradise whydahs. What is the advantage in allowing other species to hatch out and rear one's own young? And – even more puzzling – what special aspects of bird behaviour are brought into play to make the host species accept such strange creatures as their own offspring?

Strategy for deceit

The bare bones of the story are uncompromisingly straight-forward. The female cuckoo first carefully charts the exact whereabouts of the nests of her chosen host species within her territory. She then picks a particular nest and surreptitiously observes the comings and goings of the host bird from some well-concealed vantage point. As soon as the cuckoo notices that the host has begun to lay, she prepares to act. She waits until the host has finished laying her first egg and left the nest, then she swoops down and removes the host's egg in her bill. Immediately, she lays one of her own eggs in place of the one she has stolen (this she will later eat or drop onto the ground). The whole process takes no more than five seconds.

Over the next few days, the host completes her clutch, still in ignorance of the substitution. The cuckoo never returns to the nest; on the contrary, she is soon in search of the next suitable one, laying up to twelve eggs in a season, each in a separate nest. Meanwhile, the alien egg is incubated by the host along with her own. It hatches, usually in advance of the host's, and the cuckoo chick ejects the remaining host eggs with chilling efficiency. Though blind and naked, it is extremely strong and equipped with a hollow in its back into which it can manoeuvre the eggs and heave them over the side of the nest. Once they are out of the nest, they will be totally ignored by the hosts, which then feed the usurper until it gains its independence.

Despite its apparent simplicity, this story conceals a complex system of behaviour that is fraught with potential breakdowns. Supposing the intended hosts spot the cuckoo in the act of laying her egg? Or perhaps they might recognize that the cuckoo's egg is different from their own. If the adult cuckoo gets her timing wrong, the cuckoo chick may hatch out after those of the host. Possibly the sheer size of the young cuckoo might alarm the foster parents so much that they desert it.

The first problem is often a very real one. If a potential foster parent observes an adult cuckoo near its nest, it will attack and drive off the intruder, despite the cuckoo's much larger size. The British bird photographers Eric Hosking and Stuart Smith produced dramatic evidence of such tenacity in defence of the nest by photographing small birds attacking a stuffed cuckoo. Yet, while the cuckoo was violently attacked, the indignant defenders completely ignored the human hand that held the stuffed cuckoo. Clearly the birds recognized the cuckoo as a greater threat than Man. Should the cuckoo not withdraw, the nest might be deserted, but real-life cuckoos doubtless always give in.

As to the second problem, the host may sometimes desert because it spots the cuckoo's egg as a fraud, but generally the cuckoo's ability to mimic the eggs of its host is very good. Most female cuckoos are 'host specific': that is, they specialize in parasitizing a particular host species. So there are 'dunnock cuckoos', 'reed warbler cuckoos', 'meadow pipit cuckoos', 'robin cuckoos' and so on. The preference for a particular species is largely genetically determined, and a cuckoo will parasitize the species in whose nest it was reared. This has enabled cuckoos to evolve the ability to match their eggs to their hosts' closely in colour and pattern, though they are invariably slightly larger.

This size difference does not seem to pose a problem, however. Experiments with herring gulls have shown that under the right conditions, a bird will respond to almost any egg-shaped object by incubating it. This is an example of what behavioural biologists call a simple stimulus-response situation. Yet a bird will abandon its own eggs if a larger egg is placed nearby. The larger version seems to act as a 'super stimulus'. Laying a larger egg, then, may actually be an advantage to the cuckoo, though this remains to be proved.

What is certain, though, is that the cuckoo's egg has a remarkably short incubation period for so large a bird and it usually hatches before those of the host. It is possible that the egg may start 'incubating' while it is still in the cuckoo's oviduct. Should the hen cuckoo time her laying badly, the baby cuckoo may need to remove one or more of the rival host chicks, but it has no trouble doing so, using the same technique as with the eggs. In any case, all birds feed the chick with the largest mouth; Russian biologists have observed that some birds will even abandon their own chicks in favour of an older brood placed nearby.

This is another example of a simple stimulus-response type of bird behaviour, which has the great advantage of ensuring that when food is in short supply, a pair of birds will give most of the available food to the strongest member of their brood rather than sharing it equally. This means that at least one, or with luck more, young are reared, rather than the whole brood starving to death.

As the cuckoo chick grows, usually much larger than its foster parents, its huge gape acts as yet another super stimulus prompting its hosts to ever greater efforts at satisfying its apparently insatiable appetite. Had it not gained their undivided attention by taking sole occupancy of the nest, it would not obtain enough food for sustained growth. So strong is the stimulus of the huge mouth that other birds feeding their own young nearby may be prompted into joining its foster parents and feeding the cuckoo chick.

Before long, but well after the adults have left Europe for their long trans-Saharan migration, the young cuckoo's instincts lead it to set off on its own hazardous journey to tropical Africa. Before doing so, it must take on reserves of fuel, in the form of body fat, for its long, non-stop flight. Once again, the cuckoo exhibits a fascinating adaptation. It is not by accident that the cuckoo is one of the very few birds that feeds on the hairy caterpillars of tiger and drinker moths, insects that apparently taste very bitter or even poisonous to most birds. These appear in large numbers at the end of summer. By having this food supply virtually to itself, the young cuckoo soon obtains the food it needs for its long journey. Also, when the adult female returns to Europe in spring, she can rely on a similar glut of hairy caterpillars to help her regain the reserves she needs to produce as many as twelve eggs in the course of the breeding season.

Instinct and adaptation are the keys to understanding bird behaviour. But it is fanciful to relate cuckoo habits to the understanding of human behaviour. Take, for example, the song of the cuckoo – among the simplest and loudest of bird calls, and in human terms a feature of folksong and folklore in many nations. The explanation for the cuckoo's simplicity and volume of song rests on the fact that no baby cuckoo has the chance to learn what song it should sing from its parents at close quarters. Its call must be simple enough to inherit – maybe with the memory jogged by a call from mother busy elsewhere.

Below **Resembling a sci-fi humanoid, a cuckoo chick pushes one of its host's eggs overboard. The hollow in its back helps it to manoeuvre the egg into place.** *Below right* **After removing the opposition, a cuckoo chick rests contented in a pipit's nest.**

Naturalis/Trötschel

John Mason/Ardea London

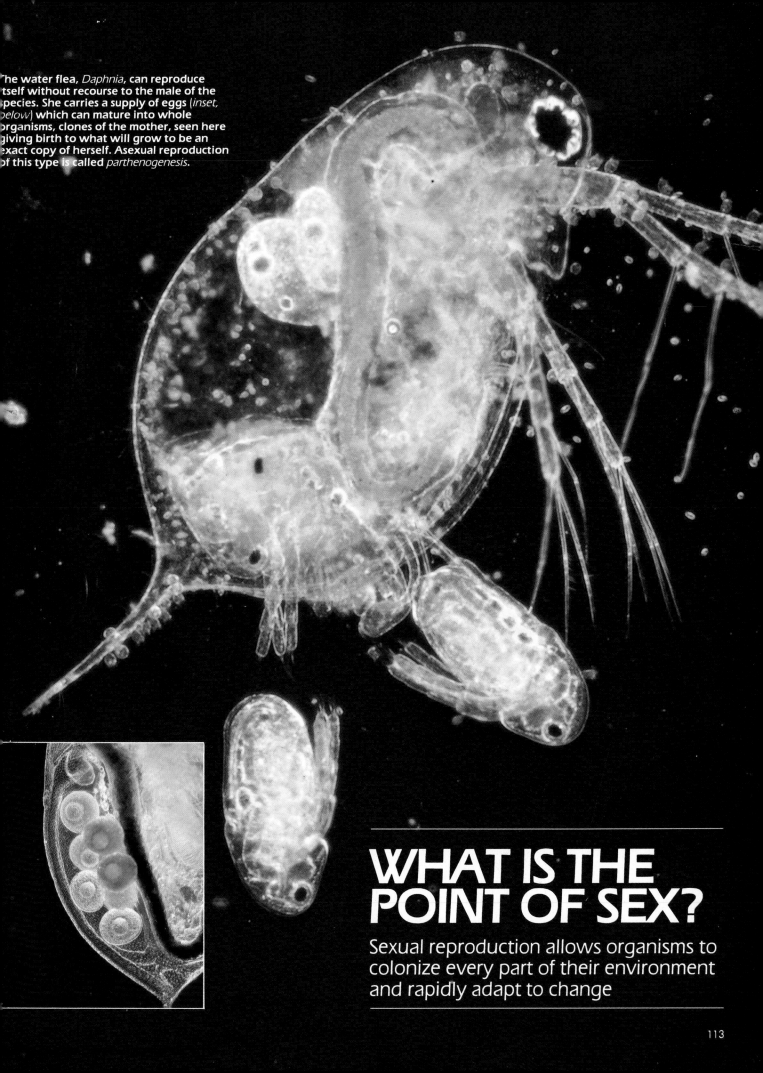

The water flea, *Daphnia*, can reproduce itself without recourse to the male of the species. She carries a supply of eggs (*inset, below*) which can mature into whole organisms, clones of the mother, seen here giving birth to what will grow to be an exact copy of herself. Asexual reproduction of this type is called *parthenogenesis*.

WHAT IS THE POINT OF SEX?

Sexual reproduction allows organisms to colonize every part of their environment and rapidly adapt to change

1. A testis cell about to divide. It has 46 chromosomes.

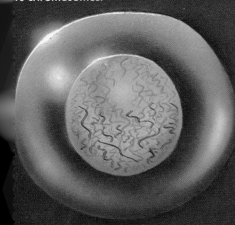

2. As the cell starts to divide the chromosomes appear as double threads.

Meiosis is the way in which new sex cells are made. The diagrams *below* and *right* shows a cell in the testis dividing to make new sperm. Only four pairs of chromosome: are shown for the sake of clarity. In a real testis cell there would be 46 chromosomes arranged in 23 pairs. A similar process take: place in the female ovaries where egg cells are produced.

3. Attached to fine elastic fibres, the chromosomes come together in pairs.

Sex is something we cannot do without. Sex keeps us off the slippery slope to extinction by constantly diversifying individual characteristics — and the same goes for nearly all our neighbours on planet Earth. But sex is a risky business. Male and female must meet and mate in the right place at the right time, and the newborn product of this union must itself grow up and survive long enough to fulfil the promise of parenthood.

Sexless techniques

A quick look round the living world reveals that although reproduction without sex is possible, it is the exception rather than the rule, and is generally an extra to sex, not an alternative. Asexual reproduction comes into play, mainly when the population needs to grow fast. It can rapidly generate numbers, but not diversity. All the new organisms are clones of their parent. Take the water flea *Daphnia*. The female water fleas make eggs which can develop into juvenile then adult — female — water fleas without being sexually fertilized by sperm from a male water flea. But when the environment gets overcrowded, this sexless method, known as *parthenogenesis*, stops working and the eggs must be fertilized to get the population going again.

Likewise, the microscopic one-celled *Paramecium* can reproduce asexually simply by splitting in half, and only goes in for

sex when overcrowding occurs. Plants, too, can reproduce without sex, as any gardener whose plot is invaded by bindweed well knows. Yet they, too, rely on sex to set seeds and spread their numbers still further afield. The inevitable conclusion is that although reproduction without sex is perfectly suitable for the short term, sex is essential for long-term survival — and wide surveys of the animal and plant kingdoms back this conclusion to the hilt.

It is easy to see how a simple one-celled creature can reproduce without sex. All it has to do is to get its DNA to make a perfect replica of itself, grow a new 'body', then split down the middle. This is fine as long as the offspring have enough space to live in and find themselves in pleasantly favourable surroundings — and as long as they go on reproducing at a regular rate and without the biological 'clerk' making any mistakes in the copying.

Simply splitting in two is, however, a much less attractive proposition for larger, more complex creatures with parts specially intended for jobs such as moving, feeding and so on. The plotted path of evolutionary history confirms that the time at which sexual reproduction became the rule coincided

with the growing complexity of body de sign. So, along with the parts equipped fo other essential life tasks, animals and plant set aside special cells, and devised ingeni ous body parts solely for the business o sexual reproduction.

Match and mix

Implicit in the way sex was devised is a mixing of genetic material from separate in dividuals. This demanded rather special be haviour on the part of the DNA. In nearly a cells, the DNA-built chromosomes are ar ranged in pairs, one member of each pai coming from the mother, the other from the father. The great asset of this matching or diploid pairing is that errors on one chromosome can be masked or dominated by the 'normal' genes on the matching

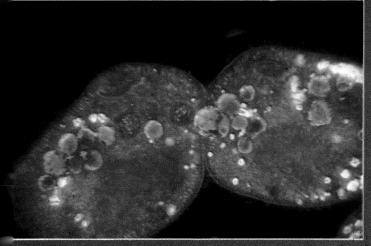

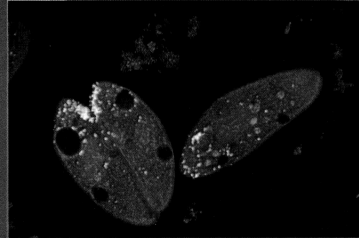

chromosome and so underwrite survival.

Sexual reproduction aims to perpetuate this advantageous state of affairs. When the sex cells are made, the pairs split up and the chromosome number is divided by two. Thus male and female sex cells contain half – the haploid – chromosome complement. And when male and female sex cells meet at the moment of fertilization the diploid condition is again restored.

Unique arrangement of genes

This reproduction in chromosome number – meoisis is its name – does more than simply separate the chromosomes. As it occurs the chromosomes become so tightly twisted round each other that when they separate DNA is swapped, or crosses over, between them. The result is that every sex cell contains DNA with a unique arrangement of genes, and this variation is increased even further when the two sorts of cells pair up at fertilization. The result is that every creature that develops fol-

4. **Each one of a chromosome pair is pulled to opposite ends as the threads shorten.**

lowing sex, be it bat, bindweed or human being is different from its parents and from its peers and siblings. Identical twins are the notable exception, but their chromosomes split after, not before, fertilization, and so they are, in effect, the products of both sexual and asexual reproduction.

Scientists are mostly agreed that it is the subtle and not so subtle variations between individuals which are the key to explaining why sexual reproduction shrugged off the pressure of conformity and won the day over asexual methods – and why it still holds sway today. Just think of a human race in which everyone was the same, and the importance of variation is crystal clear!

Best men and tangled banks

So why is variability such a good thing? The most popular, and longest held theory is the one dubbed the Best Man. According to Best Man or 'adapt or die' theory, the great plus of variation – as contrasted with the sameness that results from asexual methods – is that it gives organisms the ability to cope with unforeseen changes in their environment. That is, sex acts as a kind of insurance policy against an uncertain future. One could evisage it working, for example, if there were a vast rise in the amount of, say, carbon monoxide, in our atmosphere. Those organisms able to cope

5. **Another division takes place. Four sperm have been made from one testis cell.**

with this would have an implicit advantage over those that did not – the intolerant members of the population would die. And it would be the carbon monoxide tolerant individuals which would survive, grow up and reproduce sexually to give rise to the next generation of mostly tolerant individuals.

If the Best Man theory were true, argues Graham Bell of Montreal's McGill University, then when population drops, water fleas, for instance, with the capacity for both sexual and asexual reproduction should resort to sexual methods – which they do not in the first instance. Bell cites hundreds of examples and experiments to back his rejection of the Best Man theory on these grounds. Asexual methods, but particularly parthenogenesis were, he found, much more likely to be used to get creatures out of a tight spot. Only when their numbers increased and things improved did they underwrite their success by going for sex.

Instead of the Best Man, Bell favours the Tangled Bank hypothesis, which he has named after an expression used by Darwin in his *Origin of Species* to epitomize the complexity of any natural habitat. According to the Tangled Bank theory, the importance of the variation created by sex is that it allows a creature to take advantage of all the possible niches in its habitat – even one, to cite our previous example, high in carbon monoxide. The more variants there are, the more niches can be exploited. Like a child's postbox toy with only one shape of blocks, the creature that does not vary can only take advantage of one 'hole'. If it varies, then it has the equivalent of all the shapes to fit the holes or niches in the environment.

Chance of colonization

On Tangled Bank theory, sex is necessary when overcrowding begins because it alone can quickly reproduce new variants with a chance of colonizing parts of the environment which are as yet unsettled – again, perhaps, the ones high in carbon monoxide. Using his experimental evidence, Bell maintains that whenever sexual and asexual groups exist side by side in a population the asexual ones – the clones, who are less adaptable generally than their sexually reproduced cousins – will be much more prone to being wiped out by catastrophes.

Whatever the truth of the matter, it is certain that the secret of sex's success is twofold. First, it makes reproduction easier for large organisms, and secondly it produces the variation which is the stuff of success. And we have not let the prizes of variation go unclaimed. Plant and animal breeding, from the trial and error of prehistory to the carefully devised breeding programmes of today, have used variation to give us a wonderful storehouse of vegetable and animal foods.

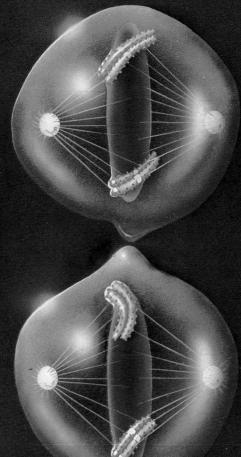

The protozoa *Paramecium* **can reproduce either sexually or asexually.**
Far left *Paramecium* **dividing asexually. The cell is splitting in two thus giving rise to a new but identical individual.**
Left **Two** *Paramecia* **conjugating sexually. In a series of complicated chromosome swaps the two cells mix their genetic material and produce in all four new individuals.**

DINNER WITH THE FAMILY

Research into what makes animals eat each other is giving biologists insight into various aspects of ecology, genetics and evolution

A robber fly with its kill – one of its own kind. Much of the knowledge biologists have gained about cannibalism comes from studies of invertebrates such as these. Cannibalism occurs in a wide variety of species, and may even form a normal part of an animal's life.

The idea of cannibalism fills most of us with horror. Even biologists usually think that to kill and eat a member of one's own species is a rare and aberrant pattern of behaviour. However, it is becoming clear that cannibalism is surprisingly common.

Cannibalism has been recorded among more than a thousand animal species. Even among Man it was widespread – though rare – until quite recently. In most societies, however, the taboo against eating human flesh is very powerful, and, despite exaggerated claims of lust for human flesh, almost all societies that practised cannibalism have done so as part of their ritual culture – for example, the Asmat tribe of New Guinea,

who ate their dead relatives because they believed that this would preserve their 'life force', or the Fijians, who considered that ritual eating of their enemies would bring strength and please their gods. Nevertheless, the very word 'cannibalism' comes from the name for a human group: from the Spanish word for the Carib tribe of the West Indies, the 'Canibales', who were regarded as notorious people-eaters.

In some animals, cannibalism is an important cause of death. A quarter of all lion cubs are cannibalized by older lions, and in some fish species, more than 90% of the young may be eaten by other members of the same species. Walleye fish (*Stizo sted-*

ion) eat each other tail first, and chains of up to four individuals, each eating the one in front, have been seen. Sometimes, cannibalism begins even before birth. In salamanders, for example, a few embryos develop teeth which they use before they are born to devour other developing young.

Obviously, then, cannibalism is a serious issue in the lives of certain animals. But what biological advantages can possibly be gained by destroying other members of one's own species?

In fact, there are several obvious benefits gained by the individual cannibal. Firstly, it obtains food – sometimes up to half its total diet. Such food may be particularly important for pregnant females. Indeed, it seems that in most species, the female is more cannibalistic than the male. It is quite common for female insects to turn round and devour their mates as soon as mating is completed: a male praying mantis, for instance, stands a good chance of having his head bitten off by the female during mating. Female spiders are even more notorious in this respect.

A second advantage of cannibalism is that it removes potential competitors for food. This occurs, for instance, in desert scorpions, allowing them to survive when food is scarce. There may also be competion for other resources. For example, in round squirrels (which nest in holes in the ground) many females can obtain nest burrows only by killing the occupants of the few suitable holes which are available.

Cannibalism of young by each other is quite common, and sometimes allows a species to ensure that the maximum number survives each generation in spite of great differences in the amount of available food. Hawks and eagles lay several eggs. In particularly favourable years, all these come to maturity. More often, however, not enough prey is available to feed all the young, and in these cases the more rapidly developing chicks kill and eat their less fortunate brothers and sisters. This mechanism ensures that in both favourable and poor years the maximum possible number of young reach maturity; many in good years, but few during lean years.

Selfish and unselfish

Recently, biologists have used the example of cannibalism to examine the theory that the behaviour of animals towards each other may depend on their degree of relatedness. At the opposite extreme from cannibalism is altruism — unselfish behaviour. Some biologists reason that altruistic behaviour is most likely to occur when the animals concerned are genetically closely related — that is, have a high proportion of their genes in common.

A familiar example of altruistic behaviour is that of alarm calls heard from flocks of birds of the same species. If one bird spots a hawk or other enemy, it will give an alarm call which warns the others. Although the altruist puts at risk its own life and its own chances of reproducing its genes in the next generation by its unselfish behaviour, it increases the chances that its relatives in the flock, who carry many of the same genes, will pass them on.

So the net effect is good for the species as a whole, or, as many biologists would put it, for that particular group of genes. And anything that is good for such a group will tend to be perpetuated by the process of evolution by natural selection. The famous British geneticist J. B. S. Haldane illustrated this idea of 'kin selection' by saying that it would be sensible for him to jump into a lake only if he could save two of his brothers or four of his cousins from drowning by so doing.

Unfortunately, biologists have a problem in deciding whether a particular behaviour is indeed altruistic, in that it is very difficult to measure the costs and benefits involved — how much does the altruist lose and his relatives gain by giving an alarm call, for example? Cannibalism, by contrast, is the least altruistic behaviour imaginable — there are few more selfish acts than killing and eating a member of one's own species. It is so clear-cut that it might therefore provide

a clearer test of the predictions of kin selection, particularly as it is relatively easy to measure the nutritional and other benefits gained by a cannibal — and very easy to measure the costs incurred by the victim! Cannibalizing an unrelated member of one's own species, biologists postulate, should increase the chances that the cannibal's own genes will survive at the expense of 'foreign' genes.

The most direct evidence that kin selection may be involved in the evolution of cannibalism comes from work with flour beetles. These are important pests of stored food, and biologists know a great deal about their ecology and patterns of population growth. In some laboratory stocks of flour beetles, cannibalism of eggs or young is the major cause of death; so much so that only about one egg in twenty reaches adulthood. Crosses between laboratory stocks with different tendencies towards cannibalism show that this behaviour is inherited.

In an ingenious series of experiments, re-

Biologists have discovered cannibalistic behaviour in some species of amphibians. *Below* A young African bullfrog eating one of its own kind in a lake in Namibia, South-Western Africa, and, *overleaf*, an African clawed toad tadpole being eaten by an older tadpole of the same species. Such behaviour may bring greater breeding success or individual survival for the cannibal.

Sexual and social behaviour

Bruce Coleman Ltd./Jane Burton

Right **At the opposite pole from cannibalism: altruistic, or unselfish, behaviour, as a greater flamingo protects its young from a marabou stork on a lake in Kenya. Such actions may bring danger to the individual, but a net advantage to the genetically related group as a whole.** *Far right* **A female European green orb spider eats her mate.** *Below* **Cannibalized great white shark.**

ARDEA/Ron Taylor

searchers offered beetle eggs as food to beetles from a laboratory strain with an initially low cannibalism rate. The beetles readily accepted eggs from unrelated beetles, but they were much more reluctant to cannibalize eggs which might have developed into their own brothers and sisters. After eight generations, the cannibalism rate in the population offered unrelated eggs was twice that among the beetles offered the eggs of closely related individuals. Kin selection was therefore involved in the evolution of this behaviour; beetles are reluctant to eat their own genes, which are carried by their close relatives.

The same seems to be true in mammals.

Lemming males will kill and eat the offspring of unrelated males, but never attack their own young. This is also the case in male house mice. The effect is so strong that pregnant female mice exposed to a male who is not their mate may terminate their pregnancies and reabsorb the foetuses. This has presumably evolved in response to the certainty that these foetuses would be killed and eaten by the strange male at birth.

Misleading conclusions

It is tempting to think that all behavioural interactions between individuals in species which form social groups – such as lions and monkeys – are also due to kin selection. Some sociologists have even suggested that the roots of human conflict can be traced to an evolutionary history of kin selection. It is certainly true that lions are much more likely to kill and eat cubs from outside their own group than from within it. It might seem reasonable to go on to assume that the individuals in a pride of lions or in a cooperatively hunting group of social apes are indeed close relatives, so that their generous behaviour to each other and their aggression towards outsiders result from their having so many genes in common. However, recent detailed studies of patterns of mating in wild lions and genetic tests of relatedness in wild monkeys have shown that in both these complex animal societies members of a social group are *not* particularly closely related to each other. Kin selection cannot therefore always be used as an explanation of social behaviour towards 'friends' or aggression (which may include cannibalism) towards 'strangers'.

However, one thing is very clear. Although it is comforting to think that animals are in general kind to other members of their own species, the study of cannibalism reminds us that nature is indeed often red in tooth and claw. Meanwhile, the prize for the most ingenious way to avoid getting eaten for dinner has to go to the species of spider who escapes the female's deadly embrace at mating by handing her a neatly spun silk parcel. She unwraps it instead.

Bruce Coleman Ltd./Udo Hirsch

WHEN MOTHER IS FATHER

Few male animals play the major role in care of the young, but in those that have evolved such role reversal, there is an advantage to the species as a whole

The natural world exhibits virtually every imaginable form of reproduction. Though it is normally the female that produces the eggs or young, there are examples of bisexual reproduction, as in the earthworm, and even sexless reproduction in various primitive invertebrates. There are large females and small males; males that are eaten by their mates; males that mate with virtually every female they can find; and females that show the same reaction to males. So it is not surprising that there is a place in nature for the comparatively simple business of role reversal between the sexes.

Such a situation is easily observed in certain birds. Though in many species of bird it is the female that takes the main, or even the exclusive, role in nesting, incubation and care of the young, there are plenty of exceptions. For instance, some birds adopt a communal approach to breeding, in which the care of the chicks, which are reared in a single nest, is shared among a group of often unrelated individuals. Against this background, role reversal does not seem so extraordinary.

The phalaropes are a small group of three species of wading

Above **A male dotterel carefully turns the eggs, and scuttles along the ground in imitation of a rodent to distract predators.**

Trevor Marshall/Ardea Photographics

Oxford Scientific Films/David Thompson

The male three-spined stickleback of Eurasian lakes and rivers makes a model parent. He builds a nest (*top left*), hidden among waterweed, from pieces of weed which he glues together with a sticky secretion from his kidneys. He then induces a female to enter the nest to lay her eggs, which he fertilizes. Depending on the temperature of the water, the eggs take between five and twelve days to hatch; throughout this period, the male waits by the nest (*centre left*), fanning fresh, aerated water over the eggs to keep them in prime condition and prevent fungal infections. After the eggs hatch, too, the male guards the baby fishes, driving away any potential predators such as snails (*bottom left*).

Oxford Scientific Films/G. I. Bernard

birds in which role reversal is the norm. The red-necked phalarope, for instance, breeds in the Arctic and sub-Arctic tundra of the far north during the brief summer season of plenty. The female is, for a start, more brightly coloured than her mate and it is she that selects the breeding site. She then takes the initiative in courtship; male phalaropes have even been seen cowering submissively while two females squabbled over him. Soon, the female lays her four eggs in a nest which the male constructs for her. From this point, she takes no further interest in her mate, the eggs or the chicks that hatch from them. Amazon-like, she flies to a nearby lake or marsh where she whiles away the time with other females that have similarly set up their mates on the first stages of parenthood.

The male, similarly marked but duller than the female, starts to incubate the eggs as soon as the clutch is complete. He takes his job very seriously, turning the eggs to ensure that they are evenly warmed and taking only the shortest breaks to grab a snack between his parental duties. When the eggs hatch, he broods the chicks before leading them on to an adjacent marsh where he teaches them to feed. Always attentive, he guards them and, for a while, broods them at night.

The story is broadly similar with the other birds which show

role reversal. Males of several other long-distance migratory birds, especially some northern waders, also take full charge of the business of nesting and rearing their offspring. As well as in the two other species of phalarope, this lifestyle is practised by a couple of species of stints and the dotterel, which is a European mountain-based plover. The hen dotterel selects her drab-coloured mate from a group of males, then chases him away from the others and induces him to mate with her. Some hens may lay two clutches of eggs in separate nests; the eggs are then incubated by two different males. Later, the hen may help in tending the chicks, but it is the male that has evolved a special 'rodent-run', in which he drags himself along the ground, looking just like a rodent, in an attempt to distract an approaching predator from his brood. In most birds, it is either the female or both parents that practise such deception.

Female jacanas and Old World painted snipe as known to establish and defend territories, behaviour normally associated with male birds, while some buttonquails in Asia have such aggressive females that Indians use them for 'cock-fighting'. A hen buttonquail attracts a male with her booming call and then courts him, circling him with her tail raised and chest puffed out, stamping up and down while she continues to boom. Female

Above left **A male red-necked phalarope broods a clutch of eggs in his summer home on the northern tundra. After laying them, his mate takes no part in incubation or care of the young. As with the two other species of phalarope, she is more brightly coloured than the male. Role reversal can be seen in amphibians as well as in birds and fishes. The glass frog** *Centrolenus fleishmani* **is an example:** *above,* **a male glass frog photographed in Costa Rica guards his eggs. Another example is provided by the frog** *Colostethus trinitatis,* **seen,** *left,* **carrying his tadpoles to safety, photographed in Venezuela.** *Right* **Looking like a knight in a chess-set, a male seahorse shows the brood pouch in which he keeps the eggs laid by the female. They hatch into as many as 100 miniature adults four to five weeks after laying, and the male forces them out one at a time, with jerking movements of his body, resting between each effort.**

arred bustardquails even develop a bright courtship plumage pecially for the breeding season, like the males of many birds.

Biologists have sought explanations for the evolution of such rrangements. In general terms, all 'normal' behaviour within a articular species can be explained in terms of the advantage to he species as a whole. This can be demonstrated in the case of he red-necked phalarope. Though the Arctic summer is very ountiful, with almost 24 hours of continuous daylight each day n which the birds can search for food, it is also very short. Phalaropes do not arrive in northern Britain from their wintering grounds on the West Africa coast until the second half of May, ut by the time they have crossed the Arctic Circle it is well into une before they are established in their territories. Even so, before August is out, the days are already getting too short for efficient feeding and the birds must depart southwards once more. So they have less than 12 weeks in which to accomplish breeding.

A phalarope's eggs take four weeks to hatch and the chicks a urther four weeks to gain independence. That leaves less than our weeks for mating, forming the eggs inside the female and aying them. Clearly the schedule is a tight one. But it is all the ighter because, on arrival, both male and female have just

completed a prodigious migratory journey which has used up almost all their food resources. Both must feed continuously to recover, the female to build up enough energy to form the eggs, and the male to perform the equally demanding task of incubation. Clearly, a neat division of labour between the sexes has a distinct advantage to the species as a whole, so natural selection has evolved a role-reversal system of reproduction.

It is not just the birds which feature this approach to breeding. Among fish, males quite often take a major role as parents. The male three-spined stickleback, for example, is a model father. Male seahorses are even equipped with a brood-pouch in which they look after the eggs laid by the female. Although many amphibians are rather poor parents, the males of some frogs guard the eggs or young with great devotion.

It would be too easy to generalize about such behaviour and attempt to use it to either justify or oppose proposals for human role reversal. Evidence gained from the animals should not be used as grounds for making what are basically ethical decisions about the roles of women and men in human society.

THERE'S NO PLACE LIKE HOME

From termites that make huge air-conditioned mounds to birds creating tiny nests of nothing but their own saliva, the animals are busy building

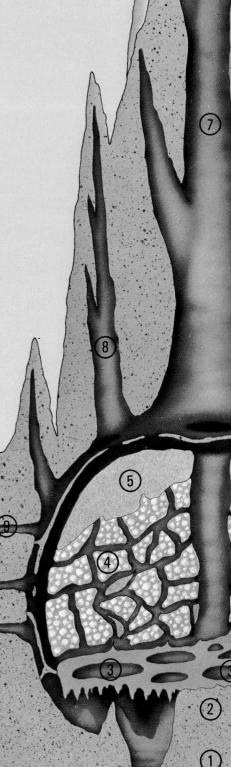

Below left Towering up into the trees, this bizarre structure is a nest, or *termitary*, built by workers of the species *Macrotermes bellicosus* in West Africa. *Right* A termitary of the species *Nasutitermes triodiae* in eucalypt woodland in Australia.

Bruce Coleman Ltd./Peter Ward

Left *Nasutitermes* **workers building a covered roadway across a broad path in Trinidad, West Indies.** *Bottom* **A low-lying** *Macrotermes* **nest in Sudan, Africa, is split open to reveal the chambers where the termites cultivate fungi for food.**

Left **Cross-section through a mound of the African termite** *Macrotermes bellicosus,* **home for as many as a million or more individuals. It is built of pellets of sand or clay mixed with saliva. The underground nest is built on a supporting pillar (*1*), with a spiral base plate (*2*) above. At a higher level are chambers for rearing larvae (*3*) and 'gardens' (*4*) in which the termites grow fungi for food. There are also food stores (*5*) and the royal cell (*6*) for the huge queen. The mound is equipped with a central chimney (*7*) and side chimneys (*8*): these form a heat-regulating and air-conditioning system. Foraging tunnels (*9*) allow the insects to obtain food and building materials without the risk of drying up.**

We are not the only species on this planet to practise architecture. Many animals, too, are accomplished builders. Their sheer ingenuity at using the materials to hand and their technical abilities are astounding.

Among the most remarkable builders are the termites, some of which live in huge, complex and self sufficient colonies inside imposing mounds. The termites pay a price for their impressive skill, however: if they are removed from their dark, humid refuges, these whitish, soft-bodied insects soon die – sometimes within a few hours of being exposed to the open air.

The most ancient of all the social insects, whose closest relatives seem to be the cockroaches, the termites number about 3,000 species, almost all of them tropical. The most primitive termites feed on wood as they tunnel it out of timber, digesting the cellulose with the aid of microscopic protozoans in their guts.

Other termites build nest mounds from soil or their own faeces mixed with their saliva. The blind, white, wingless workers are the architects, mixing particles of soil or faeces with saliva and then shaping them into small pellets with their legs and mouthparts. They then press each pellet firmly in place; it soon sets into a hard, cement-like substance. First of all, the insects build the tall vertical pillars, and then join these by slender arches and roofs.

Though blind, termites are extremely sensitive to light, and are quick to seal it out by plugging up any holes in the mound. They are also highly sensitive to air currents, and create elaborate ventilation systems. As they build up the nest mound, the convection currents produced by the growing structure act as a kind of invisible scaffolding system, around which the insects build solid walls.

Some tropical Australian species build grotesquely shaped mounds that may reach almost eight metres above the ground. Australia is also the home of the compass termites, which build slender tapering mounds, up to 4m high, and always oriented on a north-south axis. This ensures that the knife edge of the mound, with its minimal surface area, absorbs as little heat as possible during the searing Australian noon.

Fungus gardens

Relatives of the compass termites store grass and other vegetable food in their nests, while the most advanced termites, notably those in the African genus *Macrotermes,* actually cultivate fungi in special subterranean 'gardens' – just as we grow mushrooms in cellars.

Some of the fungus-farming termites build nests that are totally underground, while others construct tall chimneys above

the underground portion. The *Macrotermes* nest begins as an underground chamber, where the termites set up a fungus garden around the royal cell. As the nest grows, the termites build a dome above the fungus garden which contains new fungus chambers. Among the largest and most complex of all termite nests, *Macrotermes* mounds may top 7 m high and measure 30 m across when completed, and contain over a million termites.

Like humans, termites have through their building been able to become largely independent of external conditions, but – again like ourselves – this independence has brought its own problems. To keep their fungus gardens productive and their huge populations healthy, they have to ensure that the humidity and air temperature within the mound remain within critical limits.

Natural humidifiers

The termites cope with the humidity problem by a variety of ingenious methods. Some Saharan species dig right down to the water table, as much as 40 m below the surface, to encourage moisture to evaporate into the nest far above. Others carry moist pellets of clay into the nest.

The construction of the mound itself helps to maintain humidity: the thick walls prevent evaporation, and they are covered with a thick layer of sand and clay that is impervious to moisture.

Temperature control is equally impressive. The thick walls of the mound insulate the termites from fluctuations in the outside temperature; termites living inside tree trunks or underground are similarly protected. Removing the heat that they themselves produce and from the metabolism of the fungi in their gardens calls for a more subtle approach. The termites also need to maintain an adequate supply of oxygen and remove the poisonous carbon dioxide which they and the fungi produce.

Built-in ventilation system

Mounds such as those of *Macrotermes* have an elaborate ventilation system to cope with this problem. Warmth from the insects and the fungi rises up through the nest into the main tower. Air circulates and passes into the side chimneys along capillary ducts which run close to the outside walls. Here oxygen can diffuse in and carbon dioxide diffuse out, so that, in effect, the termite mound acts as a giant 'lung' for the whole colony. As the air passes through the capillary duct system, it is cooled. The result is that a constant supply of cool, oxygen-rich air flows into the nest at a rate of about 12 cm per minute, and the temperature inside stays at a steady 30°C. So efficient is the system that the temperature fluctuates by an average of less than half a degree over the year.

Not all African termites build large mound nests. Some construct delicate nests on tree trunks, often protected from heavy

rains by overhanging canopies. Underground nests, too, can be intricate. That of *Apicotermes gurgulifex*, for example, from the Congo, is like a giant pine-cone built about 50 cm below ground. Inside, it consists of an intricate arrangement of horizontal galleries separated by floors as little as 1 mm thick. Ramps lead from one floor to the next, and these are guarded against insect invaders by soldier termites – sterile adults with huge heads and jaws.

The outside of the nest is peppered with tiny openings which lead into the galleries. Far too small for the termites to pass through, they probably serve as a gas exchange system like the ducts in the *Macrotermes* chimneys. They are protected by tiny roofs, which help to prevent rain from entering the nest. The insects leave and

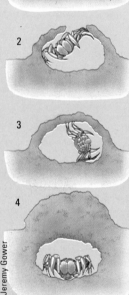

Right **Malaysian soldier crabs live between the tide marks on coastal sand flats. As the tide rises and the crabs are about to be covered with water, each animal builds itself a little air-filled burrow in which it hides in safety, supplied with oxygen, until the waters recede. It starts building by pushing tiny pellets of wet sand upwards and outwards (*1, 2*) until it is totally enclosed by a thin dome (*3*). The crab then makes its shelter more secure by scraping pellets of sand and mud from the floor and plastering them on the ceiling (*4*).**

Jeremy Gower

enter the nest by tunnels that open in the top of the nest.

Ants, bees and wasps – which belong to the great order *Hymenoptera* – also build impressive intricate structures in which to live and raise their young. Like termites, ants are all communal – not one of the 10,000 or so species lives alone. Army ants manage without a nest, but all other species make nests of varying degrees of complexity.

Red wood ants are familiar examples of ants that build imposing mound nests a metre or more high, the result of months of hard work by millions of individuals. Weaving, or tailor ants from South-East Asia use living green leaves to build their nests. They find a place where two leaves grow close together, then draw the leaves together and use their own larvae as living tools to spin silk to bind the leaves together to form a nest. The larvae are then installed in the home they helped to build. The ants keep on building new homes as the leaves die, so

hey are always on the move.

The black jet ants nest in rotting wood, constructing papier-maché-like partitions of 'carton' from wood and saliva. Fungi often penetrate the carton wall, reinforcing it and providing food at the same time.

Some ants in South-East Asia and Africa build huge egg-shaped nests high up in trees, using a mixture of carton and soil which the workers carry up on countless laborious trips from the ground. The nest is started as a single small flake attached to the bark. Other flakes are added and cemented firmly in place to form the first cells: then layer upon layer of inter-connecting cells are built. Eventually, the only flakes left visible as reminders of the construction method are small 'porches' jutting out over the many entrance holes. In some

African species, the carton is as hard as the wood on which it is built, and the nest may take 20 years to complete.

Bee and wasp nests are familiar to most people, but not all of them build homes of this type. Leaf-cutting bees fashion nests from pieces of leaves which they cut with surgical precision with their large mandibles, while mason and potter wasps build beautiful little flask-shaped nests in walls and sand-banks, or attached to plants. They make the nests of clay and sand grains glued together with their own saliva. The female wasp stocks the flasks with caterpillars which she first paralyzes with her sting, then lays a single egg suspended from the roof above the caterpillars, which will eventually serve as a food supply for the developing wasp larvae.

Mud-dauber wasps build long half-tubes of mud, subdivided into separate compartments, in each of which the female lays an egg. The food supply left for the young in this case consists of paralyzed spiders.

Underwater retreats

It is not just land animals that build homes to protect themselves or their young. Malayan soldier crabs, for instance, live between the tide marks and bury themselves as the tide rises in little air-filled shelters around which they construct walls and a roof from small pellets of sand as the tide recedes.

Various marine worms build beautiful, intricate tubes to protect their soft, delicate bodies, while the caddis larvae of freshwater rivers and streams construct ingen-

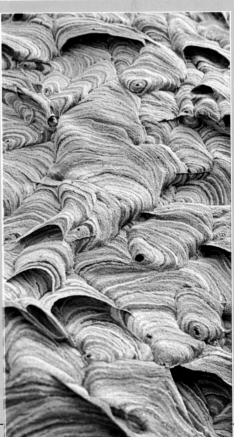

Above left **Nest built by ants of the species** *Azteca chartifex* **on a tonka bean tree in Trinidad.** *Left* **This delicate house of shells protects a** *Limnophilus* **caddis-fly larva from predators in its pond.** *Above* **A female potter wasp with her row of tiny nests, built of clay mixed with saliva, in Veracruz, Mexico.**

Above right **Various mammals make nests, but that of the harvest mouse is the most intricate.** *Right* **Part of the outside of a common wasp's nest.** *Below* **A male satin bowerbird waits to woo his mate at the bower he builds, decorates with blue objects and even paints with a dye he makes by crushing berries.**

Bruce Coleman Ltd./John Markham

Heather Angel

iously camouflaged homes consisting of sand grains, tiny stones, empty shells, leaves or twigs glued by strands of sticky silk from their salivary glands to a silken cylinder which they weave around themselves. On the animal's last abdominal segment is a pair of strong hooks which it latches onto the silken lining of the case to drag it along as it moves about in search of food.

Birds' nests

An old French proverb says that Man can do everything except build a bird's nest. Certainly, birds build some of the most sophisticated and beautiful natural structures, ranging from the tiny, delicate nests of swifts glued to a cliff-face by saliva (and in the case of the edible nest-swiftlets of Asia built *only* of saliva) to the huge communal nests of the weaverbirds. In each case, the bird carries out the entire operation using only its bill and feet – an impressive achievement.

Some of the smallest and daintiest of nests are built by the hummingbirds of the New World. Typically as tiny as the bird themselves, they are built of the lightest materials, including moss, lichens, hair, feathers, leaves and flower petals, often held together by sticky spiders' webs. The nest of the vervain hummingbird from the West Indies, for instance, one of the smallest birds in the world, is about the size of half a walnut shell.

Precarious homes

African palm swifts also build extremely delicate nests, consisting of a small pad of feathers glued to the underside of swaying palm leaves. So precarious is this home in high winds that the bird glues the eggs to the nest: nest, eggs and incubating bird are sometimes turned upside down.

The long-tailed tit of Europe and Asia builds its elaborate bottle-shaped nest from mosses and lichens, held together with cobwebs, and lined with huge numbers of feathers – over 2,000 in some nests. Building normally takes about three weeks, but can be completed in as little as ten days.

The tailor birds from South-East Asia are small warblers which earn their name from their habit of sewing two adjacent leaves together, using cobwebs or plant fibres as thread, and using their bills both to make holes in the leaves and pull the thread through them. Into the space so formed,

Oxford Scientific Films/M. J. Coe

Bruce Coleman Ltd./Günter Ziesler

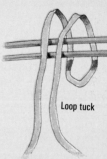

Loop tuck

Left **A giant communal nest of the social weaver-bird dominates a tree in the Kalahari region of South Africa. Built of dry grass, it may hold over 100 pairs of birds, each having its own nest chamber.** *Below* **Oropendola nests hang from the trees in Peru.** *Below right* **A young emerald hummingbird in a nest measuring only 2.5 cm across, built of lichens, moss and cobwebs.** *Below far right* **A Eurasian long-tailed tit at the entrance to its bottle-shaped nest, made of the same materials as the hummingbird's, and lined with as many as 2,000 feathers.**

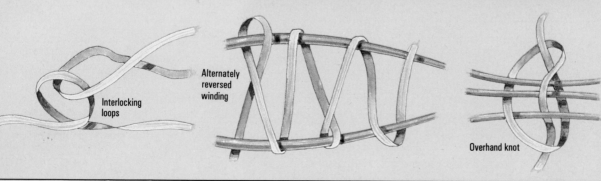

Chris Lyon

Interlocking loops

Alternately reversed winding

Overhand knot

Left **Some of the intricate methods used by weaver-birds in nest-building. The birds hold strands of dry grass with their feet and knot or weave them into place with their bills. As usual with animal architects, their actions are purely instinctive.**

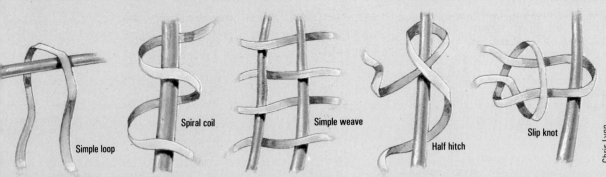

Simple loop

Spiral coil

Simple weave

Half hitch

Slip knot

Chris Lyon

Left **Further examples of weaver-bird weaving and knotting.** *Right* **The village weaver builds a kidney-shaped nest with an entrance at the bottom. It knots twigs together with grass (*A , B*), then makes a circle (*C*) from which the nest is hung (*D, E*).**

they build their nests of plant material.

Oropendolas, from Central and South America, are among the most accomplished of bird architects, building bag-shaped nests up to 2 m long, with an entrance hole at the top, which are suspended from tree branches so that they sway in the wind like stockings on a washing-line.

Native Bread Oven

Another dramatic sight in tropical America is the nests of one of the ovenbirds, or horneros. Small, unpretentious-looking birds, they build extremely strong, bulky nests of sun-baked clay or reinforced mud which resemble a native bread oven. Most ovenbirds have a very long breeding period, and may remodel their 'ovens' for up to nine months, adding or subtracting material and generally improving them. Despite this, they always build a new 'oven' each year.

Among the most impressive of all nests are built by the weaver birds, of which most of the 100 or so species live in Africa. These small, sparrow-like birds construct large,

elaborate nests by knotting, twining and weaving long pieces of grass, palm fronds and twigs, using the bill and feet. It seems hard to believe that the intricate pattern of movements involved in building the nests are inherited and instinctive — as with all animal architects. Some weavers can complete a nest within a day.

Weavers are gregarious birds, and the social weavers of south-west Africa build their huge nests side by side hanging from branches or telegraph poles. Some of these communal nests have the size and appearance of a haystack. The entrances to the individual nests are on the underside of the colony. Sometimes the nests are so heavy that they break the branches from which they hang.

Decorated bowers

Perhaps the most remarkable of all animal architects are the bowerbirds of New Guinea and Australia. The males build extraordinarily complex, highly decorated 'bowers' where they perform elaborate displays for the females before mating. Some

species make 'lawns' on which to perform, decorated with large leaves, shells, insect remains or chips of tree resin, while others build moss-covered stages, their roofs decorated with fruit, berries, fungi and charcoal. The golden bowerbird constructs a tall tower of vegetation up to 2 m high, surrounded by smaller towers and decorated with moss, berries and flowers. The satin bowerbird builds a sturdy, roofless bower of sticks surrounded by blue pebbles, feathers and other objects, and even decorates it with a blue 'paint' made from the juices of berries — sometimes using a wad of bark held in his bill as a brush.

Next time you gaze up in awe at the Eiffel Tower or St. Paul's Cathedral, reflect on the sobering thought that animals were building structures perfectly adapted to their surroundings, using no machines, millions of years before the first humans discovered the shelter of caves.

Oxford Scientific Films/D. H. Thompson

Aquila Photographics/E. A. Janes

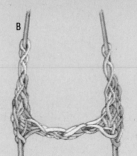

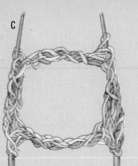

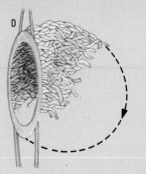

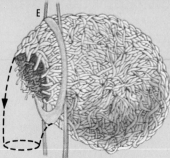

A   B   C   D   E

THE LITTLE HOUSES ON THE PRAIRIE

Study of prairie dogs – not dogs at all but ground squirrels – has revealed that they have elaborate social rituals enabling them to co-exist peacably within their 'towns', some of which once contained as many as 400 million animals

There once was a time when the prairies of the Great Plains stretched over vast areas of North America, forming an almost continuous sea of grass. This was the home of huge herds of bison and pronghorn antelopes, until European settlers pushed westwards, bringing their own herds of cattle and destroying the wild animals that competed for grazing and robbed their crops. The settlers took little notice of the smaller animals, but one could not be overlooked.

The animal in question was the prairie dog, and some of its colonies could be so enormous that they were measured in square kilometres. One colony in Texas covered an area 380 km long and 160 km wide and was home for an estimated 400 million prairie dogs. Such enormous 'cities' no longer exist, but smaller 'towns' of one thousand or so animals are still scattered over the prairies. Zoologists are discovering that each colony is held together by intricate social bonds and an interdependence with the physical environment.

Prairie dogs are ground squirrels – rodents like marmots, chipmunks and woodchucks. The misleading name was coined

from the barking calls. Prairie dogs lack the bushy tails of tree squirrels and look rather like outsize hamsters, about 40 cm long, of which some 9 cm is tail. The five species are very similar, all having yellowish-grey or brown fur. The two most abundant and widespread species are the black-tailed and white-tailed prairie dogs. Biologists have made extensive studies of the black-tailed species to gain an understanding of the social system which enables their colonies to function without chaos.

The highly social prairie dogs differ from most rodents, which live mainly solitary lives. Other rodents of open country, such as the marmots of alpine meadows and ground squirrels of the Arctic tundra, may live communally to a degree, but none approaches the social organization of the prairie dog.

The basic unit of prairie dog society is the *coterie*, a clan of animals who maintain friendly relationships among themselves but are hostile towards members of neighbouring coteries. The average coterie has one adult male, two or three adult females and their offspring. When there are two or more males, one is dominant and the others keep out of his way. Exceptionally,

Colin Newman

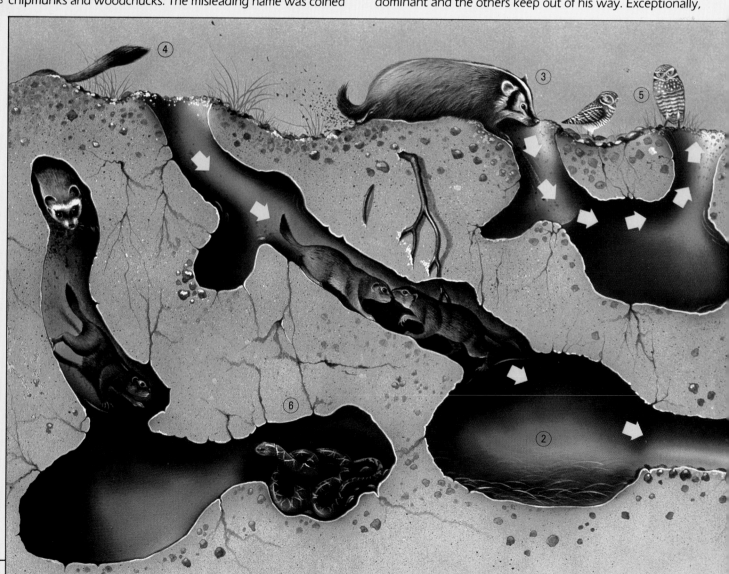

there may be 20 or more youngsters, but some coteries dwindle until there are only a few elderly adults left and they are taken over by encroaching neighbours. Even when this happens, the territory boundaries of a coterie remain intact, despite the change of inhabitants. The boundaries are as rigid as a garden fence is to human householders.

Trespassers keep out

The key to the integrity of the coterie territory is the defence of the burrow entrances. If these are defended against trespassers, the surrounding area will be inviolate, and a considerable portion of a prairie dog's daily activities is devoted to maintaining the bonds within the coterie and checking trespass by others.

When two prairie dogs meet, they put their heads together, open their mouths, and 'kiss' with teeth bared. The 'kiss' may be prolonged into a 'cuddle', as one animal rolls onto its back and is groomed by the other. Then they stretch out side by side and relax before going off to feed, still with their bodies pressed together. Although it appears a charming sight, the initial 'kiss' is, in fact, a threatening gesture indicating that the prairie dog intends to defend its territory. If both are members of the same coterie, they recognize each other and behave in a friendly fashion, but when strangers accidentally meet within a territory they react aggressively. The interloper lacks confidence and retreats rapidly.

At the boundary of the territory, a prolonged ritual ensues. Perhaps one prairie dog has strayed across the boundary while feeding, but at the boundary itself neither prairie dog is totally confident. They approach each other, then stop. One turns its rump to the other and raises its tail; the other advances and sniffs the exposed scent glands, like a real dog. Then they exchange roles, and a scuffle may ensue. More sniffing takes place, and more scuffling, until a decision is reached as to the exact position of the boundary, and the prairie dogs withdraw into their own territories.

As well as these personal encounters, there is a general advertisement of territorial ownership vocally. At odd intervals, but more especially after a boundary dispute, a prairie dog gives vent to a two-note, harsh call, not really resembling a dog's bark, and best transcribed as *AH-aaah*. As it calls, the prairie dog rears up on its hind legs, nose to the sky. The first syllable is given with an intake of breath as it rears up and the second as an expiration as it descends. The whole performance is called the '*jump-yip*' display. Sometimes a prairie dog rears up with such exuberance that it leaps into the air and even falls over backwards.

The integrity of the coterie is maintained from day to day by the rituals just described, but for it to continue over the years young prairie dogs must learn their place in society. This is true culture: the transmission of knowledge from one generation to the next. When prairie dogs first leave the nest and meet other members of the coterie, they are treated with extreme tolerance. They play with other youngsters of their own age and any of the adults will 'kiss' and groom them. They are part of an extended family, and only rarely will an adult not tolerate the attentions of a youngster which may be climbing over and under it in an effort to solicit grooming. The young can even wander into neighbouring territories with impunity.

Within a few weeks, however, the restrictions of adult life begin to encroach on the childhood idyll. Trespassing is no longer tolerated and the young prairie dog is chased back home. It

Oxford Scientific Films/Marty Stouffer/Animals Animals

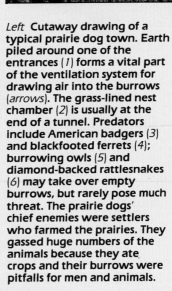

Left **Cutaway drawing of a typical prairie dog town. Earth piled around one of the entrances (*1*) forms a vital part of the ventilation system for drawing air into the burrows (*arrows*). The grass-lined nest chamber (*2*) is usually at the end of a tunnel. Predators include American badgers (*3*) and blackfooted ferrets (*4*); burrowing owls (*5*) and diamond-backed rattlesnakes (*6*) may take over empty burrows, but rarely pose much threat. The prairie dogs' chief enemies were settlers who farmed the prairies. They gassed huge numbers of the animals because they ate crops and their burrows were pitfalls for men and animals.**

Above **Prairie dogs usually build their towns in treeless, windswept areas. The adult in the foreground is standing on top of a raised 'volcano' entrance: other 'volcanoes' can be seen in the distance. They help in ventilating the burrows by creating a difference in air pressure between them and the lower 'mound' entrances, so that air is sucked through. They also serve as dikes against sudden floods. The area looks as if it was hit by a miniature air-raid, so peppered is it with entrances. The prairie dogs strip the ground of grass so that it is colonized by weeds, whose flowers and seeds form the animals' staple diet.**

learns that not all prairie dogs will treat it in the same way and that the type of treatment depends on whether or not it stays within the invisible boundary around its home burrow.

At about this time the youngster starts to perform the 'jump-yip' display and the 'kiss'. If it does either in a strange territory it is quickly sent packing, so it learns to associate these rituals with friends and safety. Later still, it will know that a prairie dog that does not respond must be chased away.

Time for change

By the end of its first summer, the prairie dog has taken its full place in social life, but there must be a change in the coterie. Unless it can adapt to the increase in numbers as the young grow up, the society would collapse under the strain of overcrowding and the exhaustion of food supplies. In most animal societies, the young animals are driven from the parental territory as they mature, but prairie dogs have found an alternative solution to overcrowding.

Between March and May, when the females are busy with breeding, they defend their nest burrows against all-comers, including members of their own coterie. The old freedom of movement within the territory disappears and the boundaries lose some of their significance. Adults not concerned with breeding and yearlings start to wander through the town during the day, but they continue to return at night.

The wandering may take them beyond the outskirts of the town, where they feed and dig new burrows, or they may merely lead into neighbouring territories where the coteries are weak in numbers. These forays are different from the accidental excursions described earlier. The intruders are aggressive and

stay to fight the occupants until they can drive them from their homes or teach them to accept their presence. When the new generation of pups are coming above ground, their wandering elders spend more and more time away from the coterie. Eventually, they spend the night in their new homes, and, thereafter only rarely make fleeting return visits.

The prairie dogs need an organized source of food to allow their dense 'urban' lifestyle. The animals actually modify their environment to achieve this end. Their favourite foods are the flowers and seeds of herbaceous plants, especially in summer, though they also eat some grasses. The prairie dogs even practise a form of weed control, cutting down and leaving plants to wither in the Sun. As yet, this interaction between the animals and their environment has not been studied to the same extent as their social system.

Ventilated burrows

The prairie dog burrow is a marvel of engineering. Researchers think that the raised rims of soil around the entrances act as lookout posts or defences against flash-flooding after rainstorms. The burrows themselves are U-shaped, measuring between 10 and 30 metres long and descending to a depth of I-5 metres. There are two entrances at either end of the 'U', and sometimes a third, too. The rims of soil and the entrances are of two distinct types. One is a low, rounded 'mound', the other is a taller, steep-sided 'volcano'. If an entrance is destroyed, it is rebuilt in the same pattern. By throwing smoke candles into burrows, researchers have found that a mound is always connected to a 'volcano'. What is more, if there is a slight breeze blowing, a plume of smoke always appears at the 'volcano' and never at the

Bruce Coleman Ltd./Wayne Lankinen

Bruce Coleman Ltd./Jeff Foott

Bruce Coleman Ltd./John M. Burnley

Left **Prairie dogs are vegetarians, feeding during the hours of daylight on weed flowers and seeds, as well as on grasses.** *Above* **A family group, or** *coterie,* **emerges from its burrow at the Wind Cave National Park, South Dakota, USA.** *Right* **Sounding the alarm: an adult stands tall, resting on its hind legs and throwing back its head as it gives the two-syllable bark that has earned the prairie dogs their common name.**

'mound' to which it is connected.

The 'mounds' and 'volcanoes' of prairie dog burrows serve to drive a current of air through the burrow for ventilation in accordance with the *Bernoulli principle*: if a fluid moves horizontally, its pressure must decrease whenever its velocity increases. This is the same principle that explains the lift of an aircraft wing, where air moves faster over the upper surface than over the under surface and creates a pressure difference beween the two. The burrow is ventilated because wind speed is reduced at ground level by friction, so the flow of air is greater past the taller 'volcano' than the lower 'mound'. Low pressure is created in the 'volcano' and air is sucked out.

Calculations have shown that without this aid, there wouldn't be enough ventilation to keep even a single prairie dog alive in the burrow, but with the raised entrance system, the slightest breeze of 0.45 metres per second will produce a complete change of air in 10 minutes. The importance of wind in ventilating the burrow may explain why prairie dogs prefer the most treeless, windswept parts of the prairie.

Dealing with predators

One apparent drawback of living in large groups is that the prairie dogs attract large numbers of predators, such as hawks, rattlesnakes and coyotes. American badgers, which are more carnivorous than the European species, dig into the burrows to extract their prey, and the black-footed ferret is so tied to a diet of prairie dogs that it is never found anwhere else but in their towns.

Despite having so many enemies, a prairie dog has a much greater life expectation than most rodents. Most mice, for instance, are lucky to live through their first winter, but young prairie dogs live under the umbrella of an efficient warning system. The animals' habit of cropping the plants around the burrows enables them to see well in all directions, especially from the tops of the burrow rims. While sentinels are not deliberately posted, with so many animals in the town there will always be someone on the alert. Individual black-tailed prairie dogs spend less time on the alert than do white-tailed prairie dogs, which live in less dense colonies. The more pairs of eyes to keep watch, the less time need be spent by each animal looking out for danger, because there is a greater likelihood that one of its fellows will be on the alert. Biologists have also shown that this is true in flocks of birds.

When a prairie dog is alarmed, it runs to the burrow extrance and gives a variant of the 'jump-yip' display, continuing to bark until the danger is past. Other prairie dogs look alert and may run to the burrows. The chances of a predator catching one unawares are very slender.

The balance between prairie dogs, the prairie vegetation and predators which has evolved so subtly over millennia has seen a drastic change over the last century. As European settlers encroached, the prairie dogs became a nuisance. They ate grazing needed for farm stock and when the prairies were turned into farmland, the prairie dogs ate the crops. Before long, gassing campaigns had eliminated many towns, so much so that the Utah prairie dog became a species officially listed as vulnerable to extinction. The future of these unusual animals now depends on maintaining sufficient nature reserves on the prairies.

Above **Gazing out over the prairie, two adults stand sentinel over their township against danger from any quarter. Special sentries are not needed, with so many animals in the town.** *Left* **Two adults 'kiss' at a town in Albuquerque, New Mexico. Despite its tender appearance, this ritual is really a threatening gesture by which one animal shows another it means to defend its territory if needs be.** *Right* **An adult basks in the sunshine.**

Bruce Coleman Ltd./Joe Van Wormer

THE DAM BUILDERS

Many years ago vast tracts of North America and Europe were flooded by the activities of beavers. Today the beaver population is much smaller but they still leave their mark on the countryside

Anthropomorphism is a common pitfall in the study of animal behaviour. It is very easy to fall into the trap of crediting an animal with unusual intelligence because it is doing something which would test human skills.

A bird's nest of woven grasses and twigs perched in a hedge is a marvel of construction, which the most dextrous human fingers would find extremely difficult to recreate. Yet a bird has only its beak as a tool. However, it can build a perfect nest with no previous experience, indicating that nest-building is purely instinctive and requires

no intelligence on the part of the bird. Mammals, on the other hand, are much more intelligent than birds and they are more likely to do 'clever' things.

The beaver's engineering activities are truly remarkable feats and they have been considered in the past to be the result of a very high level of intelligence. The animal fells trees and uses the trunks and branches to build dams and lodges that withstand flood waters and provide a secure retreat. It seems, however, that the beaver makes these remarkable constructions with as little intelligence as a bird building its nest.

The range of the beaver is across Europe and North America. There are two species, *Castor fiber* and *Castor canadensis*, but they are so similar that it is simpler to speak merely of the beaver, and some zoologists consider that there is only one species.

The European beaver was once widespread across the northern half of the continent, including the British Isles, but it was hunted for its dense fur and for the glandular secretion with which it marks its territory. Known as *castoreum*, the secretion was widely used as a medicine in earlier times, and modern research has shown that it contains salicylic acid, the principal ingredient of aspirin.

Until recently the European beaver had become confined to the Rivers Rhone (in France) and Elbe (in Germany), southern Norway and Russia, but it has been reintroduced to many parts of Scandinavia, the USSR, Germany and Switzerland. It is said the Russians have even liberated beavers in remote areas by parachute!

The demand for beaver fur hastened the European colonization of northern North America as trappers reaped a rich harvest. The beaver soon started to decline and became extinct in many areas. Today the

Air vent

Beaver lodge

Food store

Dry floor

Tunnel entrance

Tunnel exit

Left An incomplete beaver lodge. Beavers build elaborate dam systems and lodges (*below*). The water on the lodge side of the dam is higher than on the down-stream side and protects the lodge by turning it into a little island. The beaver can enter and leave its lodge via two underwater passages.

Right (*1*) The first step in building a lodge is to dig a burrow in the stream bank. *Figure* (*2*) The beaver piles branches on top of the burrow to form a lodge. *Figures* (*3*) and (*4*) The dam can be built in various ways. Sometimes a log is used but very often stakes are driven in first.

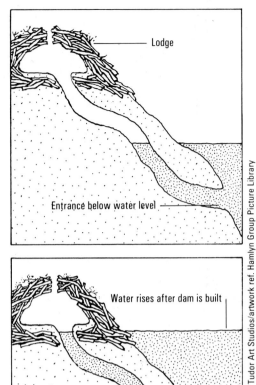

Lodge

Entrance below water level

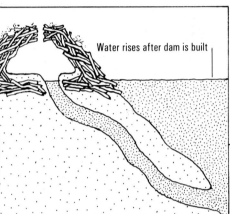

Water rises after dam is built

Tudor Art Studios/artwork ref. Hamlyn Group Picture Library

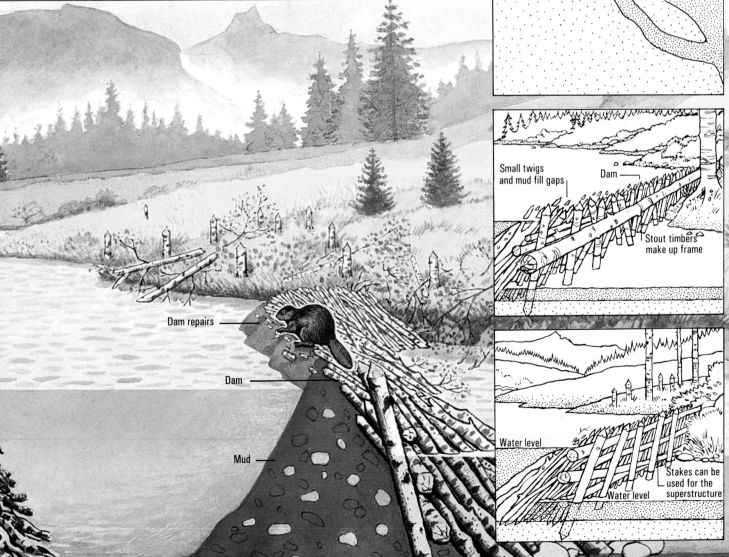

Small twigs and mud fill gaps

Dam

Stout timbers make up frame

Dam repairs

Dam

Mud

Water level

Water level

Stakes can be used for the superstructure

beaver has regained some of its lost ground with protection and reintroduction programmes. Indeed, numbers need to be controlled in some regions.

The beaver is the most aquatic of all rodents. Its nose and ears close when it dives and it can stay submerged for 15 minutes. When swimming on the surface, the beaver propels itself with its hind legs, assisted by sculling movements of the flat, paddle-shaped tail. Underwater, it swims with hind legs moving together and the tail moving up and down.

The life of the beaver is centred on water, either a river or a lake, but it comes on land to find food, which is made up of leaves, twigs and bark, mainly of aspen and willow, and low-growing land and water plants. Beaver society is made up of a colony consisting of an adult pair, their young – the kits – and yearlings. Although they live amicably and sleep together in a single nest, they work independently at feeding and engineering.

To get leaves and twigs, the beaver has first to cut down a tree. It was once believed that the beaver deliberately made use of assistance from the wind to topple trees in the direction of the water, but

Leonard Lee Rue/Bruce Coleman Ltd.

trunks are left in a felling area pointing in all directions. However, the beaver is aided unconsciously by the fact that it prefers to work where the wind is blowing towards the water's edge. This is so it can better detect approaching danger; also the slope of the bank encourages the tree to fall towards the water.

The industry of a beaver colony is amazing. An American colony of ten beavers felled 1584 trees in the course of four years. Any tree less than 12 centimetres in diameter can be chewed through in under half an hour! Trunks of one metre in diameter are sometimes tackled. The beaver chews at an angle of 45° to the horizontal; the upper incisor teeth act as an anchor while small bites are taken with the lower incisors. When several cuts have been made, the beaver turns its head almost upside down and attacks at the opposite angle to remove chips, in much the same way as a lumberjack works with an axe.

Felling takes place at night and each beaver works alone in bouts of five or ten minutes. In between, it rests and sharpens its teeth. Like all rodents, beavers have incisor teeth that grow continuously as they wear down. The front face of the tooth is lined with hard enamel and the softer dentine behind is worn away to leave a sharp cutting edge. The sharpening process is assisted by the rodent grinding the enamel of one set of incisors against the dentine of the other.

Provisions for the winter

During the summer, tree-felling is abandoned because there are plenty of low-growing plants to eat. It starts again in autumn when the beavers lay in provisions for the winter. Logs and sticks are piled up underwater near the burrow entrance so the beavers can continue to feed even when the water is covered with thick ice. The animals carry leaves and small sticks, either by pushing a mass along the ground or holding it in the forepaws and walking on the hindlegs. Large logs are dragged by the mouth and the going is made easier by constructing runways and canals, which are deep furrows leading to the nearest open water. One canal of unusual length stretched 400 metres from the waterside.

Logs and sticks have also to be transported to the water for the construction of the lodge and dam. These structures are not built by every beaver colony and beavers will often live in a burrow deep in the river or lake bank. The burrow is furnished with an underwater entrance, a feeding chamber just above water level and a dry sleeping chamber on a higher level. The burrow may be converted into a lodge by adding sticks and soil to the top. Where the banks are low, a sleeping chamber can only be made by excavating into the pile from the inside.

Building is performed in a very stereotyped fashion. The beavers dump material in an untidy fashion on top of the structure

Above left A beaver lodge is a safe haven from predators, Surrounded by water, the only way in or out is under water. Even in winter the lodge is safe (*above*). The beavers also have a secure underwater food store that keeps the family fed.

Far left It is always obvious when beavers are about because of the way they cut down trees. The animals chew at 45° to the horizontal, and the front teeth act like an anchor. After several cuts, the beaver turns its head and cuts at the opposite angle.

Left centre Beavers are amazingly industrious animals, constantly cutting down trees and branches which are used either as building materials or as food. The animals come on to land to cut the wood and then swim with it to the lodge.

Although beavers live in family groups they always work alone (*left bottom*). This beaver is fixing a breach in the dam. It will use mud or sticks and will only stop when the sound of running water ceases. *Below* Dams can be massive structures.

and then fill up any crannies or gaps by dropping a bundle over it, or pushing in a finer material and compacting it with paws and snout until a smooth, gentle incline is made. The structure is strengthened by pinning it with long sticks. Grasping one end of the stick with its teeth and guiding the other end with a paw, the beaver works it firmly into the existing mass.

The characteristic pile that makes up the lodge serves to protect the burrow from erosion and keeps out the frost. Providing there is a good snow cover, the temperature in the nest remains above freezing even when the temperature outside drops to −35°C.

The dam is built in much the same way as the lodge, through the stereotyped dumping of vegetation and stones. It is strengthened with pins until a long, triangular pile is built from bank to bank. Beav-

ers work on the upstream side, clambering up the pile to deposit material and fill crannies. What seems to be an intelligent deployment of building material is no more than a simple reaction to the sound of running water.

Wherever water is spilling through or over the dam, the beaver adds material. This is so instinctive that a captive beaver will pile sticks against a loudspeaker transmitting the sound of running water. One of the signs that a pattern of behaviour is instinctive rather than intelligent is that the animal does 'stupid' things when faced by unusual circumstances. The sound of running water is a sensible guide to dam building under natural conditions but a beaver that tries to plug a loudspeaker is clearly not fully aware of all its actions.

There is no reason to disparage beavers for lack of intelligence; it is remarkable that

their behaviour has evolved by natural selection in the first place. The result has been not only an animal superbly adapted to its chosen environment, but also one that can adapt its environment for its own purposes.

Few species other than human beings can manipulate the environment to their own ends. The dam, lodge, winter foodstore, canals and runways are part of an environmental engineering programme. The dam transforms a shallow stream into a deep pool which gives the beavers a place to store their winter food, increases the radius of navigable water and makes it easier to transport food and building materials. It also gives the beavers a safer refuge from predators. When the pool freezes over, the water level drops naturally or because the beavers cut a sluice in the dam, they can swim safely under the ice in search of food to supplement the winter store.

The beaver pool has wide effects on the ecology of the surrounding country. It raises the water table, slows drainage in summer and prevents the worst effects of flooding by maintaining a steady flow of water in headstreams. By their systems of dams and pools, they not only hold the water directly but distribute it through the surrounding soil which acts as a vast spongy reservoir. In this situation, forests flourish – despite the beavers' tree felling – with a dense scrub and undergrowth that many other animals will enjoy for food and shelter. The pool itself becomes a haven for waterbirds and fishes. These attract predators and the whole web of life is enriched.

Wayne Lankinen/Bruce Coleman Ltd.

Left **Beavers are powerfully built animals. They have flat paddle-like tails that propel them when swimming. The beaver is the most aquatic member of the rodent family and can close its nose and ears when diving.**

Beaver young, called kittens or kits, live with their parents in the lodge until they are old enough to provide their own shelter (*below left*). *Below* **The beaver family feeding together is a rare sight, seen only if there are kits.**

Jen & Des Bartlett/Survival Anglia Ltd.

DEATH IN THE AFTERNOON

Like Dr. Jekyll and Mr. Hyde the beautiful dragonfly has two faces – as a larva it is a ruthless killer

Left The beast becomes a beauty. The Golden-Ringed Dragonfly sheds its larval shell and takes to the air.

Above Although it may spend as long as six years in the larval stage, the fully formed dragonfly dies within weeks.

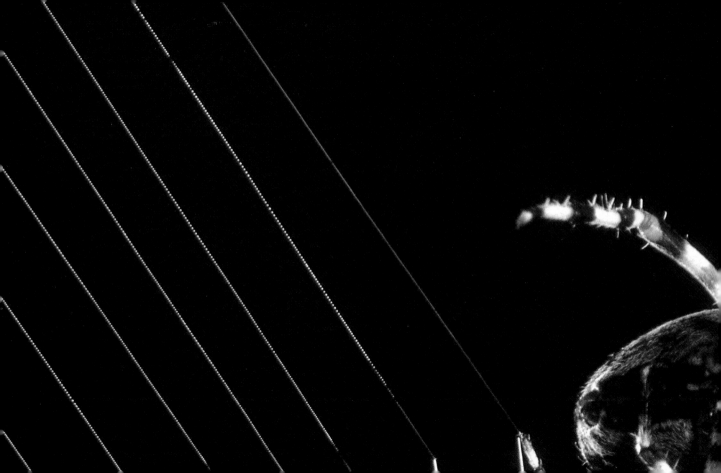

WON'T YOU STEP INTO MY PARLOUR?

Spiders build webs with silk stronger than steel.
Now we unravel the secrets of these deadly traps

Next time you decide to sweep away a cobweb on a wall, pause to spare a thought for its extraordinary qualities. The spider silk of which it is made is stronger than nylon or terylene, and has a higher breaking point than ordinary steel of the same thickness. It is also highly elastic, so a falling spider is not pulled up abruptly. Despite its strength, spider silk is very light, and a dragline extended right round the Earth would only weigh a mere 320 grams!

The silk is a high-polymer protein with the molecules coiled when it is a liquid inside the spider's silk glands. As it is extruded from spinning organs called spinnerets at the rear of the spider's body, the molecules are stretched so that the silk sets as a fibre. Side-chain amino acids are regularly arranged along its length in a semicrystalline structure that gives the thread great strength.

The spider can control the speed at which it lets out the silk, and it can stop in mid-air if need be. All spiders spin a dragline thread as they walk along, which they anchor as they dab their spinnerets on the surface at intervals, like a mountaineer belaying a rope. Then, if the spider is blown off course, or needs to jump to avoid a predator, it has a safety line to hang on to. Usually, the heavier the spider, the thicker the silk. A dragline can normally support one and a half times the weight of the spider that laid it – so spiders seldom have climbing accidents.

Spiders are the next most successful group of land invertebrates (animals without backbones) after the insects, with about 35,000 known species, and new ones still being discovered: in 1981 alone, over 50 were described. Silk, in particular its use in trapping insect prey, probably plays an important part in their success. All spiders are carnivores, the majority eating insects. Not all spiders build webs, however: some actively hunt, stalk or ambush their prey instead. The web-builders have the advantage of being able to exploit the abundant supplies of flying insects, which their non-web-building relatives are denied.

Many spiders build three-dimensional webs of no particular form, ranging from a few threads to a large tangle. These rather conspicuous structures are built from the same sort of silk as the draglines. Only a few such webs have sticky threads. Cobwebs consist of these types of web.

Orb weavers

By contrast, the *orb web* (a misnomer, for it is not spherical) is a two-dimensional geometric design shaped like a cartwheel. Orb webs are probably invisible to insects, for their catching rate is higher than the 3-D types. They are also gummy, and any insects touching them usually stick fast.

There are 3,000-4,000 species of orb weavers, the best known being the common garden or cross spider, *Araneus diadematus*.

The orb web is superbly designed for catching flying insects. It consists of a frame of several fibres to give strength which are fixed to vegetation by even stronger anchor threads, and a number of radical threads emerging from a meshed hub and crossing the frame fibres. All the supporting threads are made of dragline-type silk, with an elasticity of about 30%. Their strength and 'give' enable the web to withstand the impact of flying insects – or strong winds. They support a closely spaced spiral of sticky threads that catches the insects.

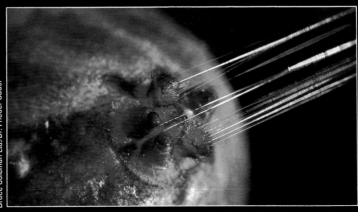

Bruce Coleman Ltd./Dr. Frieder Sauer

Far left **A garden spider** *Araneus diadematus* **spins the sticky spirals that will form the insect-trapping part of its intricate orb web. The spider produces silk – both sticky and non-sticky types – in glands, from which it is extruded through spinnerets (close-up** *left***) at the rear of its body, then manipulated with the hind legs.**

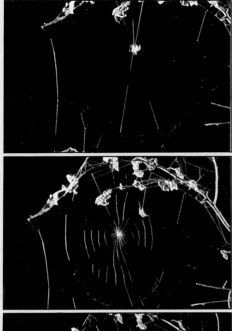

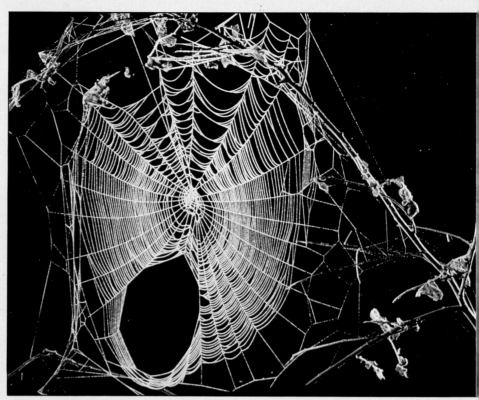

Oxford Scientific Films/J. A. L. Cooke

Left **Stages in the spinning of an orb web by the garden spider. First the primary radii and basic frame are laid** (*top*). **Then** (*centre*) **with radii and temporary, non-sticky spiral (around the central hub) in place, the spider spins a permanent sticky spiral.**

Left, bottom **A further stage in laying the sticky spiral, and,** *above,* **the finished web. The whole process takes only 25-50 minutes, and the spider builds a new web each day as the silk is damaged and struggling prey, rain and dust render the 'glue' less effective.**

Sticky-silk thread is produced in different glands from those that make dragline silk. It is finer, and even more elastic, stretching 500-600% in some cases, for the side-chain amino acids are not arranged in a regular crystal and can be pulled apart without breaking. Glue is manufactured in a further set of glands. The great elasticity of the sticky threads allows them to stop flying insects gradually, thus decreasing the likelihood of their snapping. Unfortunate victims struggle to free themselves, but their movements usually make them stick to even more spirals. Junctions between the sticky spirals and the radials are not bonded, but at many of them the spiral can slide giving them even greater flexibility. Spiders' webs can restrain larger insects than artificial webs of the same dimensions, probably because of their flexibility.

The web restrains the prey until the spider, responding to the vibrations in the threads caused by its movements, comes out to bite the insect, swathe it in silk, or both. The spider can then cut its prey out of the web and eat it at its leisure.

Spiders do not respond to immobile prey, but can tell the direction of live insects by analyzing the vibrations they produce. If uncertain of the exact location of a small insect, the spider plucks its web in the approximate direction to sense its position accurately. Biologists used to think that the elastic web would not transmit vibrations well, but recent research using laser Doppler vibrometry has shown that the web does transmit longitudinal vibrations, to which spiders are particularly sensitive.

The method of spinning an orb web is similar in most species. The best studied orb web builder is the common garden spider *Araneus diadematus*, which takes 25-50 minutes to build a complete web. Researchers persuaded garden spiders to use a wooden frame in the laboratory. They started by walking along and laying a dragline. In its natural environment, the garden spider usually begins by letting silk from its spinnerets blow out in the wind until the far end catches on some object, forming a bridging line. In this way, the spider can build a web across a stream or other obstacle. In some species, such as *Araneus cereolus*, a West African relative of the garden spider, the bridging line may be as much as 8 metres long. This spider builds webs up to a metre in diameter.

The garden spider then normally drops vertically to the ground or to vegetation and fixes the thread to form a 'Y'. This 'Y' is

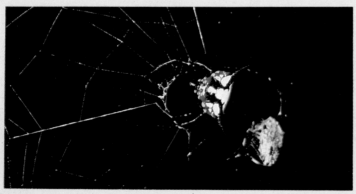

Brian Rodgers/Biofotos

Oxford Scientific Films/J. A. L. Cooke

Heather Angel

turbed, spiders never build incomplete webs. If the radii are burned as soon as they are laid, the spider lays more until the radius silk is exhausted, and it then tries to lay spirals on a deficient base. The bridging line of the garden spider may vary in length, but the catching area varies little. The spider lays threads cutting off corners or sharp angles of the frame, so defining the catching area. It is at this stage that somehow the size of the web is determined by the amount of silk in the glands. Spiders that have been fed the drug physostigmine, which stimulates extra silk production, spin larger webs than normal.

A daily task

The fine silk of the spiral is easily damaged, while the gum is washed away by rain and struggling insects, or clogged by dust. After 24 hours, the orb web is no longer an efficient insect trap, so it is normally rebuilt daily, at a time characteristic for each species. The spider eats the silk and uses the digested amino acids to rebuild silk for the next web. The garden spider and the Argiope spiders leave the frame intact and eat just the radii and spirals. Spiny-bellied spiders eat almost the whole web, leaving just a 'Y' to start the next one. Some tropical spiders, such as *Araneus cereolus*, were never known to build webs until naturalists discovered that they build them at dusk and completely destroy them at dawn. In temperate regions, there would not be

the basis of the web, and the hub will be where the three arms of the 'Y' meet. It is as though a wheel were started by fixing three spokes together to form the hub. Outer frame threads come next, each with its own radial thread attached to the hub. Sometimes the spider will produce additional frame and anchor threads to reinforce the web. The spider continues by filling in extra radii, which are always laid next to an existing radius at an almost constant angle, though longer radii have smaller angles between them. With a few extra turns on the hub, the spider then starts on the temporary spiral, moving towards the frame. On completing this, it turns, and travelling inwards, lays the sticky permanent spiral, using the temporary one to get between the radii. It then eats the temporary spiral — a neat arrangement.

The coils of the permanent spiral are evenly spaced. A spinning spider probes the previous radial or spiral threads with a front leg and pulls out silk with its fourth (hind) pair. Longer-legged spiders build larger webs, but mesh size is related to the weight of the spider: heavier species spin thicker spirals laid in a coarser mesh. This is an adaptation to the size of insect caught rather than one for supporting the spider, which walks on the radials. Heavier spiders can deal with larger prey: average-sized garden spiders weighing 0.2 g seldom catch honey bees, but a large West African *Argiope* deals with them adeptly.

Intricate geometric patterning is not the only fascinating feature of orb webs: the regulation of their size is equally remarkable. At the end of web-building, the silk glands are almost empty, but unless dis-

Above left **Linyphia spiders build a hammock-shaped web (white sheet at bottom) supported by a maze of threads above and below. When insects blunder into the upper scaffolding they fall onto the sheet, which, though not sticky, traps them long enough for the spider to run out and kill them.**

Below, opposite page **One of the spiny-bellied spiders, a brightly coloured** *Gasteracantha* (*far left*) **from Papua New Guinea, binds its prey with silk in its orb web. The tangled web at** *left* **was built by a species of** *Nephila* **from Trinidad – the spider is in the centre of the web. The leaf-curl spider (***below left***) fashions a retreat from a leaf that has fallen into its web, while the web of the orb weaver** *Argiope* (*below*) **features a cross of white silk across the hub, the** *stabilimentum.* **This probably camouflages the spider, especially as it vibrates the web, blurring its outline.**

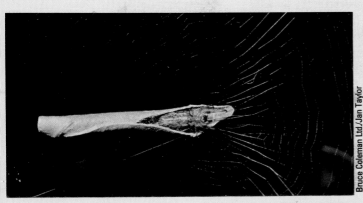

Bruce Coleman Ltd/Jan Taylor

Oxford Scientific Films/J. A. L. Cooke

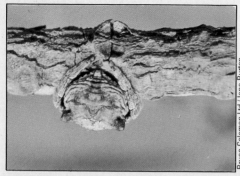

Dr. Janet Edmunds

Bruce Coleman Ltd./Jane Burton

Dr. Janet Edmunds

Oxford Scientific Films/Mantis Wildlife Films

Oxford Scientific Films/J. A. L. Cooke

Above far left **By day the spider** *Caerostris* **escapes detection by mimicking a bump on a twig: at night, it builds a web a metre or more across, which it dismantles at dawn.** *Above left* **A female wolf spider** *Pisaura mirabilis* **guards her newly-hatched young in a silken nest. Wolf spiders do not build webs, relying on speed to catch prey.** *Above* *Segestria* **spiders weave silken tubes in holes, with radiating trip wires to alert them to prey.** *Far left* **Australian bolas spider** *Dicrostichus magnificens* **with its remarkable weapon: a single silk thread with a blob of sticky silk at the end. The spider holds the thread with a leg and swings it out to trap flying insects.** *Left* **The ogre-faced spider** *Dinopis* **with its box-shaped web.**

enough time at night during summer, and there are not so many nocturnal insects, so the spiders usually leave their webs intact during the day.

A variety of designs

There are considerable differences in web shape between species. The catching area is normally oval, with the hub above the centre and the first spirals forming incomplete loops to fill the space more evenly. The web of the garden spider is inclined slightly to the vertical, but the angle varies and more inclined webs have a more circular outline. Webs of spiny-bellied spiders are built at a considerable angle and are more nearly circular. *Zygiella* spiders build webs in the corners of window-frames. These have no spirals between their three radials. The middle radial forms a guide-line to the spider resting in its lair at the edge.

More dramatic variations have recently been discovered in the tropics. An incredibly long ladder web, about 1 metre or more long and only 15-20 cm broad, has evolved

twice. In New Guinea, the spider *Tylorida* spins a web with the hub at the top and the bottom elongated, while in *Scoloderus* from tropical America and Florida the situation is reversed, with the ladder above the hub. Biologists believe that these fly-paper-like webs are used to catch moths whose scales powder the glue, so allowing them to escape from normal webs. It seems that the moths drop down these ladder webs, losing scales as they fall, until they are left with too few scales to prevent the glue from holding them.

Reduced webs

At the other extreme, there are spiders with reduced webs. *Wixia* from Florida builds a small asterisk-shaped web, with no spirals, and a few radials attached to the ground, equipped with sticky ends to catch walking insects. *Poecilopachys* from Australia and *Pasilobus* from New Guinea build horizontal webs with few radials, spanned by very adhesive threads that hang in loops. The joint at one end is strong,

but that at the other breaks freely when the loop is hit by a moth. The victim is held fast by the glue and flies completely ineffectually, as though tethered, until it is seized by the spider.

The web is reduced even further in the bolas spiders of America, Africa and Australia. These produce single threads with sticky blobs on their free ends. The spider holds the thread with one leg and swings it towards passing insects, especially moths. Unlike other silk, the glue-covered thread is flattened and coiled, acting like a spring. Researchers have found that the bolas spiders produce a chemical that imitates the scent produced by female moths to attract mates. One bolas spider was found to catch only the males of two species of moth which actively flew towards it.

Another unusual web has recently been found in tropical America: *Synotaxus*, which belongs to a family of spiders that normally build cobwebs, has evolved a sticky rectangular two-dimensional web. About four parallel dry threads support dry

Above **Dew spangles spiders' webs on heathland in autumn. Spiders are highly successful animals: for instance, a British meadow in late summer may contain more than five million spiders to the hectare.**

Heather Angel

cross-connections that in turn support sticky threads. The method of construction is quite different from that used by the orb weavers. This is a beautiful example of *convergent evolution*, where unrelated species have evolved structures that are similar in function and general appearance, but different in detail.

Using spiders' silk

Spiders have evolved silk with properties as remarkable as any manmade material. Cloth has been spun from their silk, but the totally carnivorous spiders are not easy to feed and are often cannibalistic when kept together, so it is easier to obtain silk from silkworms fed on mulberry leaves. Also, spiders' silk lacks lustre. Traditionally, cobwebs were used by surgeons to staunch bleeding, the fine threads catching the

blood cells and helping clotting: researchers are currently re-examining the effectiveness of this technique. Spiders' silk is also used for cross-wires in delicate optical instruments.

Biologists have carried out a variety of experiments in which they have induced spiders to build webs under the influence of drugs and in outer space. In an attempt to delay web-building from the unsociable (to the researchers) time of 2.00 am, a garden spider was fed a small amount of amphetamine. It produced an abnormal web at the usual time. Smaller doses made it build a slightly irregular web, while with larger doses, it built very distorted webs. Under the influence of the hallucinatory drug psilocybin, spiders produced a smaller, coarser-meshed web. With larger doses, few spiders built webs at all. Surprisingly, small doses of LSD increased the regularity of the webs, which were built more slowly, with the appearance of more care being taken.

Biologists hoped to learn much from

experiments such as these about the physiological properties of drugs and the mechanisms spiders use in web-building. Unfortunately, the results did not yield the expected insights, and the research ceased.

In a recent experiment, two spiders built webs when released in the orbiting US Skylab. Some webs were similar in size and regularity to pre-flight webs, though others were highly abnormal. As expected in space, with no gravity or weight, the webs were nearly circular and the thread was thinner. When first released, these spiders floated at the ends of threads, but they soon adapted to running on the frame instead of trying to drop.

Perhaps one day a use will be found for spiders' silk so that it will be worth the effort of keeping them in captivity. In the meantime, we can leave them in their webs to catch insects, and marvel at the sophistication of their lures.

THE KISS OF DEATH

Sex can be deadly in the animal kingdom. Some spiders turn to liquid in their mate's embrace. And mantises lose their heads

Kim Taylor/Bruce Coleman Ltd.

Mata Hari used her legendary powers of seduction to assure success and survival — at the expense of besotted male admirers. And females of other species use their charms in the same way. Female spiders make notoriously deadly spouses. Next item on their agenda after sex is a good meal: they eat their mates.

Biologists have found much to wonder at in the complex love life of insects. But, bizarre as many of the arrangements seem at first sight, every one has a purpose.

Nearly all male spiders, for example, are much smaller than the females. (An extreme case is the *Nephilia chrysogaster*: the female body measures some 5 cm in length while the male is a mere 2.5 mm.) This size difference reduces the chances of the male spider escaping from the lethal embrace.

Within a few days of the final molt, which brings him to maturity, the male spider has to build himself a sperm web a few millimetres in diameter. He then taps his geni-

The Wolf Spider (*above*) **takes a placatory parcel — a wrapped fly — to his female. If she is eating when he mates with her, she is less likely to eat him. The Garden Spider** (*series right*) **is less prudent. He approaches the huge female** (*main picture*), **who drops into an attitude of submission** (*1*). **But during the embrace, she rises up** (*2*). **He misses the cue to run for his life, and she wraps him in silk** (*3*) **and eats him** (*4*).

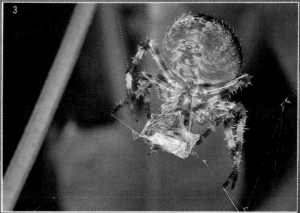

John Markham/Bruce Coleman Ltd.

Jane Burton/Bruce Coleman Ltd.

The lethal courtship of the Green Orb Spider. Minus one leg – from a previous mating – the male caresses the female's legs (*1*). He inserts his semen-charged pedipalps (*2*), and though he has lost two more legs to his hungry lover (*3*), he is undeterred. Four legs down, he hangs in the web (*4*). Another sex session ends in death (*right*).

tals against the strands so that the web becomes coated with seminal fluid. The male spider then scoops up the fluid with his palps which, when charged with the liquid, are inserted into the female. Laboratory experimentation has established that the spider finds this process rather more exciting than it sounds.

In order to achieve mating, the male spider either creeps under the female from a frontal approach or climbs on to her back, leaning over to insert one palp at a time. If the male succeeds in evading the death clutches of the female, he will recharge with sperm and set off in quest of another female. But what tends to happen all too frequently for the male is that the female bites him, injecting venom. The poison contains a digestive enzyme which breaks down his tissues into a liquid form. Then the female drinks him.

The female spider apparently shows no hesitation in attacking either a former or potential mate – and many males escape only as a result of devious means. Their chances of survival depend upon whether or not the female has just eaten and feels re-

plete at the time of the encounter.

Web weaving spiders are shortsighted so their courtship relies on tactile contact. When the male arrives at the female's web he will shake it slightly to produce vibrations. The female takes this as a sign that some prey has approached her web. Her gastric juices start working. The male apparently senses the threat and starts to stroke the female's forelegs.

Waiting till she's eaten

One of the web weaving spiders, *Aranea diaderma*, has been seen to bind up the male by spinning a web around him – then eat him – despite the fact that his palps were still inside her. The male *Meta segmentata*, another web weaver, evades the kiss of death by waiting until he has seen the female devour some other prey. Then he creeps up from behind.

Crab spiders of the families *Thomisidae* and *Sparassidae* do not spin webs and are shortsighted. This means that the male of the species can easily stumble upon the female with little warning. When this happens he has to grab the female by one of

Left A mantis loses his head. The male stalks the female until he is close enough to jump on to her back, then begins thrusting down his abdomen in an attempt to copulate. His mate turns back over her shoulder and starts munching on his head.
The crafty female firefly of the genus *Photurus* (*below far left*) lures males of the *Photinus* genus to their death. The male *Photinus* emits flash patterns characteristic of his species (*below left*), and the *Photurus* female mimics the *Photinus* female's response. The male flies in to mate — a fatal mistake!

Ric Gallup

her legs so that she cannot reach him with her jaws to administer the death bite. These spiders become sexually excited quicker than any others. So if the male succeeds in pinning down the female, he will probably be safe — unless she happens to be very hungry or pregnant, in which cases food becomes the priority.

Spiders of the genus *Xysticus* have a particularly deathly sex life. A female was observed to bind up and devour a male while he was still caressing her. The males of two species of this genus, *Xysticus viaticus* and *X. lania*, make sure of their escape by binding up the female in a prolonged tickling and stroking phase so that she cannot move after mating.

The male *Drassodes lapidosus* has to contend with one of the fiercest spiders in Europe. He kidnaps an immature female and imprisons her in a silken 'tent' until her last molt has taken place, signifying maturity. Mating then follows.

The aptly named jumping spiders perform a dance in front of the chosen female as part of their courtship. *Ballus depressus*, for example, executes an almost hypnotic

dance to minimize the threat of the female. But such a show does not impress the female of an American species, *Phildippus morsitans*. She kills the male while he is engaged in his mesmeric spectacle.

Perpetuation of the species at the expense of the male is well known in the spider kingdom. But the kiss of death is seen in other species too.

Praying mantis

Such is the reputation of the praying mantis — so called after its characteristic pose — that it is often known as the 'preying mantis'. The photograph at the top of this page tells the story.

Male ants die shortly after mating while the females collect enough sperm from the now obsolescent male to last their lifetime.

Bees illustrate ruthlessness of Nature in assuring the survival of the species. Drones, which are produced throughout the summer, exist only to fertilize the queen of their own colony or another colony. On her nuptial flight, the queen bee flies away followed by a swarm of drones. As she departs, the queen emits a pheromone to in-

itiate sexual attraction. Drones up to 10 km away respond to her 'sex perfume'.

As mating takes place, the drone can eject sperm only by generating an intense pressure in his abdomen through muscular effort and by the fluid pressure of blood. As a result of such pressure, the drone's reproductive organs virtually explode and are forced out into the body of the queen. The mating pair fall to the ground. The queen then extricates herself from her dead mate. The remains of the drone's genitalia are later removed from the queen — usually by one of the workers.

These behaviours do not necessarily imply a deception — more an indication that the survival of the species must take priority over all other considerations.

But positive deception is shown among fireflies. When male fireflies are ready to mate, they make use of their bio-luminescent powers to send light signals to the females of their species. Each species has its own flash code. Different flash durations, different rates between the flashes, different rates of repetitions — as well as different intensities of the flash — distinguish each code. The female of the species answers in her own code.

This seems straightforward enough. But the females of some species of the firefly genus *Photurus* mimic the signals of the females of the *Photinus* genus. When the male *Photinus* sights what he believes to be his own species' signal, he flies in and repeats his signal. For some 15% of male fireflies, this is a fatal mistake.

The female *Photurus* continues emitting the false signal, drawing her duped would-be mate to his death. She makes a meal of him without the dubious benefit of sex first.

SAVE THE SIRENIANS

Though not as famous as whales, sea cows — the sirenians — face similar problems. Their love of flowering plants — if it proves useful to Man — may help to save them from extinction

Francois Gohier/Ardea London

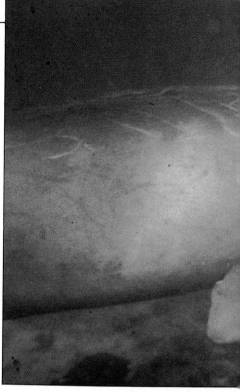

Alan Power/Bruce Coleman Ltd.

Christopher Columbus discovered 'mermaids' as well as America on his first voyage into the unknown. His comment was that they 'are not so beautiful as they are painted, although to some extent they have the form of a human face'.

The creatures he described turned out to be *manatees*. They resemble a cross between a dolphin and a hippopotamus, and the only link we can find between this marine mammal and the mermaid of mythology are the paddle-like tail and the human-like breasts of the female. In fact they were hardly likely to set pulses racing, even among Columbus' sailors.

The Portuguese crew were probably already familiar with the manatees from previous voyages of exploration down the coasts of West Africa. Not many years later,

as European mariners pushed into the Indian Ocean they met the *dugongs*, which are related to the manatees. The physical form of the dugongs has excited similar comparisons with mermaids and they are called *arusa t'albahr*, brides of the sea, in Arabic.

The manatees and dugongs are sole survivors of the mammalian order *Sirenia* or *Sirenians*, whose nearest relatives are the elephants. Again, it is strange that these unprepossessing animals should have a name which means sirens, and be linked with those sweetly singing creatures of Greek mythology.

There are three species of manatee. *Trichechus senegalensis* which inhabits the rivers and coast of West Africa, *Trichechus manatus* which lives in the Caribbean, from

Florida to French Guiana, and *Trichechus inuguis* which is wholly freshwater in its habitat and lives in the rivers of the Amazon basin. The single species of dugong, *Dugong dugon*, is wholly marine and lives around the coasts of the Indian Ocean and the west Pacific, from Australia to China.

Both manatees and dugongs look rather like seals, with stout streamlined bodies, and forelimbs modified as flippers. However, their skin is almost hairless and, instead of swimming with hindflippers, they propel themselves with the aid of tail flukes. The manatee has a broad, paddle-shaped tail and its face has none of the round-eyed seal's appeal. Ears, eyes and nostrils are placed on top of the head, as in most aquatic mammals. The dugong is hardly more attractive. The snout is turned down, rather than straight, and the tail is divided into two flukes like a dolphin's.

Steller's sea cow

There was, until about 200 years ago, a third sirenian. When a Russian Arctic expedition under Captain Vitus Bering was marooned on the island which now bears his name in 1742, huge herds of placid animals were discovered. The animals grew to about nine metres in length, and lived in the shallow coastal waters. They became known as *Steller's sea cows*, after Georg Steller, the naturalist on the expedition.

The sailors killed a few of the sea cows for their meat and skins and, after the expedition was rescued, news of these easily-caught animals spread and hunters soon arrived. The population of sea cows was never very large, and it was confined to the Bering Sea. By 1768 not a single one was left.

The extinction of Steller's sea cow leaves unanswered many questions about its lifestyle. Georg Steller's notes are tantalizing,

Manatees (far left, right, **and** below) **and dugongs** (left) **are the sole survivors of the order Sirenia – their closest relatives are elephants. The dugong is wholly marine – its down-turned snout enables it to eat bottom vegetation. The manatees shown here are all of the species** Trichechus manatus, **which lives in the Caribbean, from Florida to French Guiana. The Amazonian and West African species are rarer – the latter is virtually extinct.**

Jeff Foot/Bruce Coleman Ltd.

because they describe an animal which lived almost entirely on seaweed. Although sheep sometimes graze on seaweed at low tide, the only other animals to specialize in such a diet are invertebrates and small fishes. So Steller's sea cow was unique as a seaweed-eating mammal, and it must have had a very specialized digestive system.

It must also have been well-adapted to survive in Arctic seas. Despite their layers of blubber, living sirenians are not very good at regulating their body temperatures, and are restricted to warm tropical and subtropical waters. The manatee's natural northern limit is Florida, but one group has managed to push farther north by colonizing a stretch of shore which is warmed by the water from a nearby power station.

Shy animals

The manatee and dugong have not received the same attention from scientists as have seals and whales. This is partly because they are difficult to keep in captivity, and partly because they are generally shy and difficult to study in the wild. And they have not caught the public imagination as have other marine mammals.

Manatees and dugongs spend their lives in the water, but they are not as well adapted for submarine living as the seals and whales. Their blood does not have the high oxygen-carrying content and other diving adaptations of most marine mammals. It is, however, quite suited to the sirenian's lifestyle.

Whereas seals and whales actively pursue food in the open sea, often at great depths, the sirenians live in coastal waters and rivers, rarely travelling any great distance. They feed on plants growing in shallow water, so there is no need to dive to any great depth or to swim at high speed. Neither animal can come on land, and the calves are born in the water.

The diet of the living sirenians is almost as unusual as that of Steller's sea cow. They feed almost exclusively on aquatic or semiaquatic flowering plants. Manatees living in fresh water have the greatest variety of diet, because they can crop the lush growth of grasses, rushes, waterlilies, pond-weeds and other plants that clog slow-flowing tropical watercourses.

Stealing fish

Sea-dwelling manatees and dugongs are restricted to frogbits, eel grasses, and turtle grasses (not true grasses) which grow on the shore between high and low tide-marks. Manatees have been known, on occasion, to steal fish from nets. They suck off the flesh, leaving the skeleton intact.

The high water-content of lush aquatic plants means that large amounts of food have to be eaten each day. Dugongs in captivity are known to eat 10 per cent of their own body weight per day, and manatees as much as 25 per cent. The animals congregate on rich grounds which provide easily-gathered food. The sea cows are well named — herds, sometimes numbering several hundreds, placidly eat their way across aquatic 'meadows'.

Food is gathered into the mouth with the aid of the huge, mobile rubbery lips which contribute considerably to the sea cow's distinctive appearance. The down-turned snout of the dugong is an adaptation for feeding on bottom vegetation, whereas the manatee can cope with floating plants, and will hitch itself on to the bank or rear up to pluck leaves from overhanging branches.

Although their food is soft, a large amount of sand and grit gets taken in with it. This leads to problems with excessive tooth wear. To combat this, the dugong retains its milk teeth until they have worn away, rather than shedding them in infancy — so that the permanent teeth will last longer. The manatee's solution is to use its molar teeth in sequence. As the teeth in the front wear out, they drop out. New ones appear at the back of the jaw, and the whole row moves forward.

Aquatic herbivores

The feeding habits of the manatee and dugong have attracted the attention of zoologists because they are the only mammalian aquatic herbivores, compared with the vast array of terrestrial grazers and browsers: sheep, goats, cattle, elephants, hippopotamuses, horses, antelopes, deer, voles, rabbits and so on.

There is also the possibility that they could be of economic use. If this can be demonstrated it might make it easier to save both species.

Their existence is currently threatened by overhunting, as well as by being accidentally drowned in fishing nets and wounded by collisions with powerboats.

A sirenian carcass is a very valuable commodity for a community in the developing

Alfred G. Milotte

It took Man about 25 years to rid the sea of one type of sirenian (*left*). First discovered in 1742 off an island in the Bering Sea, the Steller's sea cow was hunted to extinction by 1768.

Francois Gohier/Ardea London

Right A manatee calf suckling. One of the problems of captive breeding to extend the population is that the female only calves every 2 to 4 years, and the calves take several years to reach maturity.

In the winter, the manatees which spend the summer off the Florida coast gather around the hot springs of central Florida (*right*). This sign is designed to prevent collisions with the sea cows.

WARNING

MANATEE AREA

PROCEED WITH
CAUTION

Manatees feeding in the Crystal River, Florida (*right* and *inset*). **The only aquatic herbivores, sea cows congregate in 'aquatic meadows', and eat their way through up to 25% of their body weight each day. This could be of economic use to Man – the manatees could clear blocked waterways of weed – and might thus increase their chances of survival.**

Jeff Foott/Bruce Coleman Ltd.

world. The meat is prized for its delicate flavour, the fat is rendered into oil, the rib bones are so dense they can be carved like ivory, and the skin makes a durable leather. So the massive beds of marine plants which are totally unexploited at the moment could perhaps be turned into sirenian ranches to produce marketable products.

Clearing the waterways

There have also been various schemes to use sirenians to clear waterways of weed. In fact, manatees have been used for water-weed control ever since 1885, when they were brought into the Botanic Gardens of Georgetown, Guyana, to keep the ornamental pools clear. A larger scale project was started in 1952, when four manatees removed plants from a reservoir and its feeder canals. As each manatee died, it was replaced from the wild. Over 200 have now been employed.

A group of manatees will systematically clear a raft of weed by cropping at the edges. They are not selective about which plants they eat, and since they consume up to 25 per cent of their body weight each day, they make a significant impact on the weed. In one instance, two manatees cleared a 1.7 kilometre stretch of canal in 17 weeks.

It might, therefore, be thought that manatees would provide the answer to a serious problem in tropical countries. The huge lakes forming behind the new dam schemes and irrigation canals become choked with dense mats of floating plants, especially water hyacinth, water lettuce and salvinia. Growth is so thick that navigation by boats is virtually impossible, and so fast that eradication by other means has proved extremely difficult.

However, although manatees have proved that they can remove the weed and keep the waterways open in certain conditions, there are drawbacks in these instances. The new man-made lakes are so huge, and the plant growth so rampant that thousands of manatees would be needed to keep them clear.

Transferring manatees from elsewhere would effectively destroy the wild populations, and captive breeding would never

Jeff Foott/Bruce Coleman Ltd.

provide enough animals. A female manatee calves only once every two to four years and the calves take several years to reach sexual maturity. The manatees would also need continuous guarding from poachers and vandals, and there would bound to be continuous loss from hazards such as getting caught and drowned in fishing nets and sluice gates.

It seems likely that manatees will only

be useful weed clearers in limited circumstances. Still, one such project is underway. In 1982, 16 were released in the lake behind a hydroelectric dam at Curua Una, on the Amazon. Their penchant for aquatic plants may prove to be the manatees' saving grace.

EGGS WITHOUT NESTS

Somewhere on this shell-strewn beach a seabird has laid an egg. The puzzle is to find out exactly where the egg is located, to identify the bird that laid it and to estimate where the beach may be. A thorough visual search reveals a spotted egg typical of the white-fronted tern *Sterna striata*. This name then gives the clue to the beach's location; it must be on the New Zealand coast, or on a beach on Chatham or Auckland island, since these are the only sites at which white-fronted terns breed and set up colonies. This egg, laid in a 'nest' which is merely a scrape amongst the mollusc shells, has probably been temporarily abandoned while the pair responsible for it were either searching for food or fleeing from the photographer. Normally, both male and female of the species help incubate the egg, a process taking up to three weeks. The downy chick that hatches out has a speckled plumage which makes it as well camouflaged as the egg from which it came, and which is vitally necessary to prevent it from making an easy meal

for a carnivorous predator. The chick is fed on fish by both parents for 4 to 5 weeks until it is ready to go fishing for itself. But because the parents have to fly long distances over the open ocean for food, the chick is likely to be the only youngster in the family since family size in terns is limited by the nearness of food supplies.

Even in their first year on the wing, young white-fronted terns will undertake the 2,000 km migratory journey to the warmer coasts of Tasmania, Victoria and New South Wales to avoid the worst of the winter. Only when they return from this sunny sojourn do the terns set up breeding colonies. Then, as spring advances, the males make their ceremonial approaches to the female. Fish in beak, a male will court a potential mate, but he will only be accepted as a breeding partner after a mock aerial fish fight. Finally mating is achieved, an egg laid and the life cycle is complete.

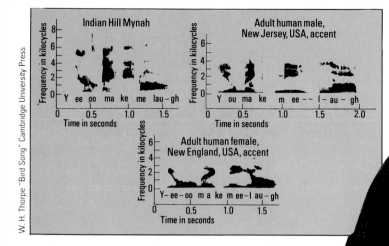

ALL OF A TWITTER

Songs invented by birds millions of years ago still give us some of our best tunes. How do the birds do it?

A nightingale opens its bill and pours out a medley of notes that has inspired musicians and poets since Man found the time to devote to such arts. Its song has been described variously as a virtuoso performance, a masterpiece of improvization and an outpouring of pure joy, yet the nightingale had been producing such sounds for millions of years before Man appeared, and continues to do so with total disregard for human descriptions. There seems little doubt that it was the sounds of birds that inspired early Man to develop song, and thereafter instrumental music, as an art form.

Birds are capable of producing the most extraordinary range of sounds. The lyrebird of eastern Australia not only has a well-developed series of calls of its own, but can also produce remarkably realistic renderings of many of the noises of the dense forests in which it lives. It has incorporated the calls of other birds and mammals into its own repertoire over many generations, but with the coming of human technology to the wilderness, the lyrebird now faithfully reproduces the sounds of chainsaws, axes and bulldozers with equal ease.

Parrots are renowned for their imitations of the human voice – particularly such clichéd phrases as 'Pretty Polly' and 'Pieces of eight'. The Indian hill mynah is perhaps the best mimic of human speech, capable of uttering not only sentences that are intelligible (to humans at least) but also at least four of our vowel sounds perfectly.

A quick glance is enough to show that the hard bills of birds simply cannot function in the same way as our flexible lips in producing sounds, while anatomical dissection shows that they also lack our resonating cavities of throat, mouth and nose. How, then, does a nightingale produce its exquisite song, or a parrot talk like its owner? Could it be that the bird's sound production system is more akin to a musical instrument than to the human voice?

Early anatomists discovered that Man produces his vocalizations via a system of resonating membranes – the vocal cords – located in the voice-box, or larynx. Though birds do have a larynx, this lacks vocal cords, and is capable of playing little, if any, part in voice production. Instead, they have a well-developed *syrinx* situated where the trachea, or windpipe, divides into its two bronchial tubes. Though varying from one species to another in

details, the basic plan is that the lower rings of the windpipe and/or the upper rings of the bronchial tubes are partly or completely replaced by membranes. It is these soft, elastic membranes that vibrate to produce the songs and calls of birds, just as the membranes of the larynx vibrate in Man and the membrane of a loudspeaker vibrates to reproduce sound in a radio or hi-fi system.

A vibrating membrane produces sound that is amplified when passed through a sound box. Yet to vary the pitch and timbre, the tension and position of the membrane must be controlled in some way, or, alternatively, the size and shape of the box must be altered. The reed of a clarinet, for example, vibrates to produce a sound that is changed by the length of the barrel of the instrument which, in turn, is determined by the positions of the fingers covering the various stops. For a bird to produce notes in such a way would require a remarkably elastic neck that could be varied, in the case of a small songbird, by up to four times its original length. Clearly, this is neither likely nor possible and the analogy between the bird voice and other musical instruments falls down.

Muscles for controlling sound

The movement of the membranes, and indeed that of the whole structure of the syrinx, is controlled by a battery of muscles. Some are on the outside of the syrinx, and others on its inner wall. Among the inner groups of muscles, some have actually moved during thousands of years of evolution from the virtually defunct larynx, whereas in Man they have stayed put while the larynx has developed into the main organ of sound production. Birds may boast an impressive number of inner muscles – up to nine pairs in some songsters. They are attached to the bronchial rings or half-rings of the windpipe, and control the vibration of the membranes, which in turn controls the pitch of the notes produced.

To utter the vowel sounds so characteristic of human speech, we need to use our separate resonating chambers. Scientists studying speech discovered that to some extent these chambers work independently of each other. They did this by examining a simple sentence, using a sound spectrograph. This device breaks down sounds into their component pitches and displays them

W. H. Thorpe "Bird Song" Cambridge University Press

Best bird mimic is the Indian hill mynah (*left*). Sonagrams at *far left* compare the same phrase uttered by mynah and humans. Parrots (*below*) are famed for their imitations, and the Australian lyrebird (*right*) can imitate almost any sound it hears, from chain-saws to musical instruments. Up to 80 per cent of its song may consist of 'borrowed' sounds.

J. R. Brownlie/Bruce Coleman Ltd.

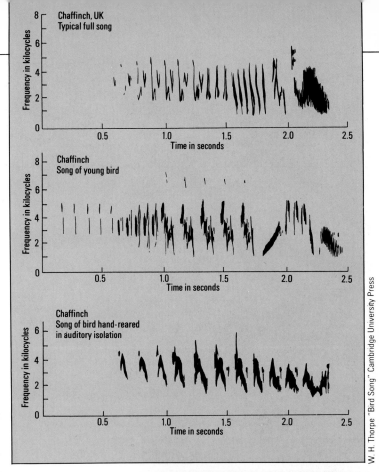

Chaffinch, UK
Typical full song

Chaffinch
Song of young bird

Chaffinch
Song of bird hand-reared in auditory isolation

W. H. Thorpe "Bird Song" Cambridge University Press

Above **Sonagrams of the song of the male chaffinch (*right*) show that although a young bird can imitate the end flourish (a part that must be learned), a bird reared so that it cannot hear other chaffinches sings only a vague song.**

Avon & Tilford/Ardea London

visually, just as white light can be broken down into its constituent colours, or wavelengths by the prisms in a spectroscope. Since its adoption by ornithologists during the 1950s, the sound spectrograph has revolutionized the study of bird song.

When the bird-song researchers analyzed the same sentence uttered by a hill mynah, they found that not only did the bird produce similar vowel sounds to ours, but that they were formed by several distinct chambers working independently, just as in Man. Just as the human larynx is capable of producing complex speech patterns, so too is the syrinx of a bird. But while human speech — and human song, too — is produced in a harmonic form (where notes of a higher frequency are added to a pure note), birds normally produce separate, individual sounds at the same instant. This apparent internal duetting is quite remarkable, though we would never have known of its existence without the sound spectrograph. Although ornithologists know that many birds produce two or more distinct sounds at the same moment, they do not really understand how they achieve this impressive feat.

Crawford H. Greenewalt, an American ornithologist specializing in the study of bird song, has proposed a model that takes as its foundation the position of the syrinx at the junction of the two bronchial tubes. These, he postulates, can function independently and thus simultaneously. In this way, birds are able to produce one note via one bronchial tube and a different note via the other. Attractive and simple as this explanation may be, it

does not by any means satisfy other experts or fit all the facts.

Birds such as the reed warbler, a common summer visitor to Britain and Europe, are quite capable of producing different notes that overlap at exactly the same moment in time. The American wood thrush utters no fewer than four distinct notes overlapping at a particular point in its song. Clearly, in this case, the bird is using more than two vibratory membranes, leaving Greenewalt's model quite insufficient. As yet, no-one has come up with a satisfactory explanation for this phenomenon, though further research will doubtless reveal more examples, possibly of even greater complexity, of these vocal gymnastics.

What is clear, however, is that the ability to produce two or more sounds at the same time makes any analogy with either a musical instrument or the human voice quite inappropriate. At our present state of knowledge, a better parallel might be with a choir or a band.

Simple bird 'song' consists of the repetition of call-notes that are produced virtually automatically, with little or no variation, either between individual birds or individual performances. Such 'songs' are characteristic of birds that are primitive in an evolutionary sense, such as the divers and plovers. The more advanced 'songbirds', such as thrushes and warblers, produce a regular pattern of notes that is repeated and varied to produce a song that is both pleasing and apparently creative. It is this 'creativity' that biologists find so intriguing, for intensive study of their behaviour has shown that birds usually act in a clearly determined, instinctive way to stimuli. If, however, it is true that

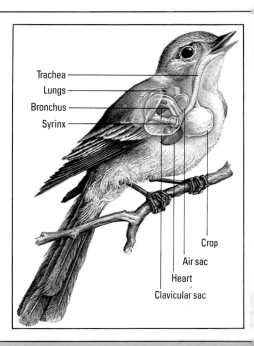

Left **The wood pewee. View into its body** (*right*) **shows position of syrinx. Diagram A** (*far right*) **shows how pressure of air in sac forces membrane into passage. Muscles alter tension in membrane. These two forces determine width of passage and thus frequency of note. In B, tension is increased, making membrane vibrate faster and retract, opening passage, increasing intensity of song. In C, tension is so great membrane can't vibrate across whole passage and intensity drops.**

A. D. Brewer/Ardea London

Trachea
Lungs
Bronchus
Syrinx

Crop
Air sac
Heart
Clavicular sac

Right **and** *far right*
A well-balanced melodic line from the song of the wood pewee. The musical notation is shown to the left of the sonagrams for comparison.

A   B₁
ah–di–dee   pee–ah–wee

the brain of a songbird modifies the pattern of notes it sings, then such a simple, stimulus-response theory cannot totally explain its behaviour.

By accepting that the bird's brain selects and arranges the variety and combination of notes, we are likening this supposedly 'simple' creature to a musician. Jazz improvization consists of just such arranging without a predetermined score, though once again a band rather than a single soloist might be a better analogy. Perhaps a group of jazz *singers* might be an even better analogy; some researchers have likened the song of the European woodlark to folk-song. One woodlark produced no fewer than 103 melodic lines, at a speed of up to 80 separate notes per second, during a five-minute burst of song. A German musicologist, using a series of pitch-pipes, managed to persuade a blackbird to imitate each note he produced. In this way, he led this particular individual to sing in all keys: as prodigious a feat as that performed by a group of bellringers ringing all the changes, with the added difficulty of having been produced by a single individual.

Spanning four octaves

Biologists have discovered many more examples of such a sophisticated ability for producing sounds among songbirds. One of the finalists in any 'bird-song Olympics' would surely be the brown-headed cowbird, a North American species of unprepossessing appearance. Researchers investigating its courtship song found that the frequency range covered by two consecutive phrases was wider than in any other bird song. It extends from 0.75 to 10.7 kilocycles per second, spanning nearly four octaves! In the second part of the first phrase, the cowbird sings with two 'voices' simultaneously, with an impressive frequency range between them. This phrase, which to our ears sounds rather like 'glug', consists of five widely different subphrases. The second phrase, which has been written as 'gleeee', opens with one of the shortest notes ever recorded for a

bird. It lasts a mere two milliseconds or less, and consists of only 12 sine waves. The 'sliding' sound, or glissando, in the middle of the 'gleeee' is one of the most rapid ever measured, spanning the range from five up to eight kilocycles per second in only four milliseconds.

We are inclined to see – and hear – everything in the world of animals within our own, limited, frame of reference. We may listen, enraptured, to the song of a blackbird or a nightingale, because they happen to sing within the ambit of our own musical experience, but find the songs of other birds unmusical, monotonous or even downright unpleasant. But this subjective judgement ignores the fact that we cannot hear the rapid and extremely subtle modulations in the songs of birds such as the brown-headed cowbird. We hear them as if they were 'smeared' together to produce a note that has a different, unpleasant quality. The human ear can easily resolve a trill whose frequency is 30 cycles per second or less, but when the frequency is 100 cycles per second or more, all we hear is an unpleasant buzzing note. Although our frequency discrimination is about the same as that of birds, our time discrimination may be as much as 100 times poorer. It is very likely that birds hear every detail of the rapid modulations in their songs, and that the information content of even a simple song is immense. This explains how birds can not only distinguish the songs of their own species from those of other species, but also of individuals within the species – using as clues subtleties that are imperceptible to a human audience.

Their virtuoso performances make it clear that birds use a staggeringly sophisticated system of sound production. Biologists have gone a long way towards explaining how this sound system works. And they have also investigated the question '*Why* do birds sing?' Along with the whales and dolphins and Man, birds have chosen sound as their medium of communication. Many other animals rely on scent or visual signals. Sound messages have the advantage of directness. They can pass through dense

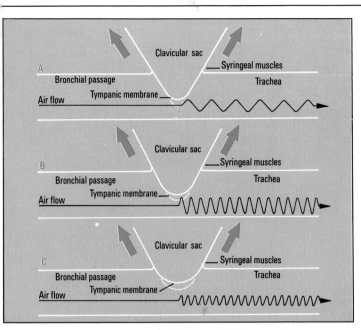

forests, over high hills and round corners.

The main function of bird song is to provide a clear indication of territorial rights. Although females sing in a few species (such as the European robin) and a few species (such as the American mockingbird) sing in winter, bird song is primarily a method by which the male of the species advertises ownership of his breeding territory both to rival males and to prospective mates. The message to the males is 'keep out', while to an unmated female, part of the complex information within the song can be translated as 'come on in'. The songs, as any experienced birdwatcher will confirm, form an immediate means of identifying the singer. Since one chaffinch sounds just like another, it is reasonable to assume that their song is inherited. However, experiments involving rearing birds in complete isolation have shown that while the first part of the song is automatic, the final part has to be learned. Also, researchers have found that chaffinch song varies from one part of its range to another.

Birds clearly have a system of sound communication that is equal, if not superior, to that of Man. It seems that the only thing that stops them developing a fully-fledged language is the size of their brains.

W. H. Thorpe "Bird Song" Cambridge University Press

Below **The European reed warbler can sing two songs at once.**
Below right **Young American wood thrushes learn to sing by copying adults.**

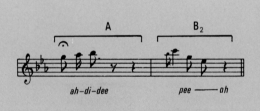

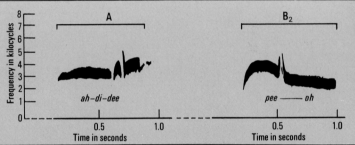

Jack Dermid/Bruce Coleman Ltd.

WORKING WITH NATURE

Conservation and wildlife research is constantly
showing us the benefits of trying to co-exist
with nature and understand our role on planet Earth . . .

THE RESOURCE-FULL OCEAN

We've been eating fish for thousands of years, but now the oceans promise to yield a new harvest of drugs and other products

In 1981 a research team from the University of Southern California, USA, announced the successful isolation of didemnin, a powerful anti-viral agent obtained from sea squirts at the bottom of the sea. During laboratory tests on tissue cultures, didemnin has shown promise as one of the most effective anti-viral drugs available by proving toxic to a variety of viruses, including influenza viruses, some of the viruses causing meningitis, rhinoviruses responsible for the common cold, and the herpes strain responsible for cold sores and other more serious lesions. Didemnin, which also seems to have powerful anti-tumour properties, is now the subject of extensive research on animals.

This discovery is just one of those being made which will lead to the harvesting of marine resources whose very existence remained unsuspected until relatively recently. It seems that many marine organisms, ranging from humble bacteria to seaweeds, horseshoe crabs, and even sharks, may make a significant contribution to the health and wellbeing of Man.

Microorganisms as slaves

Smallest and simplest of all marine organisms, bacteria may be used to fight pollution. In some cases, microbiologists have succeeded in isolating organisms capable of attacking pollutants. The bacteria are encouraged to do this by imprisoning them within tanks containing the polluted water. With nothing else to eat, they consume the pollutants, leaving the water safe for re-introduction into the sea.

There are also other exciting possibilities concerning marine microorganisms. Recently, a research team headed by Dr. Akira Mitsui of the University of Miami, Florida, USA, has searched for innovative ways of using marine blue-green algae (tiny seaweeds) and photosynthetic bacteria in the production of human food, animal feed and fuel. One aspect of this work is the production of hydrogen by these creatures, rendered significant by the energy crisis. The discovery that a number of photosynthetic microorganisms can convert solar energy into hydrogen gas has opened new doors in the search for fuel.

After many years of patient work at sea in the tropical Atlantic, more than fifty strains of microorganisms capable of producing hydrogen gas have been isolated, of which various blue-green algae and one photosynthetic bacterium seem promising candidates for use in applied hydrogen production. The development of large-scale hydrogen production is now under way.

Furthermore, many species of blue-green algae are able to 'fix' atmospheric nitrogen,

Prof. A. Mitsui, University of Miami

Left **Seaweed products are already used in the manufacture of food and other products. 'Farms' of giant seaweed in the Pacific Ocean may one day supply us with food and fuel, and** (*inset*) **tiny blue-green algae are being coaxed into yielding up their hydrogen gas.**

Ron & Valerie Taylor/ Ardea London

incorporating it into their tissues at high rates, and this has implications for agricultural fertilizer production. One promising avenue is the mass culture of nitrogen-fixing blue-green algae as a substitute for animal protein feed at fish farms. Several species of such microorganisms are proving to be as good, or even better, for shrimps and fish than traditional feeds, and their mass culture could well bring a significant breakthrough in aquaculture technology and economics.

Versatile seaweeds

Seaweeds have long been harvested and used by Man for a variety of purposes. Agar was the first commercially significant seaweed product, with its best known use in bacteriology as a gelling agent for culture media. *Alginates* extracted from seaweed are widely used in food manufature, as are the *carrageenins* derived from red algae such as Irish moss. Biologists are also testing giant kelp farms in the Pacific Ocean to provide food and fuel. The giant kelp *Macrocystis pyrifera* grows at an impressive rate and is an efficient converter of sunlight energy. It is already a valuable crop and its extracts are used in products as diverse as toothpaste, pills, ink, cardboard and paint.

Research on marine life also helps to throw light on medical problems. The attachment of seaweeds and other marine organisms to ships is known as *marine biofouling*, the study of which has borrowed much from medical research, and now promises to repay the debt. Research workers at the University of Delaware, on the Atlantic coast of the USA, have found that the attachment of marine bacteria to exposed surfaces in seawater can be largely understood by studying how human blood platelets respond to prosthetic implants such as heart valves. In return, further research into how to prevent biofouling of ships' hulls will have important implications with regard to such seemingly unrelated phenomena as thrombus formation, rejection of artificial implants, wound healing, blood clotting, and the functioning of intrauterine contraceptive devices.

College of Marine Studies, University of Delaware

Above Sharks, such as this man-eating great white trapped in a net, have skeletons made of cartilage, which may have wound-healing properties: they may also aid research into cancer and sperm storage. *Left* Spinning a filament of chitin, extracted from crab shells. It is being tested for a variety of uses, especially as an animal feed supplement.

Ron & Valerie Taylor/Ardea London

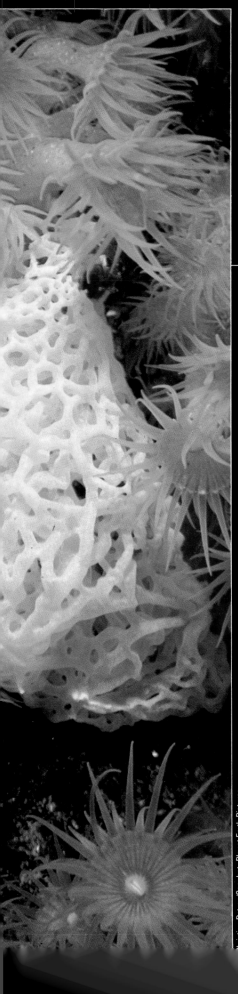

Christian Petron/Seaphot: Planet Earth Pictures

Far left, below **Sea squirts like these yield didemnin, being tested as an anti-viral and anti-tumour agent, while sponges and anemones** (*centre*) **may one day give us important antibiotics and other medicines.**
Left **A spotted puffer fish from the Pacific Ocean. The deadly poison it contains has been tested as a muscle relaxant and in the treatment of migraine headaches and arthritis.**

Kenneth Lucas/Seaphot: Planet Earth Pictures

Other research workers at Delaware University have focused their attention on possible uses for *mucopolysaccharides*, found in many marine animals. These substances are made up of long chains of amino sugars associated with proteins. *Chitin*, the best known, is found in the shells of crabs and other crustaceans. One of the most promising uses for chitin is as a purified nutritional supplement for whey in feeding poultry. Enormous quantities of whey left over from cheese-making are discarded every year because of its high lactose and protein content, which causes severe digestive problems when fed to chicks. If, however, whey is fed together with chitin the side-effects are eliminated. This is probably because the chitin introduces bifidobacteria which create the lactase enzyme needed to break down the milk sugar in whey.

Medicines from the sea

Land plants, and even animals, have for a long time provided humanity with important drugs and other medicines, ranging from aspirin to insulin for diabetics. Now it looks as if we may find what we need in the oceans, too.

Another mucopolysaccharide, cartilage, forms the skeletons of sharks, rays and skates instead of bone. Researchers have found that cartilage preparations can accelerate wound healing and possess anti-inflammatory qualities: they believe that the active components are complex substances known as *chondroitins*.

Sharks may be important to medical science in other ways, too. For some reason few sharks have cancers, and preliminary studies have shown that shark blood can inhibit the growth of viruses, bacteria and cultured human cancer cells. Proof that sharks are resistant to certain carcinogens would have important implications for human cancer research. Another intriguing aspect of shark biology is the ability of the female to bathe the male's sperm in a secretion which preserves it for many months. Biologists may be able to improve the preservation of human sperm in sperm banks

by studying the shark secretion.

Tetradontoxin is another compound which has been isolated for clinical study. Although found mainly in the deadly puffer fish, it is also produced by the Californian newt. Tetradontoxin, the most powerful of fish poisons, is used in neurological research, and has been tested in Japan for treatment of arthritis and migraine headaches. It has also been investigated as a relaxant for muscle spasms and as a palliative in cases of terminal illness. It is, however, too toxic for use as a general pharmaceutical agent.

Treatment of arthritis

Researchers in New Zealand have found that the green-lipped snail contains a natural drug with useful effects on the body's neuromuscular system, as well as an ability to combat viruses and bacteria. This is under investigation worldwide for its possible applications in the treatment of arthritis. Several other species of marine mollusc could yield similar substances.

Exploitation of the sea's natural resources, and the know-how to ensure that the delicate web of ocean life is not endangered are in their infancy, and there is much to learn. Why, for instance, do some motionless or slow-moving marine organisms not become fouled with other animals or plants? Could the manufacturers of anti-fouling paints for ships or oil-rigs learn from them?

Scientists are currently isolating natural substances from marine sponges and other animals such as hydroids, jellyfish, corals and sea anemones. In time, they should be able to determine the exact chemical structure of those that prove to have important medical or industrial applications. Already they have extracted thirty-five compounds with antibiotic, anaesthetic, anti-tumour and anti-leukemia properties from sponges alone. It may not be long before humanity begins to benefit in a big way from this unexpected harvest from the sea.

THE TIGER RETURNS WITH A VENGEANCE

A few years ago the tiger was earmarked for extinction. But then came 'Operation Tiger', a conservation plan which has succeeded beyond original hopes. Now hungry and homeless big cats are stalking new prey . . . Man!

In the course of 40 years, the number of tigers in the world crashed from 100,000 to a bare 5,000. Then, in 1972, one man, Guy Mountfort, began a crusade. 'Operation Tiger' became the greatest international effort ever made to save a single species from extinction. The irony is that the success of the operation is marred by the deaths of innocent people – victims of the cat who came back. Not since the days of the British Raj has Man been such easy meat for the tiger.

Solitary animals

Tigers are solitary animals, meeting up only for mating. Most of the tiger's day is spent resting in vegetation near water: the distinctive markings are good camouflage. They kill only once or twice a week – and then may eat up to 30 kg of meat in a night. Prey can include a one tonne jungle bison, a young elephant, or even crabs, fish and locusts. Massive strength in their forequarters enables them to carry a carcass their own weight with ease: a tiger can scale a two metre wall carrying a cow. To dispatch a man presents no undue effort for a tiger.

Fifty years ago, India was a tiger's paradise. Huge forests covered much of the country, offering a home to large populations of deer, wild pig, wild cattle and the tigers that preyed on them. Of course tigers were hunted, but only by colonial officials,

important guests and the motley collection of maharajas and princes that imperial rule supported. Involving, as it did, a large team of elephants and beaters, tiger hunting was an expensive business and out of reach of the Indian middle class, let alone the peasantry. So a healthy population of tigers was maintained.

With the end of the Raj, the great estates of the maharajas were broken up and a new, affluent group of administrators and businessmen replaced British colonial officials. Suddenly, everyone seemed to own land; everyone had rights in the new democratic India. The result was an enormous boom in hunting and other former princely pursuits. Alongside such direct persecution, the developing India demanded timber and new agricultural land. So the forests on which the tiger depended were destroyed and reduced to mere isolated remnants. Within 20 years, the Bengal tiger was reduced to less than 2,000 animals in the whole of the sub-continent.

At this low ebb, international opinion in favour of conservation stepped in with the World Wildlife Fund's 'Operation Tiger'. With the full co-operation and financial backing of the Indian and Nepalese governments, a series of 'tiger reserves' was established, each complete with buffer zones. The total area of protection grew to 15,000 square kilometres. Homesteads and even

entire villages were moved lock, stock and barrel to provide the tigers with the natural conditions they require. Being forcibly removed from their homes did not make 'Operation Tiger' popular with local people but their antagonism did not stop the project succeeding. In return the relocated villagers were rewarded with facilities such as new houses, schools and drinking water. The forage area for domestic cattle was increased many times. Streams which used to dry up early flowed more or less constantly with clear water and employment opportunities for local people improved greatly.

A series of reserves, scattered across the sub-continent, soon held an increasing population of tigers. Within a decade the number of tigers had doubled and conservationists had apparent cause to rejoice – they had saved the tiger.

Tagging the tiger

'Operation Tiger's' first task was to learn more about the tiger's lifestyle, then devise ways to move tigers to safe refuge in well-run reserves.

Using techniques long practised by game hunters the experts steered their quarry into range of a tranquillizing dart. A long 'beat cloth' of white muslin is stretched out on either side of the beast, forming a giant V-shaped funnel. The hunter-scientist sits at the point of this V, in the relative safety of

A tiger, though not the most agile of the big cats, is more than a match for this non-human prey – a monkey. The tiger prepares to charge (*far left*), surges forward in a burst of power and grasps the monkey in its merciless jaws (*bottom left*), then settles down to its bloody feast. Made as docile as a pet kitten by a tranquillizer dart, a Nepalese tigress is collared with a radio transmitter (*left*), allowing researchers to track her at any time.

a tree-top. Then the drive begins. The team start shouting and banging. The animal tries to escape, but for some reason seems to be frightened to cross the white beat cloth which appears as white flashes among the undergrowth. It heads straight towards the hunter-scientist, and is shot with a tranquillizing dart.

The drugged beast often runs into the undergrowth before it falls unconscious. It must be found quickly, as the drug causes its body temperature to rise dangerously. If left unattended, the animal could die. So the tiger is doused with water and fanned to keep its temperature down. A pillow of branches is placed beneath its head to prevent it from breathing in dust. A radio transmitter is attached to the sleeping beast and its progress followed by foot, jeep, elephant and even helicopter.

The numerous scientific studies undertaken came to the same conclusion – that both male and female tigers have territories or home ranges within which they live and from which other tigers are excluded. A male range encompasses that of several females which mate with him exclusively. Young tigers remain with their mothers for about two years and are then driven out to seek territories of their own. Such tigers are highly mobile, moving through the ranges of established tigers or occupying marginal areas where prey is thin on the ground.

They form a population reserve, ready to move in to any vacancy that occurs.

Tiger by the tail

'Operation Tiger' eliminated much of the senseless persecution of tigers and provided a little more tiger habitat. It did not, and could not, create new reserves of habitat where none had existed before. So the Bengal tiger is confined to comparatively small islands of forest in a huge sea of agricultural land. If young tigers were to find a new home they would have to journey through the fields and villages of India, or live among the villages in belts of cover too small for their needs. By its very success 'Operation Tiger' produced a surplus of animals, but nowhere for them to go.

Confronted with a lack of prey it was not surprising that tigers once more took to man-eating to stave off starvation. In each case the victim was killed while working in dense cover, but repeated killings showed that the attacks were more than mere accidents. These man-eaters have been followed up, tracked down and killed by park officials, whose main job is to conserve tigers.

If tigers have already reached a population level that saturates the available habitat, where can the surplus animals created by the conservation effort go? And, with each tiger sanctuary being separated

from the next, often by hundreds of kilometres of unsuitable habitat, how can the surplus animals make the journey? Trapping and trans-location have been suggested, but this is easier said than done. In any case both the area of origin and the area of relocation would have to be intensively and continuously studied to ensure that a true surplus and a true vacancy existed. At present there are fewer than two areas in the whole sub-continent that meet these criteria.

Seeds of its own destruction

So the success of a magnificently conceived and well-executed conservation project has within it the seeds of its own destruction. The lesson is clear. If animals are to be saved from extinction they must not only be protected, but sufficient land must be set aside within which they can find all that they require in the form of food and shelter. Clearly in the contemporary world such areas will be limited and that, in turn, will place definite limits on the ultimate level of the population that can be achieved, no matter how good the intentions of conservationists or how large the resources they can bring to their project.

THE PROBLEM WITH PANDAS

The giant panda, symbol of the World Wildlife Fund, is threatened by shortages of its staple diet. Chinese and Western scientists are working together to save it

Right A panda chews a bamboo shoot, clutching the stem with its unique forepaw, equipped with a 'thumb'. This is really an elongated, fleshy wristbone which works against the five digits for grasping and manipulating. *Far right* Map shows present and past distributions of the panda. In prehistoric times it was more common: a drying climate probably killed off much of the bamboo on which it depends, and destruction of forests by Man conspired to make it rare and localized. *Below* One of the last refuges – Wolong Nature Reserve, Sichuan.

Giant pandas may well be bears – though many zoologists believe that they are more closely related to raccoons. They are large, boldly patterned animals, but are still virtually impossible to find. The difficulty of persuading them to breed in captivity is legendary: they have defied the expertise of the world's greatest zoos.

Adding to the enigma surrounding these extraordinary creatures, they are among the rarest of large mammals: there may be less than 1000 wild pandas alive today. They are restricted to mountain fastnesses in Central China, where the Chinese government has set up 10 reserves as part of their immense effort to protect pandas.

The first living panda to reach the West was a young male brought back to the USA in 1936. By 1938, giant pandas were being displayed at zoos in London and the public flocked to see them in large numbers.

Despite the attention lavished on them, and the knowledge gained from study of the captive animals, little was known of the pandas' life in the wild. Any hope of finding out more was dashed during the 1950s, while the struggling Chinese People's Republic sought to establish their new state, and the animals were cut off from the West behind the 'bamboo curtain'. In 1961, the

From Bruce Coleman Ltd

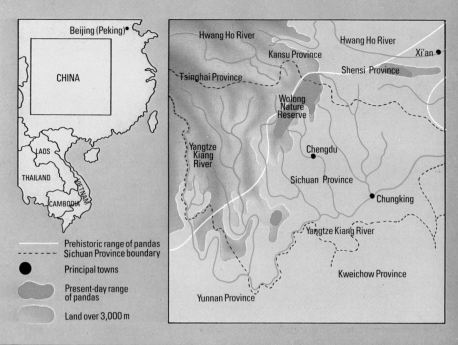

Kee Scott Design

Beijing (Peking)

CHINA

LAOS

THAILAND

VIETNAM

CAMBODIA

——— Prehistoric range of pandas
- - - - Sichuan Province boundary

● Principal towns

Present-day range
of pandas

Land over 3,000 m

Hwang Ho River

Kansu Province

Hwang Ho River

Xi'an

Tsinghai Province

Shensi Province

Wolong
Nature
Reserve

Yangtze
Kiang
River

Chengdu

Sichuan Province

Chungking

Yangtze Kiang River

Kweichow Province

Yunnan Province

Photographs WWF/Timm Rautert/Bruce Coleman Ltd.

Cover Press

Above **A programme of captive breeding is one of the ways in which conservationists hope to save the endangered panda – often using artificial insemination. Here a mother guards her newborn cub at Madrid Zoo, where it was born in September 1982.**

Left **Possessing a surprisingly inefficient digestive system for dealing with its tough diet of bamboo, a panda must spend most of its time eating to obtain enough nourishment.** *Below* **Dr. George Schaller and his colleagues at Wuyipeng Research Centre.**

panda was adopted as the international symbol of conservation by the World Wildlife Fund, though it was fast disappearing from Western zoos as animals died without breeding and no replacements were forthcoming from China. Then came the thaw in Sino-Western relations during the 1970s, and it seemed as if every Western leader would return from his visit to China with the gift of a pair of pandas.

International co-operation

Panda research took a great leap forward in 1980, when government-funded Chinese scientists teamed up with the World Wildlife Fund, and George Schaller, Director of the Animal Research and Conservation Center of the New York Zoological Society, was invited to Sichuan to join the Chinese researchers in studying pandas in their natural habitat.

Despite Schaller's impressive record of tracking down elusive, rare animals in dif-

ficult terrain, he spent two months searching in the 2000 sq km Wolong Nature Reserve before he saw his first wild giant panda. During the entire first year of his stay at Wolong, he made no more than seven sightings of the shy animals.

Although they have such striking markings, pandas spend much of their time in the dense bamboo thickets that provide them with their staple food. Not only is this bamboo 'jungle' so impenetrable in places that the naturalists were forced to crawl on hands and knees, but it clothes perilously steep crags and deep ravines and in the bitter Chinese winter these became even more treacherous when covered with ice.

When snow falls, the panda-hunters look for tracks, which they trace onto plastic sheets. By noting each footprint's idiosyncracies, they hope to be able to identify individual pandas from their tracks. But the snow cannot be relied upon and the tracks are difficult to follow or identify without its evealing properties. It looked as if panda-tracking was going to prove a slow, arduous business.

Radio to the rescue

The researchers called in Howard Quigley, like Schaller from the New York Zoological Society, to help them. He is an expert in radiotelemetry – the science of monitoring the movements of wild animals by attaching radio transmitters to them. The researchers built traps to catch the animals and baited them with roast mutton. (Though pandas eat bamboo almost exclusively in the wild, they will readily accept additional food, including meat, in zoos.)

Eventually three pandas were trapped. The researchers fitted each one with a radio-collar that transmits a distinctive signal as long as its batteries last – for a year or more. Armed with a receiver, an aerial and a pair of headphones, the researchers trek through the cold, inhospitable terrain to obtain information from the radio signals beamed back at them from the panda's collar. Once a day, they tune in to each animal and pinpoint its exact location by simple triangulation. Plotted on a map, the results will eventually reveal the size of a panda's home range, the extent of any seasonal movements, and so on.

The radio messages were also designed to reveal the animal's activity: a signal with 100 pulses a minute is given out by a walking, feeding or otherwise active panda, while only 75 pulses per minute indicate a sleeping or resting animal. The naturalists listen to the signals at intervals through the

Left A researcher at Wolong Nature Reserve follows a panda's movements by picking up radio signals emitted from a transmitter around the animal's neck. To fit the collar, the pandas are caught in traps baited with roast meat (below). Below left Weighing bamboo specimens at Wuyipeng Research Centre in the Wolong reserve, to find out more about the panda's extremely specialized diet.

day and night to obtain an idea of the panda's daily routine.

As much as 75% of the panda's time is spent eating, for bamboo has remarkably little available nutritional value. An adult panda may have to eat up to 18 kg of bamboo shoots a day, and the situation is not helped by the fact that the panda is equipped with a surprisingly short gut that hinders efficient digestion of its tough food. The result is that over 50% of the plant passes through the animal almost undigested.

Happily, however, the panda's poor digestive system helps the researchers find out as much as they can about the panda's diet before it is too late. They collect panda droppings, dry them on their camp stoves, then laboriously analyze them to learn exactly which of the various species of bamboo the animals are eating, and in what proportions; also they estimate the age of the plants.

Famine strikes

One of the chief reasons for the panda's increasing rarity has been the clearing of much of the bamboo forests on which it depends, and matters were not helped when in 1975-6 the entire crop of one of the four species of bamboo on which the pandas depend failed completely. Bamboos have extraordinary life cycles, in which they re-

produce asexually for as long as 120 years, then all simultaneously flower, set seed and die. It takes at least five years for a bamboo grove to re-establish itself, during which time the pandas starve. At least 140 died in 1975-6, representing maybe as much as 20% of the total population.

Bamboo study

Schaller and his Chinese colleagues hope that their painstaking tracking, radio monitoring and observation of the pandas will provide enough knowledge to help avoid such disasters in the future; their efforts are supported by a systematic study of the bamboo itself. A third programme aimed at saving the panda is one of captive breeding, particularly using artificial insemination, as pandas are notorious for their reluctance to mate in captivity. Peking and Chengdu Zoos have a particularly good record of panda breeding with several litters reared over the years since 1963, when the first panda cub to be born in captivity appeared.

With such a serious commitment to research into this beautiful animal – thanks to truly international co-operation – the future for the panda looks decidedly brighter than it did only a few years ago.

NEW WAYS TO STOP A SHARK

A harmless-looking flatfish can stop sharks in their tracks — and make the beaches safer for the rest of us

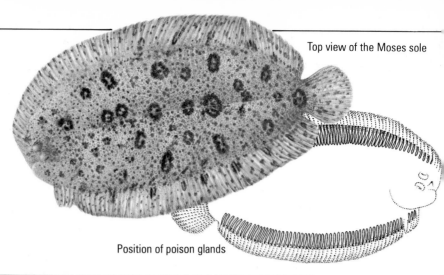

Top view of the Moses sole

Position of poison glands

The little Moses sole, found mainly in the Red Sea, can lock the jaws of the angriest shark. When attacked, this unexceptional-looking flatfish releases a milky fluid that seems to have an instant convulsive effect on Red Sea sharks — so that they cannot close their gaping mouths on their prey.

Marine biologist Eugenie Clark began studying the Moses sole in 1972 while working at the marine laboratory in Eilat, Israel. She knew that its poisonous liquid meant immediate death to sea urchins and reef fish, and later experiments showed that even when diluted 5,000 times in sea-water, the secretion from glands at the base of its dorsal and anal fins could kill every fish in a crowded aquarium. In another test, sharks offered a variety of fish as bait gulped down everything *except* the Moses sole.

The creature's ability to deter sharks has, understandably, captured the interest of researchers attempting to refine shark-repellent technology. But what is this mysterious poison and how exactly does it produce its dramatic and sometimes fatal effect on sharks?

Poisonous protein

Analysis of the sole's milky fluid and its method of action is still continuing, but by the late 1970s two Israeli biochemists, Zlotkin and Primor, had found the most powerful ingredient — a protein, which they called *pardaxin* after the sole's Latin name, *Pardachirus marmoratus*. In laboratory tests on dogfish, a dose of pardaxin added to the water was enough to send this small shark into a state of convulsion.

A further series of experiments revealed how pardaxin works. The toxin's main target seems to be the gill membranes — which perform the essential task of maintaining the body's salt balance. The shark's body has to keep constant control over the concentration of ions within its cells in relation to the level of concentration outside — in the water.

Pardaxin seems to disrupt this system. By messing up the shark's chemical balance, the little Moses sole gets the better of its huge victim by sabotaging the regulatory system which keeps what must stay, in, in — and what must stay out. out.

David Doubilet

Left **Taking a closer look — until effective repellents are found, research into the shark's unique physiology will be slow. Dead sharks reveal useful information, while marine biologists (*right*) risk their lives to study shark behaviour and sensory perception.**

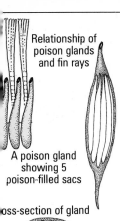

Relationship of poison glands and fin rays

A poison gland showing 5 poison-filled sacs

oss-section of gland

Left **The Moses sole** – *Pardachirus marmoratus* – has a secret weapon that drives sharks crazy. Flanking its mottled body are twin rows of glands. And the milky poison they secrete can be lethal. It means instant frenzy – then death – to dogfish, a type of small shark. And the white-tipped reef shark will convulse for minutes in its presence.

The milky toxin is called pardaxin. It wreaks havoc with the shark's electro-chemical balance by sabotaging the means by which the predator keeps control of the concentration of chemicals in its body. All in all, a powerful repellent. But there is one snag – its molecules are too complex to synthesize. So scientists are searching elsewhere for similar poisons.

Left With its gaping jaws and serried ranks of razor-sharp teeth, the shark has long been portrayed as a primitive, sharply efficient eating machine. But its evolved senses can not only detect the minutest dilutions of blood but even the electrical energy generated by the muscles of prey fish hidden under sand.

The oceans teem with creatures such as the sea cucumber (*below*) which defend themselves with lethal toxins. But it is the tiny firefly (*right*) which may hold the key to an effective shark repellent as its toxin is cheap and easy to synthesize. The molecules involved are smaller and simpler in structure than in the otherwise similar toxin of the Moses sole.

But the toxin's speed of action and the small concentrations which appear to work suggest a neural mechanism. And other experiments (carried out on frogs) indicate that the Moses sole's poison – like the venom of the black widow spider – gets straight to work on the nervous system by activating the release of the neurotransmitter, acetylcholine. This means that pardaxin directly affects the mechanism which controls muscle contraction.

There seems little doubt that the knowledge already gained about pardaxin and its mode of action will be used in the development of shark repellents.

But from a commercial viewpoint, the problem of quantity remains. The Moses sole is too scarce to be a viable source.

In the hope of finding a more practical shark repellent, research scientists are looking at other natural poisons. Wasp fish, scorpion fish and even the unaggressive-looking sea cucumber all secrete toxic substances - in self defence. And the sea cucumber's toxin may have other, unforeseen benefits for Man. This poison, which strikes directly at the nerve impulses, may in fact be an effective painkilling agent.

But shark repellent research took an unlikely turning – away from the marine world to find a source of toxin that might be commercially viable. Strangely, poison extracted from fireflies has a similar – though not fatal – effect to pardaxin. Just four fireflies per litre of water will make dogfish and sharp-nosed sharks alike, thrash around madly before their muscles lock in paralysis.

The confrontation between a firefly and a shark would be an unlikely occurrence, but this apparent quirk of nature holds a hidden advantage. The firefly poison has much smaller and simpler molecules than pardaxin – which means that it may soon be manufactured artificially, and in bulk.

Underwater warfare

The shark-sole story reflects an evolutionary arms race which has been going on for hundreds of millions of years between predators and the animals they chase. Sharks are the top predators of the cartilage-skeletoned fish world, possessing both physical power and sophisticated sensory equipment. They can hear the low-frequency underwater sound produced by a swimming or struggling prey. With their incredible sense of smell, sharks can home in on minute concentrations of blood and fish extracts – even when experimental scientists have plugged their nostrils with cotton wool! And with their strange electrical sense they can detect even well-camouflaged fish half-buried in the sand.

This electrical sensitivity might explain why scuba divers are rarely the victims of shark attack. Galvanic currents given off by the different metals that make up the tank, back-pack and regulator equipment may be so large that the shark thinks that the diver is a huge creature – too big to attack.

WOLF WHISTLES

Study of sheepdog training suggests that it refines the natural behaviour of the dog's wolf ancestors

Vast tracts of land, ranging from the Australian outback to the Scottish highlands, would be lost to agriculture but for the work of a loyal band of workers – the sheepdogs. Without these remarkable animals, sheep farming in remote uplands or extensive plains would be prohibitively expensive. About one-third of the world's one thousand million sheep are herded by border collies, but other breeds, such as the huntaway and the kelpie, are also invaluable as sheepdogs.

Exactly how is a playful puppy transformed into a skilled working dog? Shepherds accomplish this feat by capitalizing on the dog's own wolf ancestry – dogs and wolves shared a common ancestor as recently as eight thousand years ago. The farmer carefully channels the instincts and intelligence which the dog inherited from its wolf forebears.

Farmers train the dogs to respond to a few basic signals, which can be in the form of words, whistles or hand signals. The farmer may work several dogs at the same time by prefacing commands with the dog's name or by using, say, Welsh words for one dog and English for another. The commands are simple: 'stop', 'lie down', 'come towards me', 'go away from me', 'circle right' (clockwise). By combining these commands, the shepherd can manoeuvre the dog into the best position to control the sheep. Urgently repeated commands speed up the dog's movements.

Natural herders

In striking contrast to the relatively independent cat, the right breed of dog is easy to turn into a good sheep herder because it remains at heart a co-operatively hunting carnivore, with an apparently innate fascination for sheep. A young border collie tries to herd anything that moves, be it chickens, footballs, or people, and it will usually try to 'head' sheep from the moment it lays eyes on them; the dog attempts to circle round the flock to trap the sheep between itself and the shepherd.

The shepherd takes advantage of this natural tendency to head sheep in training the dog to circle left and right on command. When the shepherd moves to his or her right, the dog automatically moves to the shepherd's left, to keep the sheep between

Above **Sheepdog societies hold trials worldwide to judge the working skills of the dogs and encourage a high standard of breeding and training. Over one-third of the world's one thousand million sheep are herded by the border collie** (*right* and *above*)**. Other sheepdog breeds include the Shetland, or Sheltie** (*1*) **from Scotland's Shetland Isles; the smooth collie** (*2*)**, a plainer, more workmanlike version of the rough collie (now kept mainly as a pet); the Anatolian karabash** (*3*) **from Turkey, the Briard** (*4*)**, the best-known French sheep-herding and sheep-guarding dog; and the kelpie** (*5*)**, most widely used of the Australian sheepdogs. Kelpies are fast-moving and slow to tire, able to withstand temperatures too hot for most working dogs.**

them. All the shepherd does is repeat the command for 'circle anti-clockwise' at such moments and the dog soon makes the connection.

The sheepdog and the wolf have a lot in common. Wolves are group hunters which kill animals larger than themselves, such as moose and caribou in North America, by ganging up on their prey in a highly organized way. These intelligent social carnivores show a variety of co-operative hunting strategies. The wolves often encircle a herd and then drive the animals towards other wolves lying in wait in a wood or gulley, ready to ambush one of the herd. Sheepdogs are also expert at splitting off a few sheep from the herd. The shepherd need only indicate the ones he wants to inspire an experienced dog to take appropriate action.

One or two wolves, unable to bring down a moose on their own, may hold the animal at bay until other wolves arrive. Sheepdogs are also quite happy to guard one or two sheep; for instance, the dogs are good at mothering on – keeping an orphan

Marc Henrie

Marc Henrie

Marc Henrie

Marc Henrie

Marc Henrie

Jean-Paul Ferrero/Ardea

lamb with a ewe until she accepts the lamb as her own.

Understandably, though, one or two wolf-like tendencies, most notably the urge to kill and eat the prey, must be discouraged in the sheepdog. Biting or 'gripping' the sheep meets with fierce disapproval.

A wolf pack, composed of a dozen or more wolves, typically has a pack leader, a dominant individual who may to some extent direct the group's hunting forays. Sheepdogs probably regard the shepherd as their pack leader. The dogs keep glanc-

ing back at the shepherd for instruction, and the latter encourages this attachment. A shepherd will often train a young dog apart from other dogs for some of the time, so that the dog will come to herd sheep to him, not to a canine peer.

What wolves don't often do is drive a herd completely away from their pack mates, and it is quite difficult to convince a border collie to do this. After the sheep have been rounded up, for dipping or shearing for instance, the shepherd usually wants the dog to drive them back onto re-

mote grazing land. Most border collies need weeks of patient training before they will stay behind sheep and push them away from the shepherd. It is only after long hours in narrow lanes, with the eagle-eyed shepherd quick to remonstrate with the dog the moment it makes a move to squeeze by the sheep and head them, that most dogs reluctantly learn to drive sheep away from their master.

Interestingly enough, not all breeds of working sheepdog share this reluctance to drive sheep. The New Zealand huntaway,

BASIC SHEEPDOG MANOEUVRES

Shepherds and their dogs are able to move sheep whenever necessary by using a variety of set manoeuvres.

1. This manoeuvre is called the *outrun*. The dog is instructed to run around the sheep in a wide arc until it reaches the 12 o'clock position, when it is told to 'lie down'. A semicircular outrun is favoured, because then the dog can get itself into position without any danger of disturbing the sheep. This is always an important consideration, since disturbance can result in stress-related illnesses.

2, 3 and *4.* This manoeuvre is known as *gathering*. With the dog lying at the 12 o'clock position, the shepherd gradually backs off, calling 'come on', until he is some way from the sheep and the dog is close. Should the sheep show any sign of panicking, the dog is instructed to 'lie down'. Finally, the shepherd stands farther from the sheep and remains stationary.

5 and *6.* Turning the flock: it is possible to turn the sheep in either a clockwise or anti-clockwise direction. The shepherd walks slowly in one direction, causing the sheep to move in the other. As the dog moves to the new 12 o'clock position – directly opposite the shepherd's new position – the shepherd calls either 'come by' if the sheep are to be moved clockwise, or 'away to me' if they are to be turned in an anti-clockwise direction. Eventually, the shepherd does not have to move at all.

7. Circling is a difficult manoeuvre for the dog to learn. The shepherd calls the dog into the 12 o'clock position, then moves to the 2 o'clock position, giving the command 'come by' repeatedly until the dog has run around the flock to the opposite side to the shepherd. Because the shepherd is standing near the flock, the dog learns to run wide around the sheep. *8.* Eventually, the dog is able to circle the sheep on its own, with the shepherd standing some distance away.

9-12. The drive is the hardest manoeuvre to teach: it is vital not to panic the sheep. The best place to teach a dog to drive sheep is in a narrow lane with hedges or walls on either side. The shepherd first instructs the dog to lie down behind the flock, and then slowly moves forward with the dog at his or her side, encouraging the dog to move the sheep slowly up the lane. As the dog gains confidence, the shepherd hangs back and encourages the dog to move forward well in front of him, driving the sheep on its own. If the dog shows the slightest tendency to 'head' the sheep, i.e. to run to the front of the flock, the shepherd must discourage it by calling the dog back.

Sheepdogs can also be trained to *'go back'* to look for sheep that are out of sight. The shepherd must break the dog's concentration on the sheep which it is already working. The basic training consists of splitting the flock into two and then commanding the dog to leave one flock alone and go to the other.

David Parker. Illustrations based on Sheepdog Training Booklet, Agricultural Training Board

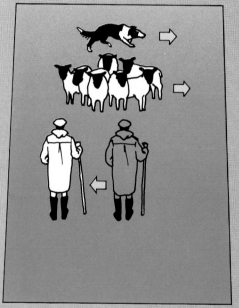

as its name implies, is a good driving dog. And even amongst the border collies so common in Britain, some dogs are much better at it than others. Farmers often have specialist dogs, using one for driving and another for, say, shedding sheep from the flock.

Wolves certainly do vary a lot in their behaviour and some may have a greater inborn tendency to drive herds away from the pack than others. Certain genes for this behaviour may be more prevalent in one breed than they are in another.

The Australian kelpie is different again. These dogs are famed for herding sheep into cattle cars and trucks in crowded lots. The dogs bark a great deal and actually climb up on the backs of the solid mass of sheep to chivvy them along.

Some countries with native populations of wolves have also developed breeds of shepherd dogs which were used to *guard* rather than herd sheep. These dogs are big and heavy, rather than light and quick. The Old English sheepdog was probably originally such a shepherd dog: perhaps it has hair over its eyes to help the sheep accept this large carnivore in their midst. Many shepherds reckon that sheep are more frightened of predominantly black dogs than they are of whiter ones — possibly because the darker dogs appear more wolf-like to the sheep.

The watchful eye

Breeding is very important because certain behaviour patterns such as the border collie's 'eye', seem to be largely inherited. 'Eye' is the dog's tendency to stare fixedly at a stationary sheep, without moving. The dog seems to adopt the stance of a hunting wolf at such times. Some dogs have so much 'eye' that they tend to stay glued to one spot gazing at the sheep instead of bringing them back to the shepherd. But a dog with no 'eye' at all may not be a very subtle worker; understandably, the sheep find the concentrated stare of the dog rather unnerving. Some dogs tend to lie down much more than others when they stop; this is known as 'clapping' and seems to be partly inborn.

Nevertheless, a good shepherd can even counteract such serious inherited defects by careful, painstaking training. A dog which has too much 'eye' for instance, can often be cured by bringing in another dog to get the sheep moving again. The dogs themselves learn much from experience; after a few years' practice a dog becomes a very skilled worker. Many dogs predict what the sheep are likely to do in certain situations and take steps to prevent disaster on their own initiative. The working sheepdog has a marvellous mixture of the instinct and intelligence of a wolf — enabling it to understand and even anticipate both the behaviour of its flock and the needs of its master.

175

THEY SPY WITH A CAMERA'S EYE

Most of us marvel at wildlife programmes. A look behind the scenes at Oxford Scientific Films shows the secret of this particular wildlife team's success — knowledge, study, technical innovation, and a lot of wasted film!

Oxford Scientific Films/Stephen Dalton

Over the years wildlife and natural science films have presented us with some of the most extraordinary and emotive images of the world in which we live. A glance at TV ratings indicates that the popularity of wildlife films is phenomenal. And it is a tribute to the people making these programmes that the huge problems they encounter and the sophisticated technology often used to solve them are hardly apparent. At its best, wildlife photography is an invisible art.

In most areas of film-making, very little is really what it appears to be. This is due to the necessity — for the most part economic — for maximum control over the subject to be filmed. Wildlife films are no exception. They constitute a highly specialized discipline in which the usual problems of film-making — money, time, equipment, the weather and so on — are compounded by the difficulty of enlisting the cooperation of the subject, which might one day be a deadly white shark, another day a microorganism living in a delicately balanced environment which cannot be disturbed.

Problem solving

A thorough understanding of the subject prior to filming, plus a rigorous adherence to the script and story-telling is the secret of successful wildlife photography according to Sean Morris, a founding member and director of Oxford Scientific Films (OSF). The technology, he says, is secondary — it has been developed as practical solutions to problems encountered along the way. Many of the practical solutions developed by OSF have since become standard tools for wildlife film-makers.

The low sandstone buildings of Oxford Scientific Films lie nestled in the quiet countryside, about 15 minutes' drive from Oxford. The outfit was set up in 1968 when five zoologists from Oxford University joined forces with Gerald Thompson.

Thompson's previous films had already achieved some renown.

A famous sequence from one of Thompson's films shows a female wasp laying her eggs in the bark of a tree. He managed to film eggs emerging from the forked tip of the wasp's ovipositor. Thompson achieved this remarkable shot by waiting until the wasp had buried her ovipositor in the bark and was engrossed in laying her eggs. He took a sharp knife and cut three sides around the wasp so as to create a little flap of the bark on which the insect was perched. Then he carefully raised this little flap until the wasp's ovipositor, with the eggs emerging from it, was clearly visible.

The wasp continued laying her eggs into thin air — in full view of the camera. This example illustrates the necessity for an acute understanding of the subject or, as Morris puts it, 'an extremely perceptive biological approach', to make such a shot possible. Though Thompson has now re-

To capture the moment at which this chameleon darted out its sticky tongue, OSF photographer Stephen Dalton had to use a very high-speed flash. A short duration of flash (1/25,000 sec) froze the action. Shooting at such high speeds requires automatic triggering devices — fingers respond too slowly. Even so, there is often a great deal of wasted film. This shot had a 'happy ending'. The butterfly escaped — leaving some of its wing scales attached to the predator's tongue.

Oxford Scientific Films/S. I. Bernard

Left **A scene from Ken Russell's film** *Altered States*. **OSF were called upon to simulate the appearance of travelling through the inside of the body. 'The body' was, in fact, just rubberized material.** *Right* **Taken from the depths of the ocean, the** *Stomias boa* **was brought to OSF's optical bench, then photographed with the aid of 'dark field illumination'.**

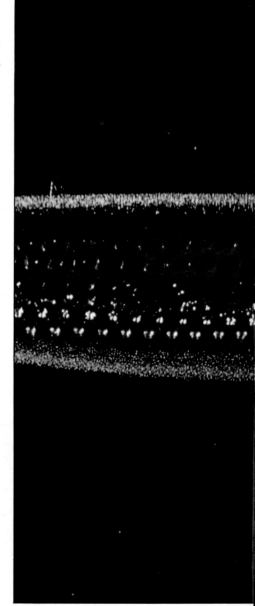

tired, much of his home-made equipment which he brought with him is still used at OSF today.

Within the walls of OSF there is a curious amalgam of high-tech and widely different natural environments as our writer discovered when he visited Morris and his team. In one studio corner a complex looking arrangement of camera, magnifying lenses and lights surrounded a cube (front and back missing) of heat-filtering glass within which the flight drill of a bee was being filmed. In another corner, on a sandy slice of 'Arizona desert', sat a Black Widow spider, leisurely knitting her nest on a twig. A camera was trained on her, though the lights were out. In another corner, surrounded by glass, was a metre-high tuft of grass. From between the stalks two harvest mice blinked. OSF had recently made a film on them.

The major concern – as in all film-making – is control. By bringing the animals to the studio set – a manageable replica of their own habitat – and allowing them to get used to the new environment, observation and photography can take place in practically ideal conditions. This may sound like a fairly simple procedure, but in reality it is only the first of a series of complex problem-solving exercises. Just finding an animal who will acclimatize well to the rigours of film-making is no mean feat.

Once the casting has been settled, the technical problems begin. Perhaps one of the most exciting aspects of natural science films is that they often show us things which the unaided human eye cannot see. This may be because the creatures who are being photographed are too small, or because 'the event' happens too fast, or both. In both circumstances a substantial amount of light is needed to capture the image on film.

If, for example, microscopic organisms are being photographed, the necessary lenses require more light than standard ones. This is due to the lenses' optical configuration and also to the need to maintain – at such close quarters – as much depth of field as possible. (This is the range of acceptable sharpness before and behind the plane of focus.)

Capturing a particularly fast event, such as the movement of a hummingbird's wings, necessitates high-speed photography. In this case, illumination has to be increased in direct proportion to the in-

These stills, from a sequence shot at pre-set 3 hour intervals, show the opening petals of an iris.
If the same process were filmed in cine, the intervals between frames would have to be much shorter – or the film would be too short and jerky. The basic principle of time-lapse cinematography is that if the camera runs slower than the projection speed (24fps), the action appears to be speeded up. In OSF's new time-lapse unit, an *intervalometer* can be used.

Oxford Scientific Films/Sean Morris

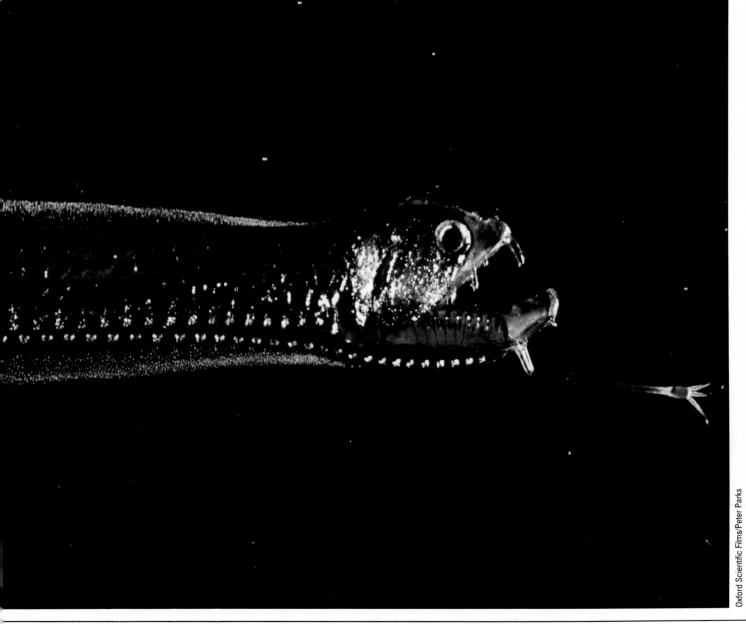

Oxford Scientific Films/Peter Parks

crease in the speed of the film's passage through the camera. The illumination levels necessary when shooting at up to 10,000 fps (frames per second) can be of the order of five times the brilliance of the Sun. Under normal studio lighting at these levels the subject would burst into flames. So lighting for this type of work is shone through a heat-filtering glass, the constituents of which have been thermally toughened and treated to absorb the red end of the spectrum. The glass allows through a concentrated beam of cold light whilst retaining the heat.

High-speed photography requires a great amount of care. When filming at thousands of frames per second, starting the camera a second too soon can result in the entire magazine-load racing through the camera before the event to be filmed actually happens. When a split second means the difference between success and failure, film-makers don't trust their fingers, so triggering devices have been developed – though they can only be used for certain situations.

These devices generally consist of two photosensitive cells with an infra-red beam between the two on a horizontal axis, and another two placed on a vertical axis. The point of focus is where the two beams cross. When the beams are broken, for example by an animal crossing through them, the camera is triggered off.

Aural triggering devices can also be used to photograph flying bullets. These techniques have been employed quite extensively, both in motion pictures and still photography, to capture moments like the darting of a reptilian tongue curling round its prey; an insect or a bird in mid-flight; a missile flying through the air and on impact with a sheet of glass. High-speed flash strobing is another trick which can produce interesting effects, such as freezing a fast-moving object in various stages of its trajectory.

Shrinking time

Most of us have at one time or another seen films in which a snail runs the 100 metres in nine seconds flat, or a plant grows from seed to flower in a matter of seconds, or clouds curl and race across the sky. Compressing time in this way is achieved by means of time-lapse photography.

Essentially this means that instead of running continuously at 24 frames per second (the same speed as film is projected), the camera films a series of single frames, with an interval of time between each successive frame. The degree to which time is compressed depends upon the ratio between the projection rate (24 or 25 fps) and the filming rate. Filming rates vary between, say, one frame per second for cloud formations, and one frame every six hours for very slow-growing plants. Normally the camera and the lights remain in a fixed position throughout the operation, even though the subject, say, a plant tendril, may be moving

Above **Small mammals, such as this squirrel, can be just as tricky to study for filming** **as trying to capture the secret life of plants and insects with the latest gadgetry.**

across the frame.

OSF have recently had a time-lapse unit made to order which not only switches the lights and camera on at programmed intervals, but – as in the case of a growing plant – will also tilt the camera up to follow the plant's progress, will subtly alter environmental conditions, and generally operate a variety of equipment connected to it.

A fair amount of the work OSF has contributed to series such as *Survival* and *Life on Earth* has involved photography of micro-organisms. Lighting was not the only major problem – the problem of vibration had to be solved. With microscopic table-

top work, the slightest vibration (the camera motor or a door shutting down the hall) would blur the subject and/or bounce it out of frame. Peter Parks, another OSF founding member, designed and built an answer to this problem which has since become standard in the trade: the *optical bench*.

This is basically a heavy, flat metal surface to which the camera is rigidly attached. Vibration cannot be eliminated completely, but on the optical bench, both camera and subject vibrate in unison. Since the camera is incapable of moving independently, the subject could easily move out of the field of view. So the object under view is placed on

a movable metal stage on top of the bench and manoeuvred in three dimensions by means of wheels placed at the side of the bench. Lights and other accessories such as background plates (photographs), magnification optics and so on, are then all attached to the bench.

An ingenious method of lighting microscopic organisms is a system OSF purportedly resurrected from Victorian times called 'dark field illumination'. The technique is vital when filming creatures such as water fleas which are transparent and would be virtually invisible without this form of illumination.

Camera, subject and light source are placed in a straight line. A large magnifying lens is placed in front of the light focusing the beam into a cone, the tip of which is on the subject. A small opaque disc is then placed at the centre of this lens, shielding the light from the camera. The subject then appears brilliantly back-lit against a black background. OSF have even managed to film the beating heart of an embryonic water flea while it is still inside its mother.

Floral viewpoint

In OSF's second self-financed production *Sexual Encounters of a Floral Kind*, completed in 1982, a bee is seen hovering with intent over a flower. Then suddenly, from within the flower we see the bee coming towards us for a landing. This shot was achieved with the use of a lens attachment made at OSF, similar to devices called endoscopes which have been developed as medical aids for peering inside the human body. Endoscopes consist either of a system of lens and prism optics that transmit an image down a long tube, or a cluster of light-transmitting fibres, known generally as fibre optics. OSF use only the former type – the latter cannot produce images of a high enough quality.

A useful addition to the OSF wildlife photographers' kit is a comparatively recent device known as an *image intensifier*. Originally developed for military use, it consists of a miniature video tube which amplifies the image by a factor of hundreds or thousands. There is inevitably a noticeable loss of picture quality, but that is the price for actually seeing in pitch darkness!

Another innovation which OSF has helped adapt for use in wildlife film-making is the snorkel lens system. This permits the camera to photograph objects from 3 mm above any surface. Like an inverted periscope, this snorkel (which is an actual lens as opposed to an attachment) can be used to stunning effect. And coupled to the Cosmoscope/Galactoscope system devised by OSF, the uses for the snorkel are virtually limitless.

Both these exotically-named camera systems are attached to a 14 metre-long tracking system (the Cosmoglide) suspended from the roof of the OSF studio. The system has the effect of miniaturizing the camera

Above **High speed flash photography 'freezes' this violet-eared hummingbird.**

Below **Each compound eye of the horsefly is made up of thousands of separate lenses.**

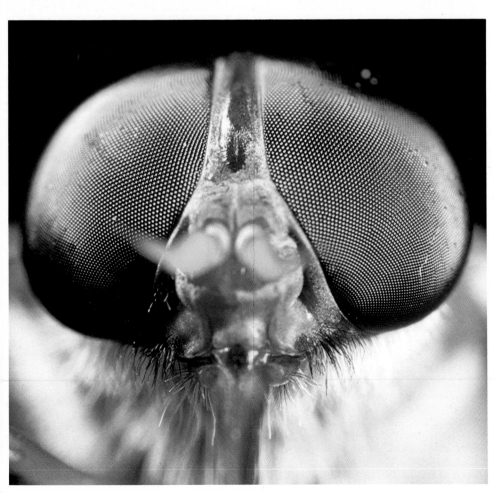

Oxford Scientific Films/David Thompson

Left **To achieve this image of a ghost crab entering its burrow, OSF photographer David Thompson had to bury himself in the Bermudan sand at the end of the burrow — armed with a normal stills camera and lens.**
Below **Back at home in the OSF studios outside Oxford, we get an insect's eye view of some of the photographers.**
Right **Close-ups — like this of a tropical tree frog — can only be taken with an extension.**

and allowing the film-makers to place the lens just about anywhere on the set below. An OSF promotional film shows the system's capabilities. The lens can track along a speeding train in close-up, submerge under water moving through algae and fishes, rejoin the train peering through its windows, spin around the front of it, and, doing a 360° turn, take to the air for a wide panoramic shot of the set as if the camera were mounted in a helicopter.

OSF has been hired to provide strange and imaginative effects for a number of feature films, amongst which are *Superman, Alien, Altered States* and *The Wall*. Commercials companies also took note of their capabilities, and with a few successful commercials under their belt, the team have now set up their own commercials production company.

Oxford Scientific Films/J. A. L. Cooke

INDEX

574
Nat

c.1

**Nature's secret
world**

DATE			

MADISON COUNTY
CANTON PUBLIC LIBRARY SYSTEM
CANTON, MISS. 39046

© THE BAKER & TAYLOR CO